"Manu Bazzano's *Buddha is Dead*, with its paradoxical implication, *Long Live Buddha*, is an extremely original work. The writer takes full advantage of his position as an outsider, in several senses, to launch a fearless attack on philosophical orthodoxy and timidity. He engages passionately with a range of ideas in Western and Eastern philosophy in order to grapple with the question of the nature of freedom – the question which is at the heart of the book. The writing style is lively and provocative, and the experience of reading the book is like witnessing a brilliant display of fireworks, or riding on a roller coaster. The reader will arrive at the final page, challenged, exhilarated, buffeted perhaps, but wiser than she or he was at the beginning." *Carole Satyamurti*

CAROLE SATYAMURTI is a poet and sociologist who lives and works in London. She teaches at the Tavistock Clinic. She co-edited *Acquainted with the Night*: *psychoanalysis and the poetic imagination* (2003). She won the National Poetry Competition in 1986. She published many collections of poetry, the latest of which is *Stitching the Dark* (Bloodaxe, 2005). Two of these are Poetry Book Society Recommendations.

"Manu Bazzano, an Italian who writes in succinct and fluent English, is a muscian, writer, Zen monk and philosopher. He has written a provocative, iconoclastic and fascinating comparative study which looks at the links between the often-misunderstood philosopher Friedrich Nietzsche and Zen Buddhism and its development and practice in the West. In his book Bazzano explores with both intellectual and practice-based insight the connection between these two very different cultures." *David Scott*

DAVID SCOTT is the author of *Easy-to-use Zen: Refresh and Calm Your Mind, Body and Spirit with the Wisdom of Zen.*

BUDDHA IS DEAD

THANKS

David Shoji Scott and Daniel Tapsell – true friends in the Dharma.

Sarita Doveton, my beloved partner.

Daniel Dohen Silberberg for mentioning Molly Bloom
in a Dharma talk.

Nigel Armistead and Subhaga Gaetano Failla, for their unconditional
love and support over many years of friendship.

Carole Satyamurti, for our invigorating discussions over
ice cream and coffee.

Stephen Batchelor, for his warm encouragement and kindness.

Tony Williams, for his humour and common sense.

Paola Prina, David Herbert and Ann Hariades for keeping
the Adlerian spirit alive.

Mark G. Payge, for genuine companionship in walking the path.

Steve Turrington, for his friendship, and for the book cover.

James Hillman for never-ending inspiration and Graham Parkes and
David Loy for their encouragement and feedback.

The drivers of the 46 bus from Gospel Oak to King's Cross.

The staff at the British Library, a secular temple in the heart of London.

The staff at Nietzsche's House in Sils Maria, Switzerland.

Tony Balazs, Joe Burton, Philip Hausmeyer, Julia Redei, Steve Tibbs,
Dorinda Talbot, Dheeresh Turnbull, Margaret Wood,
Bozenna & all the Friends of the London Zen Sangha
who have shared their practice over the years.

May we realize the Buddha Way together

BUDDHA
IS DEAD

Nietzsche and the Dawn
of European Zen

Manu Bazzano

sussex
ACADEMIC
PRESS

BRIGHTON • PORTLAND

Copyright © Manu Bazzano, 2006

The right of Manu Bazzano to be identified as Author of this work has been asserted in accordance with the Copyright, Designs and Patents Act 1988.

2 4 6 8 10 9 7 5 3

First published 2006 in Great Britain by
SUSSEX ACADEMIC PRESS
PO Box 139
Eastbourne BN24 9BP

and in the United States of America by
SUSSEX ACADEMIC PRESS
920 NE 58th Ave   Suite 300
Portland, Oregon 97213-3786

British Library Cataloguing in Publication Data
A CIP catalogue record for this book is available from the British Library.

Library of Congress Cataloging-in-Publication Data
Bazzano, Manu.
    Buddha is dead : Nietzsche and the dawn of European Zen
    / by Manu Bazzano.
        p. cm.
    Includes bibliographical references and index.
    ISBN 1-84519-149-8 (pbk. : alk. paper)
    1. Philosophy, Buddhist. 2. Nietzsche, Friedrich Wilhelm,
        1844–1900. 3. Zen Buddhism—Doctrines.
    4. Philosophy—History—20th century.
    I. Title.
    B162.B39 2006
    190—dc22

                                                2005037865

Typeset and designed by G&G Editorial, Brighton & Eastbourne
Printed by TJ International, Padstow, Cornwall
This book is printed on acid-free paper.

CONTENTS

*After a Foreword, Preface (and Precaution), and Introduction,
the text comprises one hundred and eighty-nine sections,
divided into seven parts.*

Contents

Part Six
ON NOMADIC TRUTH

Part Seven
THE INNOCENCE OF BECOMING

NOTES

BIBLIOGRAPHY

INDEX

No gain is to be made by writing out the names of the one hundred and eighty-nine sections, for their titles are oblique. The most that can be said in this description of the contents is that the final section deals with Happiness, which should be incentive enough to begin reading.

FOREWORD BY
DANIEL DOEN SILBERBERG

The title of this intelligent and provocative book echoes Nietzsche's famous assertion that "God is Dead". It also bring to mind the Zen phrase "If you meet the Buddha, kill the Buddha", which isn't an injunction to kill or even reject the Buddha. It is asking us to free ourselves of the concepts we hold that stop us from seeing the Buddha – from seeing our true self. I believe the intention of Nietzsche's famous "God is Dead' had the same freeing intention.

We get stuck in thoughts about what Zen can and cannot be. Every time Zen moves to a new location those ideas are challenged. Fortunately a unique aspect of the fiber of Zen is its ability to assimilate rather than overthrow. When in a new place the practice joins, it appreciates.

Manu's book points to this aspect of the practice of Zen and asserts that Zen can truly land in Europe by blending with and embracing its rich culture as embodied by the search for truth that is philosophy. In a sense, as philosophy and Zen meet, or as East and West meet, the old Buddha way dies so that the new one can live. From another point of view we can say this living and dying of the Buddha way is the vital life of the Buddha way wherever it goes. The book often speaks of the controversial and brilliant philosopher Nietzsche as a true philosopher and seeker of truth. Nietzsche's book "Beyond Good and Evil" brings to mind my teacher Genpo Roshi's book "Beyond Sanity and Madness" and the sixth patriarch when he says "Think neither good nor evil." It's the old life giving poison. The one that kills duality.

What this book asserts is, I think, a fine thing to do and done well. I was born in Europe and raised in a European family. I have been raised in America and am a practitioner of Zen. This book is a personal kindness to me. It allows me to embrace these two sides more fully.

We can say Buddha is dead and that is fine. We can say Philosophy is dead and that is also fine. Or we can say they are both alive. As they say in Europe "The King is dead. Long live the King."

PREFACE (AND PRECAUTION)

There is nothing to gain from Nietzsche, and there is nothing to gain from Zen. Neither offers consolation, a better future, a promised land, the whole gamut of products offered by the idolatry of salvation. They do not offer "self-development" either. On the contrary, the very self we eagerly strive to develop will instead be revealed as fictional, for both Nietzsche and Zen uncompromisingly point at what Eckhart called "intimate poverty". They are both forms of bitter medicine, but beneficial in the long run.

In a letter to his wife on 9 July 1910, referring to their common friend and fellow poet Hans Larson, Rilke writes:

> Nietzsche, with whom we have all become slightly intoxicated, he has taken as a medicine and grown healthier from it.[1]

I know that in writing this book I have *betrayed* Nietzsche, and I have done so in two ways: first, as Buddhist writer David Loy kindly reminded me in a letter, to accept Nietzsche's point is to go *beyond him* rather than embrace a "Nietzschean perspective". My book, therefore is a work of honest treason, a document to my inevitable disloyalty – to both Nietzsche and Zen: a tribute, at best, a homage – I'm tempted to say a *song* – rather than an attempt at defining either an imaginary Nietzschean orthodoxy or a comparative link with the equally elusive philosophy of Zen Buddhism. Secondly, Blanchot reminds us that we must at all times read Nietzsche with a restless, suspicious gaze and not be tempted to make use of his thought.[2] Like many others, I have *used* his thought, as I have used Zen throughout my book. I have done so as an attempt to show my gratitude: I am grateful as the patient is grateful to the surgeon, as the condemned *might* be grateful to his executioner. The patient is delivered of his illness, and the condemned person of a tedious life within the walls of a tiny prison cell. True, most people would want to live at any cost. In Dostoyevsky's *Crime and Punishment*, Raskolnikoff is intensely distressed by the idea:

> He looked upon his convict companions, and marvelled to see how they all loved life – how they prized life. It appeared to him it was prized more in prison than in liberty. What pains and tortures would not these miserable creatures endure![3]

Self-preservation, and its gang of robbers – fear, scheming, desire for gain – motivates us. But life has other designs. *Life wants to overcome itself.*

I first read Nietzsche at the age of twenty. It destroyed my belief in history and progress, introduced me to the *ABC of groundlessness*, namely, that there is no particular purpose to life, that all so-called universal values, religious, ethical, scientific and aesthetic, are man-made *errors*, necessary to make human life *bearable*.

My encounter with the Dharma, in the person of my teacher Genpo Merzel Roshi – who, incidentally, should not be held responsible for the views contained in this book – later took away a new belief that had insinuated itself in my mind: that there might be such a thing as a dwelling place, an inner sanctum, a state of oneness from which one can look at the world with newly found wisdom and compassion. Paradoxically, Zen practice started to erode the very idea which Zen is credited to strive for: enlightenment, or at least, my own idea of it.

It is dangerous to read Nietzsche at twenty. The derailment involved in taking the study of Nietzsche to heart is something from which one might never recover. And it can be dangerous to take the teachings of Zen to heart. In both cases, we must suspend, if not altogether eradicate, our cherished beliefs and opinions. "Do not search for the truth" – the *Hsin Shin Ming* states – "only cease to cherish opinions".[4]

Zen Buddhism developed in new and creative ways each time it was transplanted to new soil. From the radical scepticism of the Madhyamika School in India, it was assimilated into Chinese Taoism, later into Japanese culture, and more recently, and gradually, into Western soil; first America, now Europe.

Nietzsche represents the pinnacle *and* the overcoming of Western culture. Not only did he put metaphysics to rest by introducing *the mystery of the human body* into established philosophical knowledge; he seamlessly anticipated cultural trends and dangers of the 20th and 21st centuries.

Filtered through Nietzsche's thought, Buddhism in the West could avoid the pitfalls that had already emerged during its gestation period throughout the second half of the 20th century. I'll name but a few: elitism, esoterism, "spiritualism" in the old-fashioned, theosophical sense; a patriarchal, conservative, feudal religion ruled by males, founded on autocracy and hierarchy, on the denial of the body and betrayal of the earth, in what Nietzsche calls the "denigration of life"; a new, "oriental" belief system, with colourful and ultimately moralizing aspects: fateful, literal belief in reincarnation paired to a magical view of the law of karma, interpreted in the "eye for an eye" mode; a system of guru-worship.

In Anglo-Saxon secular societies, one notices the emergence, in the name of Buddhism, of a new Puritanism. By using Nietzsche's *hammer* – by which he *sounded out* (not smashed, as vulgarly believed) any god, old

Preface (and Precaution)

and new, and any *shadow* of god – a lot of unnecessary baggage would be suitably dealt with, to allow Zen's real work to take place.

What is then *the real work*? It might have to do more with chipping away than acquiring. It seems to have a lot to do with *appreciation* of ordinary life and *gratitude*, rather than for the search of peak experiences; and it has a lot to do with healing, within ourselves and the wide community, of *the spirit of revenge*.

Nietzsche's objection to Buddhism was that it appeared to be a form of *escapism*. Wanting relief from suffering was to him akin to avoidance, for it meant not to fully appreciate one's life.

With Nietzsche, philosophy reaches "square one". It ceases to be an academic exercise, and becomes both *radical critique* and *active appreciation of destiny*. Echoing Spinoza's *amor dei*, he called such courageous stance *amor fati*, love of destiny.

We must go way back, to the Greek philosopher Heraclitus, to find anything resembling Nietzsche in Western thought. *His is the bravest attempt made in the West to come to terms with groundlessness.* He courageously embraced nihilism to the full. In Zen, this is known as *Great Doubt*, a way that leads to pure, i.e. *purposeless*, faith.

If I had to pack into one sentence the content of this book, I would say this: *when allowed to manifest fully, nihilism overcomes itself*. If unable to embrace great existential doubt completely, an individual or a society will instead settle with dangerous surrogates: defective belief-systems, commonly accepted forms of denial, neurosis and delusion, various kinds of self-aggrandizing endeavours, patriotism, hatred of the foreign, the whole rich pageant of what Buddhism refers to as *ignorance*, whose main characteristic is the unverified belief in the true existence of a separate, self-existing "I".

Nietzsche incites us to the adventurous exploration of what he called *the open sea*. Zen gives us the tools and the anchor to avoid what Nietzsche sadly could not evade: shipwreck. The tools are *zazen*, the sound practice of everyday life and the great treasure of the teachings of the Dharma. The anchor, as my teacher is fond of pointing out, consists of the four Bodhisattva vows.

Nietzsche's ruinous fall does not in any way invalidate the authority of his findings, nor the tremendous weight they still hold after more than a hundred years since his death.

There might be light at the end of the tunnel. There is no guarantee, though. We must go and see for ourselves.

On hearing the news that the old God is dead, we philosophers
and 'free spirits' feel as if kissed by the rays of a new dawn;
our hearts overflow with gratitude, wonder, expectation
. . . at long last the horizon is free and open, even
though it may not be light; our ships may at
last venture out again, ready for any danger;
every daring feat is again permitted to those who
go in search of wisdom; the sea, our sea lies open
again, and perhaps there has never been such an 'open sea'.

NIETZSCHE[1]

Finally, there is no existence that is constant, either of our being
or that of objects. And we, and our judgment, and all mortal
things go on flowing and rolling incessantly.

MONTAIGNE[2]

No sunrise, even in mountains, is ostentatious, triumphal, and
imperial; each one is faint and timorous, like a hope that all
may yet be well, and it is this very unobtrusiveness
of the mightiest light that is moving
and overpowering.

THEODOR ADORNO[3]

Not Nirvana but Samsara is the name for the highest ideal.

LOU SALOMÉ[4]

We need to give up the hope that there is something to find.

DENNIS GENPO MERZEL[5]

Without self-nature and other-nature, who is this buddha?

NAGARJUNA[6]

To my teacher, Genpo Merzel Roshi
With deep gratitude
For tirelessly expounding the infinitely subtle teaching
of the esoteric dharma for the benefit of all.

INTRODUCTION

The European legacy affirmed in this book is not rooted in so-called "Eurocentrism", but precisely in its opposite: it is the European legacy of *exiles*. Great European thought has been shaped by exiles and refugees. Some of them were forced into exile by the political situation of their country of origin. Some, and Nietzsche is one of them, did so voluntarily. Throughout the present work, Nietzsche's spirit is evoked both as epitome of European high culture and as symbol of its demise. Both the distant past – above all Hellenism – and what was to be the future (phenomenology, existentialism, post-structuralism) are contained within his thought. What this thought also contains is, perversely, its own undoing; Zen calls this process "Great Doubt", which is also the best antidote to dogmatism, to the creation of systems, schools of thought and spiritual practices that are ultimately self-serving.

Nietzsche was a nomad without a state, a home, and a citizenship. Basel University had wanted him to change his nationality from Prussian to Swiss. He renounced his Prussian nationality, but never managed to obtain the residential qualifications necessary to acquire Swiss citizenship. For the rest of his life he was therefore stateless. In the Zen tradition, the person who receives monastic ordination becomes "homeless", for he is no longer identified with the conditioning, cherished opinions and belief systems that together constitute an artificial haven. By leaving home – factually or symbolically – he casts himself to the open sea, which is also the essential condition for philosophical enquiry.

If Zen is to plant roots in Europe, it needs to consider deeply some peculiar European characteristics. The Zen tradition has always taken on board the cultural colouring of the place into which it was planted: China, Japan, America, and now it's the turn of Europe. What are these peculiarly European characteristics? And which are conducive to and can prepare the practitioner for the "Zen experience"?

Alongside the great dualistic traditions of mainstream, Judeo-Christian religions and philosophies, alongside Cartesianism, Hegelism, the rationalism of the Enlightenment, the radical rationalism of existentialist thought and the Christian rationalism and evolutionism of Darwin, Europe has also produced a small but steady rivulet of great "heretical" thinking – heretical in the eyes of orthodoxy and dogmatism – which, originating from Heraclitus, has found its zenith in Nietzsche.

The name *Nietzsche* evokes *nothingness*. He was delighted when a

Polish friend explained to him that the pronunciation of his name was close to the Polish word for "nothing"; he was fond of thinking of himself as a "man of nothing", which was consistent with his findings that the Cartesian self is a mere construct, that there is no substance to this thing called "I". He also embodies a great harvest and, at the same time, a tremendous crisis in the whole of Western thought. The idea central to his philosophy, that of *the eternal return of the same*, was prompted by an untutored, spontaneous experience of *groundlessness*, of what Buddhists call *sunyata*. This experience was profound, unexpected and shattering; in comparison, most of Western philosophy looks pale, anemic, at best a clever exercise in articulating abstractions.

The birth of European Zen is rooted in Nietzsche's experience, the echo and the amplification of which is found, to be sure, in several other thinkers and, above all, *artists*. They all personify what Nietzsche called "a good European". What makes a "good European"? A "good European" is one endowed with the "trans-European eye", one who can look at Europe from the vantage point of the open sea.

European Zen is in its infancy, and at present owes a great deal to American Zen. The last century has already produced a generation of American Zen teachers, some of them truly outstanding. It has also provided us, at times, with some cautionary tales. At present, some of the best studies on Nietzsche come from America. Modern European thought, on the other hand, has nearly succeeded in downgrading Nietzsche's legacy to the new conformities represented by perspectivism, agnosticism and phenomenology, missing out on the *affirmative thrust* and *thorough-going mode* of his enquiry. The wayward history of modern European thought nevertheless testifies to an ever-present subterranean loyalty – almost a complicity – to the recognizable facets of true philosophy: critique, love of multiplicity, paradox and contradiction, fearlessness, and the light-footed style of the *gaya scienza*.

Amazingly, when looking deeply into the roots and origins of Western culture, what we find is *Eastern* culture. What were ancient Greek art and thought if not exquisite amalgamations of Middle-eastern, Mediterranean, and even Far-eastern components? The undisputed cultural supremacy of ancient Greece comes from its ability to absorb and handle creatively the *pandemonium* (many daemons, or voices) of several cultures and civilizations. Conversely, *resistance to diversity stems from weakness*, often resulting in chronic malaise such as blinkered patriotism.

European Zen will be the philosophy, art, and religious practice of the good European, of one who has forfeited the illusory privilege of being part of a small, narrow-minded tribe and has become homeless. Such is the homelessness of the aristocratic spirit, whose nobility is unfettered by the surrogate of social status and is forged in the rigorous and joyous discipline of freedom.

MISSION: UNTIMELY
THE TRUE TASK OF PHILOSOPHY

Philosophers as Legislators

Philosophy generates philosophers and philosophy labourers, and it would be advisable not to confuse the two, for philosophers are a rare breed. In his essay *In Defence of Poetry* of 1821, Shelley wrote of great philosophers as poets and as poets as the unacknowledged legislators of mankind.[1] Nietzsche was to echo him sixty five years later by stressing that the rule of *to each his own* should be strictly applied. To preserve, interpret, recycle and assess values is one thing; that is the painstaking, invaluable work of philosophy labourers. However, it is quite another task to *create* values: this is the endeavour of philosophers.

Philosophy labourers may produce noble exemplars, finely tuned minds capable of identifying truths in the realms of logic, art and politics. Real philosophers are commanders and law-givers.

> Is there enough pride, daring, boldness, self-assurance, enough spiritual will, will to responsibility, *freedom of will* available today for 'the philosopher' to be from now on really – *possible* on earth?[2]

A philosopher is a legislator: having dared to question deeply the very foundation of every single human value, she sets to legislate – and does so by creating new values.

Usually, we have two kinds of philosophers. Some belong to the *end* of an epoch. Their work is the swan song of an era, the message in a bottle that helps men and women of the future decipher a particular age.

In the culturally omnivorous 21st century, it is taken for granted that we can understand and easily amalgamate within a formula any culture and civilization of the past. We assume that we understand, for example, Greek tragedies and the pre-Socratic world in which they were written and performed. If we were sincere, we would admit that we do not understand them at all, for the fuller meaning of the poetic and religious world they are an expression of is hermetically sealed from us. What we manage to accede to is, as José Ortega beautifully reminds us,

> like the libretto of an opera, the music of which we have never heard; or like the wrong side of a tapestry woven by faith, showing only the multicoloured threads.[3]

If anything at all from the past is intelligible to us, it is only thanks to authentic philosophy and great art; they both help us approach distant lands without the hindrance of *hubris* and *superbia*.

Philosophers like Nietzsche, on the other hand, belong to the *beginning* of an era: their work is nearly always misapprehended, for they are *forerunners*. In his poems of "The Phases of the Moon", Yeats saw Nietzsche as a forerunner, a return of Achilles – imperfect, fierce, seeking truth and striving to overcome himself.[4] The other, poignant, point is of course that of Achilles' heel, of profound vulnerability, revealing a different type of strength.

But philosophers as such are a dying breed. Not only the word has come to mean academic, philosophy professor, but has in fact become synonymous with logician, analytical thinker, which constitutes only one of the currents within the philosophical endeavour – and not a major one at that.

Being an academic, a philosophy labourer, fulfils an invaluable task. We need people who systematize, popularize and impart both the knowledge and the enthusiasm for philosophy among each new generation. But to call a conscientious, knowledgeable, even creative academic a *philosopher* is going too far.

A Buddhist priest is not always a realized Buddha, and a country vicar is not the Saviour Himself. Moreover, a civil servant will almost certainly conform, will not challenge the views in vogue, nor for the life of him bite the hand that feeds him.

A philosophy labourer, far from being a seeker after truth – or truths – far from asking blunt, unsettling, *untimely* questions, will go a long way by using fashionable, obscure jargon, to present infinite variations on the party line.

2   *A Passion for Integrity*

Even great minds have been philosophy professors: for example, Kant and Hegel. Neither of them, however, ever challenged the status quo.

The intellectual integrity needed to pursue the vocation of philosophy is at variance with the sheepishness normally required to hold a chair at university.

> A university scholar can never become a philosopher; for even Kant could not do so but, the inborn pressure of his genius notwithstanding, remained to the end as it were in a chrysalis stage.[5]

The only exception, which Hegel loved to quote, to the irreconcilability of creative thinking and public post, would be that of Goethe. His benevolent, wise and extraordinarily broad humanity appears to equal him to a Taoist sage. But Goethe proved to be two-faced. A model of wholeness and integrity in Nietzsche's eyes, and undoubtedly one of the greatest artists who ever lived, Goethe did not show the same loftiness in matters of the world, for he achieved success by entertaining typically German vices: inveterate sentimentalism and moral insincerity.

His fault was to refrain from publicly opposing the danger of the so-called "new German philosophy" (Hegel's) in spite of having fully understood its absurdity. Why did he not oppose it? *Because it was the philosophy of the establishment.*

Goethe had the privilege of reading the works of a far greater thinker than Hegel, the young Schopenhauer, who was his devotee. He refrained from encouraging and publicly endorsing Schopenhauer, thus condemning him to the neglect and misunderstanding of his contemporaries. And this in spite of having understood that the pursuit of knowledge and wisdom did not veer towards State and public institutions (as preached by Hegel), but towards the East (as held by Schopenhauer).

Schopenhauer embodies *philosophy as vocation*: to be a philosopher after Schopenhauer, one needs to have a tremendous passion for, and a commitment to, integrity.

One would gladly avoid having to state that *a true philosopher cannot be an academic*. It sounds rigid, unforgiving, too *Bohemian*. Unfortunately, the examples of philosophers/academics we do possess too often suggest *betrayal* of intellectual integrity, and in the case of Heidegger and of his endorsement of Nazism, an appalling decline from any vestige of human dignity.

The distinguished philosophy labourers of the past chose their favourite poison and their favourite form of worship. In Hegel's case, he went as far as elevating his master, the State, to the highest rank, levelling it with God and the Absolute. No greater tribute was ever paid to the State by one of his faithful servants.

3   The Philosophy of the Knight Errant

An *un-systematic* approach to philosophy finds its equivalent in *picaresque* fiction, where the protagonist drifts through a meandering plot. The *picaresque* novel might flirt with both the tragic and the comic mode, but it *does not find resolution* in either.

An un-systematic philosophy is not an epic, nor a comic tale, a detective story, or a "social realism" saga. *All of these modes are journeys of the ego*, in other words, *ego-trips*. In the picaresque novel, as in the unsystematic philosophical text, *the ego is fragmented, dissected, dispersed* and finally *dissolved*. This is the philosophy of the *Knight Errant*, who does not belong to any church and has no credo or dogma to defend. His alliances continually shift in a world populated by masks, by "good" and "bad" characters who pass by from shadow to light and back to the world of shadows.

Above all, the picaresque novel and the un-systematic philosophy *do not chart a progress: the very idea of progress belongs to the ego*, to the dualistic mind, to the heroic and epic stance. Conversely, here we find no resolution, no redemption, and no proper ending to the meandering plot.

In short, *we are under the tutelage of Hermes*, under the enchantment of mercurial power and the dexterity of quicksilver. *We are not running after new cosmologies*, another life, another dimension; the intent is instead to *re-signify human life* and redirect it toward the wider realm of psyche, out of the narrow confinement of ego.

We are also under the spell of *Dionysian logic*, the very same that watches over events taking place in dreams, in the theatre, and in the theatre of dreams. We are in the world of *metaphor*, not in that of allegory: the former is not subject to *interpretative translation*.

The same approach, when applied to the difficult art of psychology, will shift the perspective towards the psyche, moving away from our excessive preoccupation with the human species in general and the human ego in particular. Then psychology too becomes an adventurous journey, and no longer the clinical, jargon-ridden, narrow-minded pursuit of one's own "self-development".

4 *Fatal Affinities*

Unfortunately, bohemianism does *not* offer a wholesome alternative to the salaried philosophy of academia. Not because it equates free-lance thinkers – God forbid – with artists (Adorno's fear): philosophy *is* an art form, *a form of high art*. Instead – and in this Adorno is right – it gives the free-lance philosopher "fatal affinity" to "crackpot religion and half-educated sectarianism".[6] In today's jargon, the "new age" and the reactionary spiritualism that has been in vogue since the 1980s. Our times do not encourage the birth and growth of philosophers: if not sheltered – and mummified – by academia, philosophers have to sell books for a living, are forced to come out with marketable ideas, to compete with "self-help", celebrities' biographies and popular science, as well as with the portentous output of career novelists and stand-up poets.

Like that other downgraded, dumbed-down profession – journalism – philosophers have to produce "continuous brilliance", or else perish.

The very fabric of human society, however, *requires the existence of philosophy* and philosophers. Deep within the structure of institututional, moral and religious life lies a human need for truth. And so philosophers continue to be produced: sometimes within university life, at the margins of academia, the "helping professions" and the clergy, sometimes through nomadic existence, and other times wearing an altogether different cloak. Their existence overcomes both canon and stigma, both emblazoned certainties and exhausted radicalism, in order to say what has to be said.

5 Orpheus' Gaze

For some, *philosophy alone can bring about radical change*; not religion, with its doctrines and its places of worship; not political institutions, with their self-perpetrating agendas. The individual alone can do it, the moment he or she starts to *think critically and creatively*, the moment one enters the realm of philosophy.

Engaging in thoroughgoing philosophical enquiry is not as easy as it sounds. It is easy enough to pursue logical thinking and to follow the dictates of reason alone. For Blanchot, this is akin to one who goes straight down the road without looking back: he manages to live his life with a certain assurance, albeit superficial. But the one who turns and looks back *sees terrible things* that petrify him.

> Having seen them prevents him from seeing anything else; everything else flies to pieces – principles, morality, science. The absurd is what one sees when one turns back, but more precisely it is the movement of turning back: the look back, the gaze of Orpheus, of Lot's wife, the turning back that violates the prohibition and thus touches on the impossible, for this turning back is not a power. We cannot turn back. And yet turning back is the passion of thought, the decisive exigency.[7]

What we lose in turning back is the principle of identity: we perceive the same world, but somehow, in Blanchot's words, "estranged from all order", as "the outside of all world". It is the *same*, but not *identical*. It is "the non-identical same, always dispersed and always collecting itself by dispersion, the fascinating mark of the multiplicity of reflections".[8]

Philosophy embodies the resolve to *gaze* at the absurd, to obey its demands through repetition and ritual: think of Sisyphus, having to push that huge rock up the mountain with tremendous effort, only to see it roll back again, and this *for eternity*! And how can this absurd toiling turn into faith, even into joy? But it does. Strange, but true. No guarantee of happy endings; instead, the encounter with Goethe's *daemon*:

> As soon as he sets pen to paper, he ears a voice announcing merrily: 'Well, now you are lost! – 'Then should I stop? – 'No, no! If you stop you are lost!'[9]

Philosophy is a *daemonic enterprise*: *it forever engages with the unidentified, the unfamiliar, and the strange.* To obey this vocation means to flee *isolation* and enter *solitude*.

> Here there is no guilt but neither is there innocence, nothing to bind or unbind, nothing for which "I" am responsible, since what can be expected of he who has given up the possible? Nothing, except this which is the strangest expectation of all: that through him powerlessness shall speak; that henceforth speech should utter powerlessness, nudity, impotence, and also impossibility – which is the beginning of communication.[10]

6 Abstract Thinking & Sizeable Wages

Philosophy has been wrongly equated with *abstract thinking*. Our dogmatic assumptions of what *thought* is have rarely been challenged. Gilles Deleuze mentions three influential misconceptions, our ideas of what constitutes *truth*, *error*, and *method*.

> We are told that the thinker as thinker wants and loves *truth* . . . that it is . . . sufficient to think 'truly' or 'really' in order to think with truth (sincere nature of the truth, universally shared good sense).

> We are also told that we are 'diverted' from the truth but by forces which are foreign to it (body, passions, sensuous interests). We fall into error; we take falsehood to be truth, because we are not merely thinking beings.

> We are told, finally, that all we need to think well, to think truthfully, is a *method*. Method is an artifice but one through which we are brought back to the nature of thought . . . Through method we ward off error. Time and place matter little if we apply method: it enables us to enter the domain of 'that which is valid for all times and places'.[11]

Truth conceived, in Deleuze's words, as an "abstract universal", thought conceived as "pure science": *harmless ideas*, in short, *that never challenge the order of things.*

Had not Leibniz already cautioned philosophers a long time ago? Opening new fields of enquiry is fine, as long as these do not "overthrow established feelings". Thus philosophers mutated into a *submissive species, endorsed by the State for their compliance* and their nonspecific, risk-free, and most of all "scientific" stance. They speak of truth, an anaesthetized, bloodless, non-committal "truth".

> . . . it is of course clear why our academic thinkers are not dangerous; for their thoughts grow as peacefully out of tradition as any tree ever bore its apples: they cause no alarm, they remove nothing from its hinges; and of all their art and aims there could be said what Diogenes said when someone praised a philosopher in his presence: 'How can he be considered great, since he has been a philosopher for so long and has never *disturbed* anybody?' That, indeed, ought to be the epitaph of university philosophy: 'it did not disturb'.[12]

Such misconception of truth finds place in a world where the relevance of *error* has been overemphasized; its counterpart is a *mistaken idea of truth*. Thus foolish, dishonorable discourse is possible that comprises entirely of truths. We always have "the truths we deserve". They are a "function of the sense of what we conceive, of the value of what we believe".[13]

7 *Patron Saint of Free-lance Philosophers*

Nietzsche has been perhaps the most proficient of a withered but fierce lineage of free spirits who are not afraid to endure the hardships of solitude and cultural isolation, if that is the price that must be paid for the uncomfortable truths they reveal. This is not to be confused with the anemic, tragic-romantic stereotype of tortured artists. The philosophical endeavour is not a task for everybody, for it demands tremendous resilience, self-reliance, and the capacity to bounce back in moments of crisis, ill health and doubt. Schopenhauer, who revived this proud tradition in the West, is nowadays fashionable among a new breed of pessimists in the academic world. Schopenhauer's essay *On Philosophy at the Universities* is the unrivalled manifesto of the free-lance philosopher. In his view, chair philosophy is

> burdened with the disadvantage that philosophy as a profession imposes on philosophy as the free investigation of truth.[14]

For Schopenhauer, philosophy "by government order" is diametrically opposed to philosophy "in the name of nature and mankind." Institutions *improbant secus docentes*, that is, "they reject those who teach something different". What government would pay people to contradict – directly or indirectly – "what it has had promulgated from all the pulpits by thousands of its appointed priests and religious teachers?" It would eventually undermine both government and institutions.

If in the above quote we write "scientists, logicians, post-modernists" instead of "priests and religious teachers" we get a fairly accurate picture of contemporary institutional orthodoxy. In Schopenhauer's day, orthodox philosophy – Hegelism – ran alongside the established religion: it was its justification, theoretical apology, and conceptual ornament.

Schopenhauer's position is crucial because in spite of its numerous shortcomings, it will be admiringly adopted by the young Nietzsche who was to fully personify *the philosopher as outcast*. In Nietzsche's case, his light-footedness, modesty and subtle irony replaces Schopenhauer's bitterness. With the latter, one cannot help thinking that his radicalism against academia is tinted by "sour grapes". Appointed as a lecturer at Berlin University, he proudly scheduled his lessons to coincide with those of the widely popular Hegel, and eventually lost his post.

Nietzsche welcomed his illness as a timely pretext for abandoning a life that was not truly his own, the academic life of "rummaging through old books". He was a rebel by choice, whereas Schopenhauer was a rebel out of necessity.

Left with unlimited freedom, Nietzsche created his own discipline outside the academic routine. In his early years of soul-searching, he identified in Schopenhauer, alongside Goethe and Lord Byron's fictional character Manfred, the qualities he most admired, in this case what Schopenhauer calls, "literary conscience", precisely that which an academic supported by the State usually lacks. For he renounces

all literary conscience, makes a point of deifying the State, of making it the pinnacle of all human efforts and all this because he is paid by the State and State purposes. In this way he not only turns the philosophical lecture-room into a school of the shallowest philistinism, but in the end, like Hegel for instance, he arrives at the revolting doctrine that man's destiny is identified with the State.[15]

Today it is implied that a philosopher must necessarily be an academic, a university professor, even though many remarkable thinkers have lost their university posts and their salaries: Feuerbach, Ruge, Bauer, Dühring, Marx or, like Kierkeegard, never used their degree. Whereas Immanuel Kant, the quintessential academic philosopher, in Nietzsche's view,

clung to his university, submitted himself to its regulations, to governments, retained the appearance of religious belief, endured to live among colleagues and students: so it is natural that his example has produced above all university professors and professorial philosophy.[16]

The harshest of Nietzsche's accusations against philosophy is that of *dogmatism*, by which he means propounding one's view, one's perception of the world as "the truth", as an "accurate description" of the world. It is not possible to be dogmatic, he argues, if one possesses true integrity. It is then reasonable to expect an even lower level of integrity amongst religions and spiritual paths, Buddhism included, for these often claim to aid the practitioner in perceiving things "as they truly are". It is rare to find a spiritual path that openly speaks of *blindness* and *not knowing* as highly desirable qualities.

A decent individual becomes suspicious if the great majority shares his truth, for then it becomes a middling pop-tune, a mere trend. True philosophers ("philosophers of the future") are insulted by the very fact of sharing the mob's likes and dislikes, for those are often base and murderous.

> It must offend their pride, also their taste, if their truth is supposed to be a truth for everyone – which has so far been the secret wish and hidden meaning of all dogmatic aspirations.[17]

Dogmatic self-effacement has become incredibly popular today in the world of science and the humanities, but what the self-refuting person is really saying is "This is not my own opinion, my own creation. It's a simple explanation of *the way things are*". In other words, it's a dogma. God said it, or the Buddha, or Charles Darwin. Or indeed Nietzsche or Dogen, in the case of the present work. The trouble is, Nietzsche's position is extremely ambiguous, and so is Dogen's, or that of any great Master in the Zen tradition.

8   Popular Philosophy

Totalitarianism: another name for a philosophy shared by the mob.

9   A Passion for the Unfinished

A truly philosophical discourse is constantly surpassing itself, de-systematizing the need for system building, shredding itself into fragments. *Logos* is broken down into circular, self-existing utterances, and in the rare, highly fortunate cases of philosophers who are also artists and musicians, *Logos* soars into *Melos*.

We have emancipated ourselves from fear of reason, that ghost that haunted the 18th century: we again dare to be absurd, childish, lyrical – in one word: 'we are musicians'.[18]

Cutting through a hyper-rational, hysterically coherent frame, philosophy ascends to the realm of *melody*; not the nauseous mix of populism and histrionics, but the ambivalent common ground occupied by authentic philosophers and artists. There we find style *and* thought happily cohabiting, a place where it is not necessary to abdicate to either aestheticism or conceptualization. These are both fossilized notions, shadows of God, desperate ways of *reacting* to the inexplicability and the sheer magnitude of becoming.

Thought breaks into fragments, and fragments hover into art. Today's "conceptual art" epitomizes the reverse; lacking in artistic inspiration, it attempts to precariously fill the gap by resorting to concepts.

A true artist and a philosopher move in a different direction: for them a concept is a fossil, a remnant of an experience which was born out of contradiction, which was filled with intensity and dynamism. A concept – and later a system – tries, unsuccessfully, to capture, encompass and explain.

The first movement, of fragmentation, spells out that philosophy speaks a *different language*. It no longer speaks of imagined universals, of an expected whole, but of *disconnection*, *plurality*, of *fragment*. It presupposes, in the words of Blanchot, a "passion for the unfinished". The *unfinished* remains so. That is its beauty, its meaning, its *raison d'être*.

The fragmentary does not precede the whole, but says itself outside the whole, and after it.[19]

For Maurice Blanchot, the fragmentary speech reflects the fact that we, as human beings, disappear. We can only leave writings on the sand; sounds and echoes are soon lost in the reverberation of the waves. Also, and more importantly, fragmentation *produces* becoming. Fragmentation is linked to Dionysus' dismemberment: he *is* that fragmentation.

Discontinuity, the arrest of intermittence, does not arrest becoming; on the contrary, it provokes becoming, calls it up in the enigma that is proper to it. This is the great turning in thought that comes about with Nietzsche: becoming is not the fluidity of an infinite (Bergsonian) *durée*, nor the nobility of an interminable movement. The first knowledge is knowledge of the tearing apart – the breaking up – of Dionysus, that obscure experience wherein becoming is disclosed in relation with the discontinuous and as its play. The fragmentation of the god is not the rash renunciation of unity, or a unity that remains one by becoming plural. Fragmentation is this god himself, that which has no relation whatsoever with a center and cannot be referred to an origin: what thought, as a consequence – the thought of the same and of the one, the thought of theology and that of all the modes of human (or dialectic) knowledge – could never entertain without falsifying it.[20]

14 • • • • • • • • • • •

10 The True Task of Philosophy

Philosophy's true task is to defy ignorance, to destroy inanity and delusion.

11 R.I.P.

Human knowledge and experience are laid to rest in Universities: humanity's attempts and temptations in the course of history are now safely codified and embalmed. Monks have their cloisters; dancers, actors, and singers have their theatre halls; but there are no buildings, gardens and spaces for the practice of philosophy. Philosophers are obliged to infiltrate into all of the above, feigning a membership to groups to which they do not belong, ducking in the undergrowth of academic knowledge, or hiding in the twilight world where performers and spectators meet. Often, as outcasts, they roam the streets and find seclusion in empty squares, or cut out a corner in a crowded bar.

Kindred spirits will carry on the flame of the heart, the dream of intelligence that lives on regardless of passing trends. They will do so by piercing through the shallow frame of statistics and cold reasoning that pretends to show us that man is a machine, an ape, or a god. He is neither of these, but a dignified vessel for the continuation of the dream that wants to dream itself in and out of the world as we know it, with or without the human species, a dream whose fantastically picaresque tale we glimpse at night, or during love, or deep meditation, or when caught absent-minded in the traffic haze of clangs and shouts of high modernity.

In glimpsing that dream, we may include sorrow, sickness and death. For sometimes the messenger is love, and sometimes death. And even what we call love has a depth of prostration and mourning.

12 *Mission: Untimely*

Sooner or later, philosophy comes up against the status quo, against the institutions, for these are but *organized stupidity*. This is not because philosophy is antagonistic or bitter, or indignant, but rather because by its very nature it constitutes a critique, an "enterprise of demystification".

Philosophers are burning *arrows* and shooting stars: they illumine the night sky for a brief spell, unsettling forever our badly acclimatized eyes. Dazed, in confused recollection, we turn them, after their passing, into bland, inoffensive dispensers of lofty platitudes on living and dying. Thus they join the ranks of priests and scientists as functionaries of History, as harmless "sages" whose aphoristic pronouncements adorn our unoriginal discourse.

It is not difficult to discern true philosophy: it is always untimely. It always irritates the status quo. By its very nature, it serves the time to come, and it does so by creatively re-interpreting the wisdom of old.

The threefold prejudice of truth, error and method are means of avoidance. True philosophy provides food for thought through *provocation* and *affirmation*; it forces us to think, reflect and meditate.

13 *Schopenhauer's Legacy*

Philosophy is the abiding quest for meaning, and a timeless, untimely enquiry and critique of science and religion, of morality and of the entire social fabric and its institutions. Naturally, such endeavour requires a fierce independence of mind, endurance and resistance to vertigo. We unfailingly find these qualities in all true explorers of the human condition. The true philosopher's contempt for the academic is rooted, as in both Schopenhauer's and Nietzsche's case, in the

> rich, clever, cosmopolitan man-of-affairs' contempt for the limited social as well as intellectual horizons of middle-class professors.[21]

It is easy to pathologize the haughty detachment and the despairing view of the world found in Schopenhauer, attributing it to the fact that he was brought up by an aristocratic, distant mother.

One is tempted join in Goethe's gentle mockery of Schopenhauer's need for seclusion and of his disdain of the marketplace. They were both clear-sighted about the other's failings. When Schopenhauer left fashionable Weimar for small-time Dresden, Goethe composed a couplet:

> Willst du dich des Lebens frouen,
> So musst der Welt du Wenth verleihen
> (If you want to enjoy life,
> You must attach value to the world)[22]

Schopenhauer personified the Romantic, otherworldly philosopher perfectly; his philosophy evolved in later life into pessimism, and for this Nietzsche harshly criticized him. Still, credit must be given to his clarity and courage, for his gaze at the world was unflinching. Commenting on his own work *The World as Will and Representation*, he wrote:

> The outcome of this knowledge is sad and depressing, but the state of knowing, the acquisition of insight, the penetration of truth, are thoroughly pleasurable – and, strange to say, add a mixture of sweetness to my bitterness.[23]

He gained a great reputation in England. He was praised by John Oxenford in the *Westminster Review* edited by George Eliot. He is still revered in England today, albeit in a watered-down form, his quotes employed in order to justify that old malaise eating at the heart of English thought: cynicism, utilitarianism, post-Darwinian pessimism.

Nietzsche at first idolized Schopenhauer (along with Wagner), and what followed were naturally rebellion and a need for independence from their influence. What he did inherit from Schopenhauer was the imperative of rigorously studying the self. He scrutinized himself thoroughly, not out of solipsism but firm in the knowledge that such investigation would be valuable to all. He also inherited from him an acute perception of the suffering of life. Schopenhauer had famously written that philosophy, like the overture of *Don Juan*, commences with a minor chord. Likewise, Nietzsche's philosophy might have elegiac undertones, but turns eventually into joyful symphony.

This gaiety is a mask – not a false pretence, not an exercise in histrionics. It is a necessary prop distracting us from the abyss, where the human form is revealed as an empty silhouette against the blue sky and clouds. Nietzsche abandoned metaphysics, whereas Schopenhauer still attributed value to it:

> By metaphysics I understand all knowledge that pretends to transcend the possibility of experience, thus to transcend nature or the given phenomenal appearance of things, in order to give an explanation of that by which is conditioned, or, to speak in popular language, of that which is behind nature.[24]

His view of *two kinds* of metaphysics is worthy of note: namely, one would find its evidence in itself, the other outside itself: the first would constitute the object of authentic philosophy. The second is instead for those 'who are not capable of thinking, but only of believing'.[25]

He also defined the latter as a "metaphysics for the people", a statement later echoed by Nietzsche, for whom Christianity is "Platonism for the people".

In spite of the fact that he still attributes some value to metaphysics as such, Schopenhauer's analysis of religion is thorough and sharp.

> Religions have an allegorical nature but have vested interest in not recognizing it: . . . the only stumbling stone is this, that religions never dare to confess their allegorical nature, but have to assert that they are true *sensu proprio*.[26]

Christianity's achievement consisted in bringing together these two kinds of metaphysics thus producing the "strange hermaphrodite", the "centaur", the so-called *philosophy of religion*.

An important difference with Nietzsche is that Schopenhauer attempted the impossible: giving an empirical basis to metaphysics, of what he saw as "correct explanation of experience as a whole". For him, metaphysics do not rest in concepts and ideas as mathematics and logic do. What Nietzsche did inherit from him is the disdain and contempt for joining in the fashionable philosophical discussion of his contemporaries, an activity Schopenhauer likened to "taking part in a scuffle with the mob in the streets".[27]

14   *Long Legged Grasshoppers*

The Greeks had a word for inauthentic philosophers: *Sophists*. Plato himself describes them as an example of the inconsistency between philosophy and breadwinning. The word "sophistry" means to this day laboriousness, lack of imagination, a clever but ultimately vacuous logic. It is precisely the *weed* of sophism, grown across the centuries alongside the flower of philosophy, which has given philosophy a bad name.

And if sophism is weed, philosophy is a wild plant, growing on precipices, thriving in free mountain air. It will wither away through artificial cultivation. "Those who represent philosophy in ordinary life" – writes Schopenhauer – "do so in much the same way as an actor represents a king." In another occasion, he quotes Goethe to illustrate the difference. Academic philosophy cannot but act like a long legged grasshopper:

A long legged grasshopper appears to be
That springing flies, and flying springs;
And in the grass the same old ditty sings.[28]

His attack on Hegel and the Sophists of his time is merciless: he calls
their philosophy "subsidized petticoat-philosophy", full of "hollow
word-structures". He explicitly refers to Hegelian dialectics as "absolute
nonsense." For him, one thing is to make a living, and quite another to
devote oneself to truth.

15 *Forget Them Both*

Nietzsche's vision of intellectual and artistic integrity requires nothing less
than a vanishing act, the disappearance of the I who writes, thinks and
creates.

He criticizes Wagner for he sees in him a *bad actor*, one who resorts
to seduction, overblown emotions, hypnotic trance and persuasion, the
whole gamut of affected histrionics. A good actor, on the other hand,
would need to relinquish his own self in order to allow the character to
emerge through the empty simulacrum.

In attacking Wagner, Nietzsche moves swiftly away from his musical
foundations, which were essentially Romantic, and towards a defence of
formal, autonomous art. [29]

Too much emphasis on the *individual* and *individuality* results sooner
or later in unproductive chaos, and the consequent need of seeking solace
within the familiar terrain of established dogmas. This is how we can
appreciate Wagner's later passive adherence to Christianity and his depen-
dence his own private understanding of Schopenhauer's philosophy.

Perhaps a heightened sense of individuality is a necessary requisite to
all investigation, married to a desire to move away from established ideas
and beliefs. Perhaps the first contact with Zen practice and teachings is
always tinged with Romantic, individualistic longings. Later, as studying
the self gradually turns into forgetting the self, as subjectivity – and later
objectivity – is forgotten, what shine through are practice itself, the
lineage, the teachings, and what the ancient Chinese called "the ten thousand things".

Both in Nietzsche and in Zen we find at first relinquishment of the
actor, of the self, and later relinquishment of the content: art, truth,
philosophy, knowledge, in Nietzsche's case; the Dharma itself, in the case
of Zen.

16   *Lost in Translation*

An authentic philosopher and a Zen Master are both legislators, innovators: they upset the scale of values, they create new values.

Much of what has been inherited in Japanese Zen practice has been single-handedly been created by Dogen, Hakuin, and other great innovators.

The same applies to modern, western Zen, with the first two generations of Zen Masters and teachers who are creatively applying and combining the teachings of the Dharma with elements of depth psychology, the arts, and active work in their communities.

The creation of the new is not some act of bombastic prophecy. In great individuals this is often paired to humility and subtle irony. It is tragic that so much of Nietzsche's exquisite irony is lost in translation. It is nearly impossible to reproduce his puns, his highly refined way with words.

There is another reason why a court-poet and an academic cannot be philosophers: they lack the essential requirements of solitude.

Only in solitude one becomes what one is. Hindrances to become oneself are fear, laziness, and above all, *the interiorized thinking of the mob.*

Individuality is born in aloneness. There the gifts or art and philosophy are being nurtured, and later bestowed on humanity. A philosopher needs the "essential solitude". He is neither isolated and antisocial, nor does he go around backslapping. He simply cannot retain his intellectual integrity and work for the State at the same time.

17   *Professor Polonius and the Rhododendron*

Philosophy is not a profession but, in Schopenhauer's words, "a free investigation of truth". It is like a wild plant, a rhododendron. Not wholly dissimilar, then, from the enquiry carried out in Zen practice. And even that monosyllabic, monolithic, monistic truth that the apprentice philosopher and the student of Zen is supposed to search for, might no longer (once the journey of investigation and discovery is under way), look so solid and cohesive.

It might reveal hues and nuances, appearances and dream-like, deceptive features that will set one in search of truths, in the plural, each taken *cum grano salis*.

As it is, philosophy cleverly articulates the dictates of the current, established belief-system. It does so by using the ancient art of sophistry: a cunning argument of words leading one to the no-man's land of obscurity. Lost in that arid wilderness, one is bound to reach for the first hurdy-gurdy formulas at hand, and so rely on the populist, pedantic wisdom of Polonius.

In his essay *On Philosophy at the Universities* Schopenhauer wrote:

> Their real concern is to earn with credit an honest livelihood for themselves and also for their wives and children, and moreover enjoy a certain prestige in the eyes of the public. On the other hand, the deeply stirred mind of the real philosopher, whose whole concern is to look for the key to our existence, as mysterious as it is precarious, is regarded by them as something mythological, if indeed the man so afflicted does not even appear to them to be obsessed by monomania, should he ever be met with among them.[30]

18 Roots & Wings

Studying the *roots* of Nietzsche's philosophy – the streams, rivers, and currents of ancestry that eventually gave birth to his own thought – is a riveting process for it gives us insights into the very roots of western thought, at least of a particular mode of western thought, of those who Nietzsche liked to identify as *free spirits*.

It is a thought poised on the tightrope, precariously incarnating at the same time the zenith *and* the breakdown of western thought.

. . .

In Heraclitus we find the first of Nietzsche's ancestors. Very little is known about his life, other than the fact that he was born at Ephesus, on the coast of Asia Minor north of Miletus, around the 500 BC. What matters to us here is that he is a non-dual thinker, unifying the life principle and the death principle, Dionysus and Hades.

In his often bewildering, incredibly subtle fragments, we find a depth of understanding encompassing both philosophy and psychology. He has been seen by many as *the first psychologist*.

Heraclitus looked deeply into life. Like many before and after him, he experienced it as *impermanence, becoming, and multiplicity*. What is truly remarkable about him is that he did not consider the world of imperma-

nence and becoming as illusion, as *mere* appearance. He did not chastize it. He saw no need for expiation, he envisaged no blameworthiness whatsoever in existence. Secondly, he did not fathom a better reality, a "more real", permanent, imperishable reality. There is no heaven, no *nirvana* apart from *samsara*, no eternity beyond the ephemeral. Thirdly, and most crucially, his complete affirmation of *what is* (or rather what unceasingly *becomes*) leads us *not* into a simple negation of transcendence, but instead to the very edge of an unfathomable abyss.

He affirms immanence so thoroughly that it becomes in itself a form of transcendence; a claim not dissimilar from the one commonly attributed to Zen. Heraclitus negates being altogether, while simultaneously affirming being as the *being of becoming*. Unusually for a key western thinker, in one of his fragments he acknowledges Dionysus and Hades, Love and Death as being *one* God, not two; as two aspects, we would say nowadays, of the same energy. Heraclitus, named "the obscure", is by far the most important philosopher of ancient Greece. A careful re-reading and reassesment of his thought will restore basic sanity, playfulness and depth to western thought, and will help removing it away from the hazards of dualistic thinking.

In Heraclitus, *chance and necessity are not antagonistic*. Time is a child who plays at draughts. What does a bad player do? He counts on several throws of the dice; he resorts to probability and causality in order to produce a desired number sequence. He does away with chance – a key element of both poetry and enchantment; he expects a *result*, for he fears necessity and chance. The *spirit of revenge* animates him; resentment, bad conscience, and an overriding desire to win at any cost are the result.

> But, in this way, all that will ever be obtained are more or less probable relative numbers. That the universe has no purpose, that it has no end to hope for any more than it causes to be known – this is the certainty necessary to play well.[31]

Nietzsche, following Heraclitus' example, replaces finality, probability and causality – and their grim implications – with the Dionysian relationship of chance/necessity. Some may object that this would mean reinstating pre-Socratic theories on fate and necessity, but in fact, with the sole exception of Heraclitus, the philosophy of old had *not* perceived, in Nietzsche's words, the presence of the law in becoming and of play in necessity, nor has that lesson been learned in the tradition of the West.[32]

At times Heraclitus' thought reminds one of the Upanishads; at times the similarities with Zen wisdom are baffling. Zen famously urges us "not to seek for the truth", but simply "to stop cherishing opinions". Heraclitus states:

> Human opinions are toys for children.[33]

He has more in common with early Indian mystics or with a 17th century heretic thinker such as Spinoza, than with any of his contemporaries. He is particularly sharp on fake teachers and purveyors of mumbo-jumbo; no doubt he would have had a fun-time in this day and age. "Pythagoras was the prince of imposters", he writes in fragment XXVI. Like many self-styled gurus and wise men of today, he had even founded a school! Another fragment sees him delightfully reiterate:

Justice will catch up with those who invent lies and those who swear to them.[34]

The realized man, Zen reminds us, does not ignore the law of causation. For Heraclitus, there is only one sin, and that is the sin of *hubris*, the human conceit and the desire to challenge the Gods and even Fate. But it is not possible to transgress one's limitations. Not even the sun can do that.

The sun will not transgress his measures. If he does, the Furies, ministers of Justice, will find him out.[35]

We find no trace in Heraclitus of the Platonic opposition between mind and matter, soul and body, nor anything that might later evolve into the Cartesian aberration, the *cogito ergo sum* on which mainstream western thought – and the existential misery of the West – is largely based.

From Montaigne (1533–1592), another of Nietzsche's ancestors, we learn to appreciate breezy, quintessentially European scepticism, through his unique ability of marrying doubt to faith and to profound life-affirmation.

Montaigne was also the first accomplished chronicler of the psychological life. The "art of talking to oneself", Virginia Woolf wrote, of

following one's own vagaries, giving the whole map, weight, colour, and circumference of the soul in its confusion, its variety, its imperfection . . . belonged to one man only: to Montaigne.[36]

Nietzsche loved in him the daring and light-hearted scepticism, a quality, he remarked, already possible at the times of that other – highly disappointing – thinker, Luther, who had instead squandered his talent and his intelligence by dealing with theological and political conundrums of lesser importance.

Montaigne is the European Master of Doubt. And doubt must be thorough if one is to see through it; doubt is essential in Zen practice, and it is indeed unusual to find doubt valued in a positive light in any spiritual path, for it is all too easy for critical enquiry to lapse into cynicism. It has happened countless times, and it constitutes a great part of that branch of western thought that, having succeeded in freeing itself from the prison of religious dogmas and the narrowness of the ethical imperative, has then fallen prey to *passive nihilism*, to the *bitterness* of cynicism.

The antidote to cynicism is the cultivation of sincere and profound existential doubt paired with serenity and courage. In Montaigne we find one of the highest expressions of such antidote. Montaigne is one of Nietzsche's elective affinities in his blood lineage, a lineage that, not unlike the Zen tradition, does not depend on genes but is instead a distillation of culture and life practice, which ensures the continuation of this wayward and worthy tradition.

Whether linking up with these illustrious souls through complicity or opposition, they constitute a human pantheon with which Nietzsche actively engages from the height of his solitude.

> I too have been in the underworld, like Odysseus, and shall be there even more; and I have not only sacrificed rams to be able to talk to some of the dead, but have not spared my own blood as well. Four pairs have not refused themselves to me: Epicurus and Montaigne, Goethe and Spinoza, Plato and Rousseau, Pascal and Schopenhauer. I have had to engage these figures in the course of my long, solitary wanderings . . . Whatever I say, resolve, and think through for myself and others, I look to these eight and see their eyes likewise fixed on me.[37]

Ralph Waldo Emerson's profound reflections on the subject of *fate* – his is the coinage of the expression "beautiful necessity" – originates in Heraclitus. In fragment CXIV we read:

> Man's character is his fate.[38]

Fate here is also *daemon*, a subject on which James Hillman has written wonderfully, especially in *The Soul's Code*. Far from being shrouded in fatalism, Emerson's views on fate, a direct development of Heraclitean ideas, affirms an *unconditional appreciation of chance*:

> In a large city, the most casual things, and things whose beauty lies in their casuality, are produced as punctually and to order as the baker's muffing and breakfast.[39]

The emphasis is not on the "objective" power of fate, perceived as solid and overwhelming, but on the person's response and interpretation of events.

> I cited the instinctive and heroic races as proud believers in Destiny. They conspire with it; a loving resignation is with the event.

> But the dogma makes a different impression when it is held by the weak and lazy. It is weak and vicious people who cast the blame on Fate.[40]

A necessary freedom responds to events, *conspires*, i.e. *breaths in unison* with them. That is not blind acceptance or mere resignation, but "fatal courage"

> If the Universe has these savage accidents, our atoms are as savage in resistance.[41]

We also find in Emerson a definition of what he calls *the great man*, a not so distant relation of Nietzsche's overman, of Zen's true person of no rank:

> So the great man, that is the man most imbued with the spirit of the time, is the impressionable man; – of a fiber irritable and delicate, like iodine to light. He feels the infinitesimal attractions. His mind is righter than others because he yields to a current so feeble as can be felt only by a needle delicately poised.[42]

19   *Of the Omnipotence of Dead Poets*

The benevolence and fastidious pseudo-wisdom of the well-paid, well-fed academics is suspicious. Antonin Artaud was a master in detecting in a piece of writing the workings of a satisfied stomach and in telling them apart from the unquenchable quest for truth and beauty at the heart of a true artist's work.

One would love to confidently say that the artist/philosopher needs *not* be an outcast, but the example of the last two centuries indicates the opposite. All great artists and philosophers have been tragic figures, for they had to shape their individuality and follow their calling against institutionalized mediocrity. What the State requires of them collides with what the individual has discovered.

Hölderlin, the embodiment of a true "ancient" Greek, was cast away from the refined Classicism and Hellenism of Weimar: a response from Schiller could have saved the poet's life. When Hölderlin sent a pressing call for help to Schiller before his fatal journey to Bordeaux, the latter ignored it.

> Such was Weimar's classicism: not being able to recognize a Greek in flesh and bones.[43]

It is easier to deal with a disembodied spirit than it is with one in the flesh.

Everything is permitted to a dead poet, but almost nothing to one who is alive.

20 *Beyond Romanticism*

The individual-versus-the-State controversy belongs to a Romantic constellation, and suffers from Romantic drawbacks: inspiring, tremendously adventurous (there would be no sense of the *individual* at all without the legacy of Romanticism), but still dualistic.

It is time we moved beyond the Romantic predicament, for truly there is no 'evil' out there against whom the individual must engage in combat. The effort must be instead directed at clarifying the riddle of one's own life and offer the results as testimonial to those who have not yet ventured to similarly uncharted seas, but, spurred by the example, might do so one day.

In Zen Buddhism too the antagonism is never solved; one simply moves *beyond* it. Historically, Buddhism has shown an inclination to endorse oppressive regimes and to support the status quo. But as a spiritual search, the individual who embarks onto the Zen path cannot engage in the practice without relinquishing the false consolations offered by society and the State. He retreats, goes alone in the wilderness to see for himself if there is any truth in the teachings of the Buddha. Ultimately, the State is made up of individuals; hardening one's position into stern antagonism is to fall prey to the romantic fallacy. Integrity might at first prompt one to leave aside the false protection of the herd, to refuse its rewards and consolations. But out of the same integrity, the next step is to recognize the imperfection of human, all-too-human institutions. The ox has been found, and the seeker goes back to the market place. Shakyamuni descends from the mountain, and so does Zarathustra.

21 *Apocalypse after Lunch*

To dwell permanently in splendid isolation is to repeat the mistake of the ascetic, of the tortured artist, of the otherworldly philosopher. All three are caricatures of the noble (yet ultimately flawed) triad of Zarathustra's "higher men": the saint, the artist, and the philosopher. Is there truly a difference between the two triads? The first is otherworldly, and each of the characters expresses contempt for humanity. The second triad is more closely interwoven with common humanity. Let us give it a closer look.

In the otherworldly triad we find first of all the ascetic, who kills the passions and disowns the emotions, amputating humanity from his very being. His exact counterpart is the libertine, who kills both passions and emotions by overindulging them.

Next, we find the "tortured" or Romantic artist, who looks down on the humdrum of necessity and the dreary business of having to earn a living. Life in this case is being perceived merely as leeway to achieve a handful of peak experiences, the aesthetic substitute for heaven and nirvana.

The third in the otherworldly triad is the cynic philosopher. Schopenhauer is back in fashion among contemporary pessimists. No matter how thoroughly and lovingly demolished by Nietzsche, his curmudgeonly stance has been adopted both by intelligent poets and thinkers in the past (Leopardi) and by less gifted latter-day cynics. The otherworldly philosopher is essentially a cynic and his outlook is based on a gross misapprehension of the wisdom of old. According to this interpretation, the world is nothing but illusion, but such a view betrays ingratitude.

22 *Ordinary People*

The noble triad is a refined version of Zarathustra's higher humanity, people who have momentarily come to rest in what Zen calls "ordinary mind". Here we find the saint, or wise person: one who has fully acknowledged both passions and emotions, has experienced them deeply, and has transmuted them. Unlike the ascetics, the truly wise operate quietly and almost undercover. Their spiritual strength is such that they do not crave the applause of the masses. They do not operate *within master/slave dynamics*. Their entire life is a work of art, a phenomenon of frayed beauty, a creative manifestation of *silence*. Language as such is an expression of the dualistic master/servant opposition: by definition, *the master speaks*, and *the servant hears*. Speech is here synonymous with authority. The servant can *only* hear, and his silence is seemingly powerless. However, precisely within this destitution, the potential for true mastery is found. Out of this silence and stillness come right action and right speech, and all of the eight awarenesses of the Buddha: we have moved out of the Hegelian correlation of mastership and servitude.

If expressed through the medium of Art, true mastery will communicate through a new language, a language of naked association; a difficult task, but potentially assisted by the hints provided by poetry and the poetic experience.

Here the poet, or the artist, is no longer a magician, a seducer, nor a "spiritual teacher". His art is no longer expression of malaise or of desublimation, but instead of overflowing health and strength. There is an art that belongs to the realm of the setting sun, according to the inspired vision of Chögyam Trungpa, and an art that belongs to the realm of the rising sun. In Nietzsche, "psychologist and physician" these are translated as *health* and *sickness*. The healthy artist, whose vision is of the rising sun variety, creates out of overflowing generosity and well-being. He has no time to pause and take the measurements of his godlike stature, nor of the distance that separates him from the "common people". This goes against the leading perspective – from the Renaissance to Romanticism – which sees the artist as a highly subjective genius, and his art as a thouroughly subjective affair. Instead, art and creativity filters through *in spite* of the limitation of the subjective self, often through the suggestive discourse of a *daemon*.

The philosopher of our noble triad is first of all a *creator*, not a systematizer. He *creates* new values. His style is *artistic*, it possesses the light-footedness of an accomplished dancer, the *adagios* and *crescendos* of a adventurous composer, the illuminations of un-constructed poetry. He is also a scientist, in the sense that Nietzsche gives to the word: less high priest of a new belief system than an *experimenter*, an advocate of verifiable hypotheses, of psychological insights to be tested, not to be taken as truths.

23 *In Praise of Irresponsibility*

The birth of dialectical reasoning marked in ancient Greece the end of tragedy, the conclusion of what had been a far-reaching experience encompassing both *aesthetics* and what is nowadays understood as *spirituality*. Socratic and dialectical reasoning made its entrance on the stage of the western world taking the place of tragedy. Its arrival was *timely*, for it reflected the need to impose cool *ratio* on the instincts and passions of a culture run amok. Its appearance, however, was anticlimactic, and the effect *toxic*.

Hegel did the same for the modern world: he created modern dialectic, which represents the exact *opposite* of tragic joy. He translated into a philosophical system the weapons of Judaeo-Christian thinking aimed at the *prevention* of tragic joy.

These weapons are essentially three: *resentment* ("it's your fault"); *bad conscience* ("it's my fault"); and their bitter fruit, the twisted idea of *responsibility*; twisted because it is not understood as "ability to respond" but instead as an imposition nurtured by the *spirit of revenge*. Such spirit of revenge is a powerful anesthetic used by the sufferer to numb the pain and misery of existence.

> According to my hypothesis, it is here alone, in a desire to *anaesthetize pain through feeling* that the real physiological cause of *ressentiment*, of revenge and related matters, is to be found.[44]

It is time to reassess *irresponsibility*; its synonyms include meanings describing not entirely undesirable traits: waywardness, giddiness, gaiety, and uncertainty. It is time we gave irresponsibility its *positive* sense; its lightheartedness might be of help and inspiration. We might be led into a place blessed with the absence of praise and blame, of punishment and reward. These dualistic ideas go a long way back: it was the ancient Greek philosopher Anaximander who said "Beings must pay penance and be judged for their injustices, in accordance with the ordinance of time". Against this mode of thinking, which is both miserly and miserable, Nietzsche opposes that wealth of incomparable wisdom and magnificent sense of wonder that is the philosophy of Heraclitus.

24 The Trouble with Reason

Impulses need to be employed, not enfeebled or extinguished. Reason plays an important role here, but solely as a tool of self-mastery and self-overcoming.

Reason has become a *despot* in the contemporary psyche, ceaselessly constructing universal abstracts, devising systems; for psychic health to be restored, its deployment must be urgently curtailed.

A system is by definition a fossil; it is a faint echo of what used to be vibrant thought emerging in the midst of debate, inspiration, and contradiction. Reasoning itself is firstly the shared discourse of inner experience. Its tempo and tonalities are sinuous, verbal, subject to changes of speed and intensity – an all too human response to the unfolding of phenomena within becoming.

In a subsequent stage, reasoning gives birth to rhetoric, its tempo fixated by the calculated effect of the consummate performer. Here "discourse" is already deceased, and what matters is no longer our human response to the unpredictability of becoming, but instead validation and reification of the human construct, of the net of customary ideas, a prelude to written discourse, what we commonly call "philosophy". At this stage, we still hear an echo of what used to be alive discourse. But it is already fading fast. Our common idea of philosophy is not unlike a pale dream of life within the cells of a fresh corpse. When even the last vestige of the dream is gone, a philosophical system is born.

Every system is a *simulacrum*, an altar deserted by the deity a long time before. Every system is a blatant *lie*. The painted object cannot be the object itself, but only a pale surrogate. Reason is lost, and with it philosophical discourse. The fruit of the tree of knowledge has died out, no human can benefit from it. We are left with a dead trunk in a museum. But the dead trunk is adorned, praised, and even worshipped, for many careers depend on it.

25 Artists & Professors

The professorial mistrust of creative thinkers is a common feature throughout History, and bears many similarities with the suspicion that priests of all religions have felt toward innovative, inspired individuals in their midst.

Priests and academics largely rely on fossilized dogmas and dead knowledge- that is not to say that priests and academics are uninspired archivists. Any institution must nevertheless rely on some illusion of solidity, respectability, and self-importance in order to survive. In some rare occasions the priest and the inspired thinker co-habit in the same person, but sooner or later one surrenders to the other.

There are stages in the development of an individual, and ways in which one's destiny and vocation can be creatively fulfilled. It might well be that, for some, curbing the individualistic instinct and placing themselves at the service of an institution coincides with the need, particularly in late youth, of a *fiery initiation*, a toning down of one's ego and of its ambition in favour of the community, a way of sacrificing grandiosity. It is also true that any fiery initiation, particularly of a young male, can later acquiesce in placid, stagnant conformity, often followed in middle age by one form or other of a *watery initiation*, where the individual's beliefs, his seeming solidity is shattered by depression and dark nights of the soul.

What is truly surprising is the ambivalent attitude of academia towards the danger represented by a creative thinker. The fear of being isolated by one's community, of being cast out as an outsider, a mad person, a heretic, is a very tangible and painful feeling. Craving recognition, honors, and public appraisal is the disguised form of the same fear, and it motivates some of the best minds. We have already discussed the example of Goethe, who endorsed Hegel and his vacuous philosophizing not out of any respect of Hegelism, but because it was the ruling ideology in Germany at the time. And we have seen how he failed to acknowledge Schopenhauer, chiefly because of his anti-institutional stance.

Another example is that of Jung, whose utter failure in understanding Nietzsche was unconsciously motivated by his need to distance himself from an outcast, and from the fear of being considered one himself.

Jung could not acknowledge his debt to Nietzsche. He attributed to Nietzsche *cryptomnesia*, whereby something one has read is forgotten, and later on resurfaces in one's own text as one's own words.[45] The strange thing is that precisely this very same phenomenon appears in Jung. He fails to recognize that, with regard to the acknowledgment of *autonomous personal agencies* within the psyche, Nietzsche's ideas *anticipate* his own, and it is on this point that he sees Nietzsche's worst failings. He simply cannot believe that anyone would arrive at fresh psychological insights at a time when psychology as such had not been born. 1883 (the year Nietzsche composed Zarathustra) was the time of the blooming of materialistic philosophy, so how could Nietzsche be aware of the fact that, for instance, Zarathustra was another identity, a mask, a personified voice, and that in fact all other characters appearing in *Thus Spoke Zarathustra* were different identities?

What made Jung's work notable was *personification*, his acknowledgment of other aspects of the psyche besides the "I". And it is precisely personification one of Nietzsche's great contributions, in its seed form, to depth psychology.

Jung did not see the distance in Zarathustra between the voice of the author and all other voices, particularly that of Zarathustra himself, nor the fact that Nietzsche had gone way past the Greeks in its understanding of the 'I' as *restrictive fiction*. Jung regretted the fact that Nietzsche did not know much about eastern thought. This is not only untrue, for Nietzsche knew of Indian Buddhism, but in a sense he had arrived, in terms of the 'I', at similar conclusions *by himself*. "It would be hard to think of anyone – writes Graham Parkes – who accomplishes a more deft critique of just how 'limited' and 'mistaken' [a] concept the 'I' really is".[46]

26   *You are the Night, Lailah*

In offering a critique of reason, I am not advocating irrationality, for its employment would be inadequate and its flight short-lived. Theorists of

Homo Ludens, and of life as *lila*, the cosmic play, are in the same dualistic boat as rationalists: they idealize play as a salvation as escape route from their own narrow notion of work.

What is hinted here is instead *not-knowing*, not mere irrationality. Meeting likeness with likeness: approaching the unknown, we go *unknowing*. To enter the night, we do not bring a light. Having left no stone unturned, we go back to square one. We roam happily; we go where our feet take us. Ours is a wayward pilgrimage in the words of Nigel Armistead.

In case 20, Dizang's "Nearness" of the Book of Serenity we read:

> Dizang asked Fayan: "Where are you going?"
> Fayan said, "Around on pilgrimage."
> Dizang said, "What is the purpose of pilgrimage?"
> Fayan said, "I don't know."
> Dizang said, "Not knowing is nearest."[47]

Not-knowing is not the unknowing of the plain *ignoramus*. It is knowledge *before and beyond* knowledge.

27 Is Jack a Dull Boy?

Even when he plays, there is desperation in his frolicking, that same proficient drudgery one finds in all his actions. Outside the prison cell of dualism, work and play are one and the same. Work becomes a meaningful activity encompassing the joy of play; it becomes an instinct, an instinctual gratification, not just the 'right to work', or work as an economic necessity or a social duty or a moral penance lay onto Adam after leaving Paradise.

Philosophers at the heart of Protestantism inflated and glamorized play to metaphysical proportions, seeing it as diametrically opposed, and incompatible to, the realm of work. *In a realm devoid of being*, human activity is unified, *work and play become one.*

28 Nutcracker

The anti-intellectualism of the second half of the 20th century has idealized instincts and feelings, looked down on philosophy, and favored primal screams and grunts over articulate expression and verbalization. In dismissing thought as superficial, as merely "from the head", it has promoted a lowering of general aptitude and has disheartened autonomous and intelligent critique. For the majority of people, the word "intellectual" is akin to an insult; it is synonymous with isolation, with a person who is out of touch with his feelings, instincts, and physicality; at best, an absent-minded nerd; at worst, a public enemy. The basis for such prejudice goes back to the days before advanced technical development, when thought was not yet submitted to the servile activity of working out obstacles, but was instead tantamount to creative cogitation, deep contemplation, and independent critique. A profound thinker always arose suspicion, for he could find out and reveal those lies which common folk sensed their lives might be built upon.

Autonomy of thought must be restored, if we want to resurrect human dignity and self-worth to its original glory. The task is nearly impossible, since the utilitarian mode of thought is perhaps the only one we know:

> Because thought has by now been perverted into the solving of assigned prob-
> lems, even what is not assigned is processed like a problem. Thought, having lost
> autonomy, no longer trusts itself to comprehend reality, in freedom, for its own
> sake . . . Even where there is no nut to crack, thinking becomes training for no
> matter what exercise. It sees its objects as mere hurdles, a permanent test of its
> own form.[48]

29 The Art of Joyful Thinking

Proper thinking involves the totality of one's being. One can fall in love with one thought and plunge into profound despair because of another. In thinkers like Nietzsche, thought and feeling are not two separate things. Thoughts would come to him during his six or eight hours walks through the Swiss Alps. They would harmonize with the rest of the body while it swiftly, exuberantly treaded the wayward paths above Sils Maria. He warned against thoughts arising in a closed room, while sitting at one's desk. The thought must participate in the physical joy, in the nimble dance of the solitary wanderer. This is not mere "thinking", the passive reaction of an uninspired, uncreative mind limiting itself to digest the environment's stimuli and to translate them self-centeredly into attraction and aversion. Nietzsche's thinking is not very far from *koan* study in Zen. When studying a koan, the Zen student is totally involved, he is one with the *koan*.

30 Perfectly Imperfect

The notion of perfection has to be re-interpreted. According to Robert Aitken, the ten "perfections", or *Paramitas*, of Mahayana Buddhism are "inspirations, not fixed rules. We honor them with our conduct, speech, thought".[49] They clarify Buddhist practice and deepen our understanding. They are not achieved once and for all. "Nobody, least of all the Buddha, can say, 'I have accomplished it'".[47] The ten perfections (generosity, morality, forbearance, zeal, focused meditation, wisdom, skilful means, spiritual power, knowledge) are "no more that milestones and are not any kind of ultimate consummation. Perfection is a process". [50]

31 Gods in the Machine

Self-contradiction is one of the essential requirements of a philosopher. Normally we think of it as either a sign of inconsistency betraying lack of conviction, or as Whitmanesque self-inflation.

In Nietzsche, self-contradiction is first of all a matter of *style*. There is a rich diversity of styles, each of them ascribed to a different mask; a self-contradiction akin to that of dramatists, moralists, and "teller of tales".

It has a lot to do with intellectual honesty: a philosophical system, unified and consistent, is a human artifice, brilliant at times, but less an objective explanation of phenomena and the world than an involuntary biography and an unwitting confession of one's own motives. *A worthy philosophy cannot be systematic.* It cannot be only aphoristic either, for then it would confine itself to a precarious existence among the heavily-scented shelves of the *new age* and self-help industry. Instead, it has to be self-contradictory, as it follows the twists and turns of life itself, and particularly if its chief concern is *becoming*, and does not rely on "categorical imperatives", nor on ideals or on arbitrary, dualistic divisions between permanent and impermanent, mind and body, perfection and imperfection.

The very nature of becoming, of *impermanence*, escapes our desire to express it in formulas. The human intellect, schooled in reason, is not designed to *grasp* becoming. It is trained to validate an idea of substantiality that is nowhere to be found. In his study of Nietzsche, Karl Jaspers reminds us that reason is not only *unnecessary*; it is also *hazardous*, and ultimately *impossible*. It is *unnecessary*:

> The irrationality of a thing is no argument against its existence: rather it is its underlying condition.[51]

It is hazardous:

> If humanity had actually behaved in accordance with its reason, i.e. in accordance with its opinion and its knowledge, it would long since have perished.[52]

And finally, reason is *impossible*, for there is no single all-supporting truth of reason enabling human beings to come to an understanding with each other.

Nietzsche's fierce attack on reason is an onslaught on traditional philosophy itself. It does not, however, defend mere irrationality, as many interpreters have implied. He cautions against this danger, symbolized by Zarathustra's shadow.

The attack on reason and systems in philosophy is an attack on the main foundations on which Western dualistic thought rested for centuries.

It is *seeing through*, in this case seeing through philosophical thinking itself, for whatever can be thought must surely be fictitious.

The thinker most affected by this attack is Descartes, who doubted everything but reason itself. Nietzsche goes beyond. Doubt itself must be doubted. From his standpoint, logic itself is a kind of irrationality.

The creation of a system betrays our need to dominate a "nature" we have come to loathe, because it is unreliable, dangerous, extravagant, fecund, and above all *pluralistic*.

By constructing a logical system, we fancy ourselves as the Gods in the machine. By resorting to an all-rational, ultimately mechanical interpretation of the world and ourselves, we fulfill our modern dream of self-annihilation in a predictable, explainable universe. This is perhaps the modern version of decadence, where human life is perceived as either "social" or "biological", in both cases reduced to replaceable, unessential "units" in a giant machinery.

32 *Philosophy as Temptation*

Nietzsche redefines philosophy, re-instates its claims and its field of operation, snatches it back from the claws of dialectics, rewrites it in *psychological* terms, adding to it for good measure the nuances of biography, the lyrical heights of poetry, the breadth of vision of religion.

His paragraphs and aphorisms, even his invectives, are to be read as *psychological insights to be tested, not as an exposition of the truth*. His philosophy is rooted in Romanticism, in the abysmal and pluralistic vision of great European literature (Goethe, Byron). He related directly and profoundly to those abysses. Although moving way beyond Goethe's politics and Byron's camp melodrama, he remained loyal to his project of contaminating philosophy with sweet, breathtaking life, of injecting an arid discipline with the uncertainties of depth psychology, the rapture of music and dance, the rigour of genealogy.

33 Higher Rebellion

The discovery of life's inherent absence of purpose turns lesser humanity into cynics; but if there is a hint of true greatness in one, that very groundlessness, that potentially despairing state will restore one to *innocence*.

Previous value judgments turn into holy Yea-saying. Resentment and bad conscience turn into joyful complicity with life, destiny, the self, and the world (all identified as indivisible unity). Despair turns into true hopelessness, i.e. absence of hope, a truly enviable state, for it harbours tragic joy, and a boundless freedom.

This "freedom" has little to do with the emotional, psychological, and political platitudes we normally brandish about in its name.

This *freedom is* one with *absolute necessity*, with *Ananke*. It is a form of heroism – divested, however, of Hercules' garments; it is, in Albert Camus' words, "the asceticism of the great man". It is the only true rebellion, leading to authentic honesty – one without motifs.

Camus' interpretation of Nietzsche is very convincing, and it brings to light the suffering of the man: being a proud spirit, Camus says, Nietzsche confused freedom with solitude, and eventually asceticism. Being an "addict of integrity" ("integrity that had become an instinct, a passion"), he headed for a sort of splendid isolation, endured with great courage.

Camus likens Nietzsche to Empedocles, "who threw himself down Etna to find truth in the only place where it exists, namely in the bowels of the earth".[53]

In Nietzsche's case, his invitation is to be "engulfed in the cosmos" so as to "rediscover . . . divinity and become Dionysus himself".[54]

His trajectory is an indication of where authentic rebellion might lead to: namely, *higher discipline*, a discipline that is not imposed from the outside but is the triumph of a more positive drive over internal reactive forces. Its modus is not rooted in *resentment*, the equivocation of all immature rebels, but in *self-overcoming*: it is not directly political, although its repercussions are so; instead, it is a cultural occurrence.

34 No Way Out

Before Schopenhauer, European thought was provincial. He was the first to unlock the Gate of the East, thus opening European philosophy to greater levels of depth and wisdom. Giorgio Colli attributes the fact that Schopenhauer later submitted to rationalism and pessimism, embracing some of the ideas of the Enlightenment, to his attachment to ideas and opinions formed during his youthful years. The same happened to another great thinker and poet, Giacomo Leopardi. He too settled for rationalism and pessimism. Nietzsche moved on to the next step: he showed that *pessimism, when thoroughly embraced, when seen through, leads to greater affirmation of life*. Nietzsche was able to renounce the State and society *and* be joyful. In Schopenhauer, the romantic renunciation of institutions turns into renunciation of life itself – forfeiting enthusiasm, vitality, and generosity.

His stance is one associated in the 19th century with Buddhism itself, and one wonders whether, to some degrees, the general view of the Dharma in the 21st century might still be that of an otherworldly path of renunciation, and whether a few Buddhist groups might be perpetrating that misguided view. Nietzsche denounced the path of renunciation, and Buddhism – the Buddhism he knew of – as *escapism*. Perhaps, it is only with the Mahayana tradition that the world is fully embraced. The bodhisattva does not wish to escape into another dimension, but instead lives and struggles within samsara, for the benefit of all sentient beings.

He is willing to return eternally, whether in heaven or in hell, and continue his work until the last being has crossed over to the other shore.

35 For Art's Sake

It is very distressing that Nietzsche's name has been associated with Nazism and anti-Semitism. His last intelligible words written in a letter to his old friend and colleague Jacob Burckhardt were:

Bismarck and all anti-Semites done away with.[55]

The inaccuracies of interpretation, as well as his sister's sinister manipulations, contributed to Nietzsche's name being attached to the most hideous crimes committed in the 20th century in the name of ideology.

But there are other reasons why Nietzsche's name still conjures up dark associations. One of them is Nietzsche's belief – contrary to the values held dear by modern civilization – that many of the great achievements of the human spirit have taken place in the worst atmosphere of unbridled egoism, cruelty, and violent passions. The Renaissance is the most striking example of this phenomenon, and this was, in a nutshell, his historian friend Burckhardt's idea. Nietzsche made it his own, and later applied it to his interpretation of the Greeks.

The death of God implies the deflation of politics as well as the depreciation of transcendence. This leaves only few realms where human activity can be thought of as fully human. In the place vacated by God, there are only a few things left to do: one is Art, a *transformed aesthetics* that no longer *imitates* reality, but instead *creates* a world anew. From that space not only Art proper is born (poetry, music, painting, etc.), but also religion, psychology, and more of life itself. Aristotle famously attributed great importance to politics and almost none to art. Plato rejected art altogether. Nietzsche gave art a supreme role, at first in tune with the prevailing ideas of the late 18th century, and later he moved beyond those ideas, by no longer subscribing to the sovereignty of the individual, opting instead for his swift disappearance.

On the subject of Art, Veihinger argued that Nietzsche did not read Kant properly, for the latter had supposedly anticipated some of his ideas. It had been in fact A. G. Baumgarten, Kant's teacher, to consider the artist's work, not as a pale *depiction* of the world but instead as a second world that addresses itself to sense and spirit.[56]

36 Redemption from Redeemers

The world needs redemption from redeemers. We are our own saviours, once we understand that our karma is what we are, and consciously choose our life and our destiny. Nietzsche's position is more radical than that of Buddhism: where Buddhism emphasizes *cessation* of suffering, Nietzsche speaks of embracing suffering to the point of *welcoming* it, calling it forth as a balm, a stimulant that might provoke one into existential awakening.

Accepting one's karma implies passive resignation, bending oneself to the winds of fortune, whereas *embracing* means active participation, joining in the unending creation, renewing our connivance with living-and-dying. Mere acceptance of one's destiny betrays a hint of bitterness, an unresolved grudge underneath, and a suppressed complaint.

In embracing my destiny, I am stating that it was my creation, and that I am willing to repeat the past eternally. I am grateful to every past experience, however sad or painful, for it contributed in making me who I am now.

The Nietzschean formula of *amor fati*, love of destiny, can be fully reconciled with the Zen formula *samsara is nirvana*. Zen (shorthand for Buddhism), reinforces Nietzsche's view of transcendence within immanence, of the sacred in the everyday, of eternity within the transient and the ephemeral .

37 Zen as Affirmative Art

Zen is not dissimilar from what Nietzsche calls "affirmative art", for it affirms the necessity of things and makes possible *amor fati*, the full appreciation of karma and destiny.

Reality is represented in affirmative art; no resentment is found there, but instead a profound complicity with life.

Finding ourselves in a universe where nature has thrown away the key, where the code is unknown, we have no other task but to delight in reality's ambiguity. For Zarathustra, Buddha and Jesus still had a mission to accomplish, a task to perform; they had something to do; they did not express true sovereignty. Zarathustra has no concern, no job to do, no mission. He is a dancer, a joker; he has no message, no one to save. No Dharma was ever communicated by any Buddha to any sentient being.

38 Quest for Knowledge as Fetishism

Quest for knowledge and the pretence of knowing anything are forms of prevarication and violation. Let us imagine that "truth" (or "nature") is a woman; we should show more respect, and forfeit the desire for conquest in favour of the privilege of learning the forgotten art of courtship. A woman might have good reasons for not showing us her intimate self, and, who knows, there might be no intimate reality beyond the veils of appearance. Perhaps everything already manifests generously and freely.

The Buddha turns the Dharma wheel and reality is shown in its many forms.

Wanting to know, although perfectly human, is volition motivated by our insecurity and fear. *Desiring solidity* in a bewilderingly rickety world is an understandable human aspiration, but ultimately delusional. And yet western thought, with the exception of Heraclitus, rests on that mirage.

> I shall set apart, with great respect, the name of *Heraclitus*. If the rest of the philosophical populace rejected the evidence of the senses because they showed multiplicity and change, he rejected their evidence because they showed things as if they had duration and unity . . . 'Reason' is what causes us to falsify the evidence of the senses. If the senses show becoming, passing away, change, they do not lie . . . But Heraclitus will always be right that Being is an empty fiction. The 'apparent' world is the only one: the 'real world' has just been *lied on* . . . [57]

It might be possible to be 'superficial' out of profound wisdom . . .

Modesty is needed when we are brought in the presence of truth. Only an inveterate crook would attempt to penetrate its mystery, or blindly assume that "what you see is what you get", for that is precisely *the symptom of the anti-artistic spirit.*

The naturalist/realist view of reality is mechanical, it reinforces the idea of solidity, of "things" existing *outside* the self, and the self too is seen as a *thing* endowed with substance. Nietzsche calls this view, which in our day and age is predominant, *fetishism*. Fetishism is our dogmatic *belief in things*, objects, facts, in a world where phenomena are reduced to *items*. Our language is steeped in coarse, obsolete psychology, the same found at the roots of reason and metaphysics.

Partly, Nietzsche's work has been of painstakingly dismantling the illusion of solidity, in de-constructing the edifice of western knowledge, in revealing its illusory foundations.

Zen does not address the problem of fetishism, nor endeavours to deconstruct unreality. Instead, it constantly points at the natural fluidity and interdependence of existence. The moon was always there, we just didn't notice, since clouds covered it . . . In Zen there is no mention of being behind appearance in the first place. No *other* world is created, no fiction, hence no need to destroy the fiction, or take apart the endless fabrications of the mind.

Some branches of learning take tremendous delight in spinning endless tales. There is no harm in that: it is the very task of theology, metaphysics and bad art. Such human endeavours are inspired by the creativity of the dreamworld, with one major difference. They have a primary motivation: *ressentiment*, a sour feeling of discontent and unease, the inability to feel gratitude for the magnitude of life. Above all, they betray lack of self-mastery. Theology, metaphysics and bad art are inferior to dreams, for these are spontaneous, perfectly edited images of the underworld, a realm that is not necessarily other, but which retains nevertheless ambiguity, mystery, inscrutability. Dreams do not falsify, and more importantly, they do not *devalue* reality. Most religions, when interpreted dogmatically, are, on the other hand, elaborated forms of *devaluation*.

39 *Growing up in Public*

One of the aims of philosophy is to trespass the boundary between philosophy, psychology and the arts. This bites at the heart of the "ideal", eroding it of its imaginary substantiality.

New ideas might just be re-interpreting a wisdom of old, a mode of thought that has become so alien to us, that it now sounds novel to modern sensibilities. Realization of one's true nature is at once ancient, timeless, and at the same time absolutely novel, as in the case of the revelation of the eternal return. Such thought is both distressingly new and to a certain extent ancient, for it resembles the old idea of circular time, and in particular, Heraclitus' celebratory understanding of becoming, his acute perception of the fluid, ever-moving ocean where one thought to have made out an expanse of land . . .

The plenitude of becoming is all there is. It is more than we will ever need, and it is manifesting at every instant.

In Nietzsche's time, the word for courageous critical stance and unbiased investigation was *atheism*, a term of no relevance today – and as innocuous as that other quaint designation, *agnosticism*. "Atheism" in the 19th century, *before* the Marxian credo gained popularity, meant radical dismantling of all ideals, for *every ideal is*, to the Nietzschean sensibility, *a shadow of God*. That *includes* the popular scientific mythologies and beliefs held dear in secular societies.

The point is, are we strong enough to endure living without ideals? Can we create new values out of the space left empty by broken effigies?

A Nietzschean definition of *strength* is the denial of everything that can be denied, except the will to truth. It is from such premises that great philosophy, great art and depth psychology come to light. As it is often the case, *artists* are the first at signing up for adventurous journeys into the unknown and they do so by crossing the boundaries of good and evil;

they create memorable ambiences, landscapes and characters in whom the two are not clearly defined, but who are instead "poised on the tightrope of love" on the "storm-beaten threshold".

Yeats recognized that his "masterful images" were born out of a "mound of refuse or the sweeping of a street". Rilke saw clearly that life metamorphoses into death. Thomas Mann wrote of man as "lord of counter-positions". And in D. H. Lawrence, "wicked people" are people who are not whole, while heroes and heroines are far from being pure for they have gone *beyond* the base impulses of base people.

Our latter-day, fashionable transgressors are in a different bag altogether. Their tiresome tales of desublimation *appear* to be beyond good and evil. The truth is, they are merely "controversial", with their feet firmly planted *on this side* of good and evil. They are the children of Jean-Jacques Rousseau and Augustine: they have a weakness for stripping in front of an audience, for showing how *bad* they are, and how corrupt the world is; their practice re-enacts the time-honoured diversion of doing one's dirty laundry in public.

Having lost God-given certainties, having lost moral values, they think that *value itself* is lost. What they fail to understand is that value is *created*, not given.

It would be a mistake to equate fashionable, superficial cynicism for what I call *active nihilism* in art: the latter is a thorough investigation reaching the depths of anguish and doubt and, in doing so, it inevitably reaches the "other shore" of affirmative values: it *creates* values.

There is no "glossing over" in active nihilism, nor is there self-indulgent wallowing in the mud of dualistic gloom. Why is a great work of art immediately recognizable? Because it makes the world "justifiable as an aesthetic phenomenon".

There is so much radiance in Renaissance art, a time, for both Nietzsche and Yeats, of unification of battling elements, blending coarse matter and exemplary form, giving birth, both literally and symbolically, to *polyphony*. A manifestation of Heraclitean hypotheses became manifest: *enantiodromia*, the inherent unity of elements we had perceived as opposites. This is what we mean by aristocracy. It is an aristocracy of the spirit, born out of a dignified victory over the magnificent monsters.

Cancel out iniquity, and the quality of a work of art is bland. Repress the passions, and you have a feeble individual. The "inner" life must be fertilized. The attainment is non-attainment: the regal meandering of a nobody going nowhere.

42

40 The Ape, the Priest, the Dialectician and his Lover

Contemporary culture is yet to encounter Nietzsche's Zarathustra fully; so far, it has only been acquainted with an ape, a buffoon undeservedly bearing his name. The same applies to Zen: in the West, unless we whole-heartedly commit to practice, we come to know a mere surrogate.

In Nietzsche's case, later philosophical trends (phenomenology, exis-tentialism, de-constructionism, to name but a few) made use of his insights, and unwittingly succeeded in *weaving the Nietzschean corpus into the fabric of contemporary conformity*. In the case of Zen and Buddhism in general, its existential edge has been smoothed out and replaced by either a generic "anything-goes-Zen" or by a placid, conser-vative, anaesthetized approach to living-and-dying.

Gilles Deleuze is right in asserting that one of Nietzsche's – and of philosophy in general – paramount activities is that of *critique*, and that it is a grave mistake to confuse critique with mere *grudge* and *resentment*.

> Critique is not a re-action of *re-sentiment* but the active expression of an active mode of existence; attack and not revenge, the natural aggression of a way of being, the divine wickedness without which perfection could not be imagined . . . This way of being is that of the philosopher precisely because he intends to wield the differential element as critic and creator and therefore as a hammer.[58]

This way of being is pluralistic, polytheistic, multifaceted; an authentic philosopher cannot settle with the absolutist idea of *one* God, *one* truth, *one* aspect of the mind: it embraces *many* Gods, *many* truths, *many* voices within the *infinity* of the psyche.

> Is not precisely this, godliness, that there are Gods but no God?[59]

Mainstream western philosophy, from Plato through Hegel, has always derided pluralism. Hegel compared it to a child stuttering his needs, unsure of what they might be. He thought of pluralism as an unde-veloped form of philosophy, when it is instead the zenith of critical thought, its central achievement. A true philosopher is a rare phenom-enon, and when that rare phenomenon manifests, it is often in disguise. The philosopher wears a mask, has to play tricks in order to avoid being poisoned, crucified, vilified and ridiculed. *Wearing a mask here does not mean forgery, fabrication, or sophistry, but instead using skilful means in order to outlive dangers.* This attitude is learnt from life itself; an example of life imitating matter *in order to survive*.

A force would not survive if it did not first of all borrow the feature of the forces with which it struggles.[60]

Thus in the distant past philosophers have worn the mask of contemplative priests, of religious men. Those who did not were unceremoniously burned as heretics. Nowadays, some philosophers (and psychologists too) hide behind the mask of the scientist, for fear of being accused of non-alignment with the dominant superstition of our secular age, whereas others happily hand over any residue of credibility and common sense to the unbridled, best-selling idiocies of the new-age. "They inveigh against materialism," Adorno said of occultists – But they want to weigh the astral body." "They supply simpletons with a world outlook."[61] Such charges could easily apply to contemporary, suburban spiritualists and shamans who earn a good living by selling a smart new version of that old and stinky pea-soup: the all-encompassing, universally synthesized *philosophia perennis*, and this at a time when we crucially need to emphasize pluralism, diversity, critique. But everything has its place under the sun, and these people provide an invaluable system of what Adorno called "metaphysics for dunces".[62]

That other, thouroghly post-modern, folly has also been entusiastically embraced by some pseudo-philosophers in need to fatten their bank balance: thus the abomination of *popular philosophy* was born. No wonder philosophers *have* to wear a mask. No wonder they must often retreat from the bright lights . . .

> A philosopher may be identified by the fact that he avoids three glittering and noisy things – fame, princes, and women – which is not to say they may not come to him. He shies away from light which is all too bright: for that reason he shies away from his time and its 'daylight'. In his day, he is like a shadow: the deeper the sun sinks the greater he becomes. As far as his 'humility' is concerned, he endures a certain dependence and obscurity, just as he endures the darkness: even more, he is afraid of being disturbed by lightning, he recoils in fright from the exposure of an all-tooo isolated and abandoned tree, its vulnerability to every moody storm and every stormy mood.[63]

A philosopher thus protects himself by wearing a mask until the end. His *radical critique of existing values* is too harsh, too jarring for our modern ears, lulled as we are to self-pleasing, soporific delusions, schooled in the ways of innocuous designer controversy.

The truth of impermanence and suffering expounded by the Buddha tastes bitter, and it's a hard pill to swallow. The full implications of *sunyata* (emptiness, or relativity) are *terrifying*: groundlessness and utter meaninglessness for eternity. Nothing is more unsettling, more baffling, more despairing.

In a sense, Zen Buddhism too wears a mask: it speaks of liberation and of the end of suffering. It engages its adepts into a pointless and wondrous adventure of self-discovery, all the while mischeviously eroding the life of that very self, by uncovering its intrinsic unsubstantiality, its lack of "true" existence.

To expect that a philosopher, or a buddha, manifests without a mask – or according to our expectations of what a philosopher or a buddha should look like – is to underestimate the magnitude of that universal denial of wisdom, intelligence and compassion that bears the name of "waking life". Nietzsche is at least more lenient, graciously allowing for the benefit of (mischevious) doubt:

> To express this clearly in concrete terms: until very recently the ascetic priest has assumed the dark, repulsive form of a caterpillar, the only form in which philosophy was allowed to live, creeping around . . . Has this really *changed?*[64]

4 | *Philosophy as the Language of Plurality*

Philosophy needs to be re-visioned as *critique*. It might, or it might not, use logic as one of its tools, but the inherent purity of its enquiry (always untimely, always in creative frisson and contradiction with the status quo) goes *beyond logic and the illogical*.

Critique must not be confused with reactive grudge, *ressentiment*, nor with any of the thousand disguises of the dialectic spirit of revenge. Its motivations do not reside with the Hegelian and Marxian compulsively antithetical messianism, but it serves instead a far nobler Muse: *integrity*.

In order to function in the world, through the centuries philosophers disguised themselves as scientists, priests, astrologers, logicians, or as professors. And the world has identified them with the mask: so much so that philosophers themselves have associated themselves with the role. When that occurred, priests, logicians and professors – the entire regiment of philosophy labourers – came to be regarded as philosophers.

A true philosopher is both a critic and a creator. His thinking is too profound to get caught up in monistic understanding: the way of the philosopher is *pluralistic*. In the words of Gilles Deleuze,

> There is no event, no phenomenon, word or thought which does not have a multiple sense. A thing is sometimes this, sometimes that, sometimes more complicated – depending on the forces (the Gods) which take possession of it.[65]

It is a mistake to see pluralism as dialectical. Polarities belong to the dualistic interpretation of forces. Looking back at his first published work, the *Birth of Tragedy*, Nietzsche remarked that "it smelled offensively Hegelian", i.e. dialectical and dualistic. That remarkable work invented for us, by recreating them, the Gods Apollo and Dionysus, but Nietzsche himself was later to re-examine its position and to state a hidden harmony between the two energies, in the light of the Heraclitean notion of *enantiodromia*, whereupon any drive, instinct, "voice", or energy pattern turns into its opposite, thus revealing an underlying synchronization.

The language of philosophy itself is the language of plurality: a discourse that surpasses itself. Conventional philosophy is *presupposed* rather than being given exposition: it constitutes the springboard from which the creative thinker leaps into a new language: "no longer of the whole but of fragment, of plurality, of separation".[66]

At times a philosopher will even wear the mask of the dialectic logician, in spite of the fact that nothing is further away from true pluralistic philosophy than dialectics.

42   *God Save the Ego*

Dialectical reasoning is the epitome of superficiality, for dialectics never move beyond mere *symptoms*. Dialectics muddle up interpretation with the development of the uninterpreted symbol – unfolding through oppositions, blissfully unaware of more profound, less obvious mechanisms, of topological dislocations, typological disparities. Of all reactive ways of expression, dialectics was by far the most popular in the 20th century, later replaced by deconstructionism. In the latter, the reactive forces at work are less obvious, for at first the analytical frenzy of facile perspectivism seems to work in favour of an active, more healthy intelligence. Unfortunately, deconstructionism did not deconstruct itself and ended up legitimizing good old-fashioned cynicism and armchair pessimism. In dialectics, however, the reactive forces are clearly displayed: it is the established viewpoint of *ressentiment*. Whether it was Hegel's, Feuerbach's or Stirner's nihilism, Nietzsche mercilessly attacked the superficiality of these German thinkers chiefly for one reason: *they all shared an unshakeable belief in the human ego.* They did not only substantiate its ghost-like nature; they actively constructed around it an incongruous saga of absolutist redemption through their so-called dialectical transformations.

Dialectical philosophy – a not-so distant cousin of Darwinism and Judaeo-Christian ideology – has one main objective: the *preservation* of the human species at *any* cost, and the *substantiation* of the human ego.

> The most cautious people ask today: 'How may man still be preserved? Zarathustra, however, asks as the sole and first one to do so: 'How shall man be *overcome?*'[67]

PART TWO

GREAT DOUBT AND THE DEATH OF GOD

43 *Great Doubt*

Nietzsche's intense and prolific output quickened, after his early heady detour of appraisal and appreciation of Schopenhauer and Wagner, into the terrifying existential crisis known in Zen as *Great Doubt*.

During this phase, he mercilessly dissected and unmasked all concepts, ideas and values cherished until then by humanity in the entire course of History. From 1878, with the publication of *Human, all too Human*, the pace became unrelenting, and it reached its zenith with *Joyful Science*. From 1878 to 1882, Nietzsche entered a phase of Great Doubt, and the scepticism of this period proved to be both exhaustive and exhausting. The dismantling of all values was done thoroughly, and shook him to the core. It culminated with the fourth book of *Joyful Science*: halfway through this masterpiece, he had reached the point of no return.

And then something happened. In a letter to his friend Koselitz of the 14th of August 1881, he wrote:

> I shall certainly have to live a few years more! [. . .] The intensity of my feelings makes me quiver and laugh – a couple of times already I couldn't leave my room for the absurd reason that my eyes were inflamed . . . and why? Because each time I had been weeping too much on my walks the previous day, not sentimental tears but tears of joy; and whilst weeping, I sang and talked nonsense, filled with a new vision . . . [1]

Already the style of *Joyful Science* is different: more assured, light-footed and less polemical. A feeling of freshness, of newly found, uninhibited imagination. The fourth book of this work turns a new leaf, heralds a new dawn; it starts with a serene, jubilant paragraph of appreciation of life and of good wishes for the new year (1882), of gratitude and sweetness. It introduces the fundamental thought of *Amor fati* (love of destiny), and a profound, inner healing and redirection of his creative energies. He no longer wants to "wage war against ugliness".

> I do not wish to wage war against ugliness. I do not want to accuse, I do not even want to accuse those who accuse. *Looking elsewhere*: let that be my only negation! In short . . . I only want to be, from now on, one who says Yes.[2]

This creative phase, which will find its full expression in *Thus Spoke Zarathustra*, testifies that Great Doubt, when pursued until the bitter end, turns into Great Faith, in the Great Field of Affirmation, in what Japanese philosopher Nishitani Keji's calls "the conversion from the Great Death to the Great Life".[3]

Great Faith is faith without an object. It is unconditional trust. We have many testimonies of such a phenomenon in the life of great Zen Masters, but it is an unusual occurrence in the history of western experience.

44 *Great Mourning*

The death of God signals the beginning of modernism and the start of an intense mourning. Modernism is born out of the experience of displacement, of voluntary or imposed exile. Together with the death of God we lament not merely the absence of a Creator, but the *loss of everything* that until now might have held *any* value for us: social utopia, science, love, humanity, friendship, morality, history, progress, beauty.

As Freud reminds us in his paper "Mourning and Melancholia", mourning can be caused not only by the loss of a loved one, but by that of "one's country, liberty, [by] an ideal". He wrote this in 1915, echoing the fears and horrors of the First World War, affirming the absolute necessity of *working through* the process of mourning. In a subsequent paper on 'Transience', two years later, Freud wrote that

> it will be found that our high opinion of the riches of civilisation has lost nothing from the discovery of their fragility.[4]

Or, as Jacqueline Rose put it, "mourning must come to an end so that we can believe in ourselves once more".

> No longer something to be dispatched, mourning becomes more amorphous and fluid, more interminable as one might say. Taking on the incalculable nature of mourning could then be seen as one of the defining features of modernism.[5]

Mourning is not quite the same as the overall diffuse feeling that often turns into melancholia. With regards to the pathology of melancholia, Freud suggests that it relies on failed detachment from the object and on our identification with it. When *worked through*, loss become mourning and avoids the lukewarm waters of melancholia. Melancholia is arguably a form of luxury experienced by those who try to escape the full impact of existential suffering, a comfort that perhaps neither the philosopher, nor the Zen practitioner, can afford.

Mourning is akin to Great Doubt: a strange and intense joy *befalls* those who are willing to undergo intense mourning, and the experience of profound faith awaits those who allow themselves to doubt fully. Conversely, melancholy is akin to scepticism: neither allows, respectively, profound mourning and authentic doubt. Melancholy and scepticism are both lukewarm: they never threaten to undo the self; they safeguard it instead in a limbo where loss is never fully experienced, thus never resolved.

45 Zen Desiderata

Great Faith and Great Doubt get along fine in Zen. Alongside Great Determination, they constitute the *desiderata* on the path.

What we find instead in a modern, predominantly secular culture, is shallow scepticism paired with pockets of pseudo-religious gullibility (shadow aspects of the former). If, on the other hand, a society upholds a religious creed, one will find then within it areas of flimsy "atheism". In either case, dualistic, artificial division reigns unperturbed.

Pessimism, cynicism, agnosticism are all aspects of *small doubt*, of *shallow pessimism*, of *armchair atheism*. Nietzsche's creative thinking confirms the fact that the *via negativa*, the way of doubt, when pursued wholeheartedly, turns into the *via regia*, the regal way.

Nietzsche's writings until 1881 had alienated from him all religious people and believers. From then onwards, his words alienated him from the praise of pessimists, cynics and self-styled materialist/atheist thinkers to whom he had never belonged in the first place.

46 It's the End of the World, as we know it (and I feel fine)

Forms of scepticism and atheism that came before Nietzsche were only a pale reflection of Great Doubt, and as pale in comparison are later modes of thought such as existentialism, structuralism, deconstructionism and post-modernism.

Existentialism is a form of *rationalist humanism*; with Nietzsche, however, we move *beyond the limits of man-centred existence*. The death of God is not a mere positivist stance; not the benign, rationalist reluctance to entertain religious dogma or ethereal, undemonstrated hypotheses. Instead, it is a way of registering a catastrophic metamorphosis whose implications are petrifying. We must try and imagine what took place in natural history when dry lands arose out of the sea and the countless animals that once inhabited the sea were made to live on dry land. Those animals had to radically alter their way of life, their habits: a fundamental change in their way of being.

The shift from a world based on moral and religious values (whether or not coated in liturgy or in rational/secular language) to a world devoid of God is the first radical acknowledgment in modern western thought of the *groundlessness* and *inherent purposelessness* of existence. It is similar, using the image from natural history, to the entire land descending again into the sea, forcing all the land animals to revert back into sea creatures. The shift is so profound, writes Nishitani: "not only the human mode of existence but even the very visible form of the world itself undergoes a radical transformation".

Things, animals and people "lose their substantiality"; they are *grounded on nothing*, become waves in the sea. It is the death of the Cartesian ego, it is *the end of individuality as we know it.*

In the groundlessness of existence, a new religiosity may take place, a fundamental shift in the way humans are in the world. In Nietzsche, this is represented by what he calls the *Dionysian*. In Zen, it is known as *ordinary mind*. That Great Doubt leads to a new religiosity is witnessed in many instances throughout the history of Zen. Hakuin Zenji compared it to a vast abyss opening up, "with no place to put your hands and feet. You face death, and your heart feels as though it were fire". Mind and body are dropped: this is known as seeing into one's nature.

47   *We don't want to be saved*

The death of God is the beginning of authentic *agnosticism*. Now sadly synonymous with a droopy, utterly innocuous form of atheism, true agnosticism is instead infused with a profound sense of *not knowing*.

Its other crucial aspect is a *shift from the Gnostic outlook*. According to the Gnostic predicament, the individual feels exiled among men. *Mi sento esiliato in mezzo agli uomini*, the Italian poet Giuseppe Ungaretti wrote. The self is an alien in a world vacated not only by the divine, but also by any human meaning whatsoever. As it is professed nowadays, agnosticism is a vague form of disbelief, a balancing act of incertitude and faint hope in view of the possibility of a "sensible", unfussy and cost-effective redemption.

Doing away with the Gnostic view altogether, renouncing its props and crutches, is *to give up salvation*. No more sinners or saints, but the unbroken innocence of becoming, the perpetual flower of impermanence.

A-gnosticism, the absence of gnosis, of Gnostic outlook, also abolishes the dichotomy between the artist (seen stereotypically as an inspired, highly individualized, creative rebel), and society (variously perceived as organized mediocrity or systematized horror).

The hero laughs and becomes laughable. The warrior is also a clown. That laughter, that light-footed scepticism, cures him of centuries of Romanticism. If passion is still a powerful weapon in his arsenal, it is a passion spiritualized and transfigured by laughter, irony and the sense of the cosmic play. It is a levity born out of too profound a gravity, the very opposite of the "religious" type.

The religious sensibility of the Gnostic type embraced by so many religions presents us with the familiar labyrinth in which souls are found and lost to the forces of evil. An artist working under its influence will produce stark representations of deep metaphysical anxiety and unbearable distress, only to be eventually swallowed up by the current orthodoxy. Outcasts and transgressive artists add their depictions of hell to the Church's newly painted frescos. Thus a negative theology is born out of the late Romanticism's appendix, where God is conspicuous for his absence. We see the beginning of this in Baudelaire, later in the excruciating suffering experienced by Artaud, and later still with the twilight, hungry-ghost realm described by William Burroughs.

48 *Against Silenus, Against Socrates*

What does stepping out of the Gnostic trap entail? It means cutting the umbilical chord to limbo, to life-as-we-know-it, poised between the hazard of religious damnation and the faint promise of secular redemption, between sombre Silenus and the equally dreary Socrates.

Silenus points his bony finger at us, reminding us that existence is stained by the original sin, life is shameful and imperfect, the body is mortal coil, a bag of rice, an assemblage of impurities, at the most a vehicle for transcendence. Meanwhile, Socrates seduces us to the subtle yet sterile powers of reason, the only way – according to whoever accepts this view – of narrowing down the experience of physical pain and mental anguish.

The first view, the priestly religious view simplified by Silenus, is essentially an act of revenge against life. For Silenus, life is not worth living. Best would be not to be born, to be nothing, and second best is to die soon. This view, masterly combines inane gazing at God and nothingness with malevolent jabs at the precious and precarious proximity.

The other view, simplified by Socrates, of embracing rationality as the only mode of salvation, always marks a profound crisis in human culture:

it indicates that the collective psyche has already been swamped and over-ruled by the passions, and therefore it has to cling to reason as its last resort.

Both views, and their numerous ramifications, fail to comprehend the deeper aspects of the self. What they fail to achieve is perhaps the fitting task of a depth psychology rooted in the aesthetic principles of play and immanence, in the uncovering and appreciation of what is (of what at this very moment becomes), rather than in the application of models of inte-gration and fulfilment which the forever unfulfilled and imperfect individual is supposed to grow into. A task for a depth psychology still to come, one that would be ready to study the self thoroughly, to the point where it is forgotten.

49 Cheap Thrills

We walk in the aseptic foyers of the gray buildings of knowledge with apprehension and wondrous expectation, as when before a meeting with a lover, or whilst waiting in a surgery room for a diagnosis. Soon, however, we are swimming in dead words, our lungs heavy with the deni-gration history presses on our heart, and try to extricate ourselves through the marshes and the salt, and out on the shore cutting through the entan-gled nets that cloud our vision and hinder our every move.

We were not looking for "serious philosophy". *We wanted to dance*, and enter a non-consecrated church to dream our dream of beauty and rapture. We didn't know that everything under the sky had been divided and classified; that even this thirst, this divine temptation, would find a niche in the techno-bazaar of specialization.

We approached poetry and the poet with the same apprehension, but all we found were clever words strung together by a contemptuous puzzle-maker. We hoped that science at least would restore us to the most absurd dreams of all, the dream of objectivity. It was also in vain! Thus many started deceiving themselves, and eventually settled for the neutrality that one achieves after having been neutered.

50 Saint Darwin and the Pineal Gland

Philosophy is temptation, attempt, and experimentation. It dares to ask unsettling questions; it harbours an inveterate aversion to being satisfied with borrowed answers. Science's claim had been exactly that, but it ended up taking itself too seriously, lapsing into methodical dogmatism, and thus becoming the new secular religion.

Philosophy is law giving: its clauses are written on water, in the Heraclitean flux, unconfined, vast and immeasurable as psyche itself. Its scope brims over into other endeavours, it cannot be restricted within the human mind. It is not the product of the pineal gland. It is not found in the brain, or three inches below the navel.

5 | Mr Know-it-all

The need for a system betrays our tremor of uncertainty in the face of life's unpredictability. We simply cannot abide in not knowing.

The 42-year old monk Soen Nakagawa, a pioneer in establishing Zen in the West, gave his first speech at the Theosophical Society in San Francisco in 1949. At one point during his talk, he referred to a statement by his friend Soyen Shaku who had said that after 40 years of studying the Dharma he had only begun to grasp the fact that "after all, I do not understand anything". He said that the same was true for himself: the audience was very disappointed; they just laughed at him.[6]

A knower lacks integrity. Rushing headlong to fill the uncomfortable gap of uncertainty and not knowing, he solidifies a half-truth and turns it into an "answer". Very often this is mere *nominalism*: finding a name under which to classify what we still do not understand. Nominalism is very popular in contemporary psychology, whereby we explain away a symptom by giving it a clinical name.

Will to knowledge betrays a need for linearity, for fictitious beginnings and made-up endings: the historian's fallacy of one who, looking for origins, eventually "turns into a crab". Historians look backwards, and "they end up believing backwards too",[7] as the recent nostalgic re-appraisals of the British Empire testify.

But the so-called "body of knowledge", grown grotesquely out of proportions in the greenhouse of a "system", badly deflates on its final, anticlimactic demise, when time runs out and the grain of sands sifts trough the hourglass of existence.

Fed on the *defence mechanisms of logic and dialectics*, the knowing philosopher is a pagliaccio, a straw man, a buffoon. His arguments confound and irritate. He is like a bad actor, whose histrionics astound the impressionable, who mistake them for great acting. He "lays on his opponent the burden of proving that he is not an idiot".[8] His games with words *resemble* thinking, and are effective in numbing his opponent. But dialectical reason is mankind's last resort. When employed unduly, it betrays the beginning of the end in a culture. From then on it will be a matter of a few years until it reaches complete paralysis. It constitutes, however, the staple of most university syllabuses, even though it might be hiding behind fashionable deconstructionist jargon.

On an individual level, logic is a tyrant imposed by a despairing individual upon his instincts: he feels he would otherwise be out of control. Socrates understood that the whole world needed him – his method, his cure, his personal trick of self-preservation . . . Everywhere the instincts were in anarchy; everywhere people were a few steps away from excess: the *monstrum in animo* was the general danger. 'The drives want to play the tyrant; we must invent a *counter-tyrant* who is stronger' . . . [9]

52 *Two Worlds?*

The "two-worlds" view is shared by most religions: life and afterlife, good and evil, vale of tears and blissful paradise, samsara and nirvana. The man-made separation of consciousness and matter, body and mind, constitutes the tacit, mainstream code of belief of our time, and it has not changed since Descartes.

In psychotherapy, dualistic thinking divides the self between what it is and what it wishes to be, thus fostering the *dream of change*.

Philosophy has traditionally opposed being to becoming. Being provides the ground outside the process of becoming; it provides a reference point against which to measure the flux of becoming. Being, whether as a witnessing creator and God, or as a Platonic Form, provides an aim, or goal. Humans, imperfect creatures caught up in the flux of becoming, swept away by the current, find the solace of a branch sticking out of the muddy shore of an imagined being. It gives them something to strive for, a promise of redemption and the Schopenauerian "nirvana".

By doing away with being, becoming is restored to its innocence. This impermanent life ceases to be "just" this life, the organic body of atomism and all materialisms, and becomes *unfathomable*. It is not there *for the sake of* something else. It affirms itself, for it does not lack anything. It is neither incomplete nor inferior.

The new beginning heralded by the fourth book of the *Joyful Science* is realized more fully a few years later (1883-84) with Nietzsche's most famous work, *Thus Spoke Zarathustra*. The previous year, 1882, had seen the flowering of his best hopes of finding spiritual communion with the "young Russian" Lou Salomé. In August of that year, the two lived a deep, unconsummated bond. His hopes to find in her a friend and disciple were shattered, and a cold distance grew also with his closest friend Paul Ree. In many ways, the two represented Nietzsche's last attempt at breaking away from solitude, of "going among people". The year 1883 sees him seized by depression and ideas of suicide. Determined to *turn his experiences into gold*, he starts writing *Zarathustra*, which would be completed two years later.

On the 23rd of July 1884, he writes to his friend Overbeck:

> My theory according to which the world of good and evil is only an apparent, prospectivistic world is such an innovation that sometimes I am amazed by it.[10]

With *Zarathustra*, Nietzsche introduces the voice of the Master, a vivid presence he actively engages with, and which embodies a wisdom-that-knows-groundlessness, a wisdom beyond duality.

The name he gave to the Master's voice is revealing. It is the name of a seventh-century BC Persian prophet, Zarathustra. At the heart of the religion he founded there is a conflict between *Ahura Mazda* (*Ormuzd*), God of light and good, and *Angra Mazda* (*Ahriman*), God of darkness and evil. *It was he who first introduced dualistic conception, and he himself had to see through it.*

It is the beginning of *Great Faith*. The utter loss of hope in his private life, Lou's rejection, paired with the deliberate and relentless unmasking of all values in every single field of human endeavour, made his condition unbearable.

Breakdown can sometimes lead to a breakthrough. It happened to many. It happened to Jung after he moved away from Freud. Left to himself and seized by doubts, he turned inwards and found the world of images, the "little people", *the middle realm*, the world *of psyche*.

Likewise, finding Zarathustra was a revelation for Nietzsche. Some of his friends speak of him as being truly ecstatic during that period. Resa von Schirnhofer writes:

> I too . . . was led by him to the rock lapped by the waters of the Silvaplana lake, Zarathustra's rock, in that place of exquisite natural beauty, where the dark green lake, the near woods, the high mountains and the imposing stillness together exert their enchantment.[11]

And Helen Zimmern, who stayed at the Alpenrose Hotel in ̔ ̔ Maria, where Nietzsche used to go for lunch, writes how they would afternoon and he would refer to Zarathustra saying, "as said", or "the Master said", an exquisitely Pythagorean exp efa.

53 The Abyss of Light

From an initial phase of submission, of learning, worship and surrender, Nietzsche moved to independence, to the solitary wandering in the desert of the Western psyche and Western thought. In the first phase, Schopenhauer and Wagner had been his mentors, teachers and instigators.

Having learned discipleship, sooner or later he had to move on toward his great task, experiment, and attempt: the re-evaluation of all values.

It was only after a painful sojourn in the desert of Great Doubt, through the complete loss of any hope (religious, aesthetic, scientific, and, most poignantly, personal) that life affirmation surged through with tremendous power. We witness, after countless deaths, a joyful rebirth, and a joy that is not mere "happiness", at least not in the sense of an *ascension*, but instead, as a *descent*.

Nietzsche wrote of an *abyss of light*: a most peculiar image, for an abyss is normally dark, dangerous and obscure. It is the place of Hell, it is a place of utter darkness, unconsciousness. There is no light in the abyss; the light is always upward, towards the heavens. A spiritual teacher will normally summon the faithful to an upward journey; he will invite them to ascend into the light. Instead, Nietzsche invites us to a terrifying descent, to a ruinous fall. He beckons us to an abyss of light, to a descent whose depths and perils we ignore. Zen teachings too invite us to a descent. They do not offer consolation, nor do they promise a perfected future where the agonizing imperfections of the present will be corrected, or where our destiny will be weighed up and amended by a Creator.

As a non-dual philosophy, and a practice steeped in the incommensurably profound roots of the Mahayana tradition, Zen also does not separate "I" from "destiny", self from karma.

Nietzsche took a different route, but reached a similar place: fearless acceptance of his destiny. In spite of the suffering and isolation of his particular destiny, he affirmed *I am fate*. *Amor fati*, love of destiny, became his formula, which substituted Spinoza's *Amor Dei*, love of God. *Amor fati* is a form of deep appreciation: not unlike, in fact, *Thy will be done*, a formula uttered after the *Lamma Sabachtani* of utter despair.

The madman going out in full daylight with a lantern, declaring the death of God is prepared to live with the consequences of a murder he did not commit. He is also courageous enough to succeed in transubstantiating suffering into a joyful dance.

Descending the abyss of light entails full acceptance of suffering; it means, among other things, embracing the shadow; it means facing up to oneself, readily encountering one's double; it means risking madness and displacement.

In Nietzsche's case, he did not have an anchor. In Zen, the anchor is provided by the four Bodhisattva vows.

One is still alone, travelling through uncharted lands; one still has no consolation or reassurance that everything is going to be fine. What one suspects with a strange certainty is the presence of an uninterrupted lineage, a shared blindness present in the sangha, in the community of fellow explorers.

54 *The Great Doubt: A–Z*

Zen, or more specifically C'han, is the result of crossbreeding between the Madhyamika School of the Indian philosopher and sage Nagarjuna and Chinese Daoism. The Madhyamika school, a prominent school in Mahayana Buddhism, had signaled the most radical departure from early Indian Buddhism, with various tenets being abandoned, or, to be more accurate, re-formulated *without* the ontological reality attributed to them in a process of quasi-canonization. Before Nagarjuna, *nirvana* had become an absolute reality, with an existence of its own, *separate* from the world of phenomena.

The new interpretation corrected those principles entirely, introducing a new definition (*anapeksah svabbavah*) whose core was *relativity*, or "emptiness". All the main pillars of early Hinayana Buddhism were razed to the ground, with one exception only: the principle of dependent origination (*pratitya-sam-utpada*), in its new interpretation.

Nagarjuna has used logic most thoroughly in demolishing all our assumptions about the nature of reality. His *Madhyamika karika* is a *radical critique of all metaphysics*, the very A–Z of Great Doubt. In this work, he refutes all tenets which had been previously taught on Buddhist metaphysics. Geshe Yeshe Tobden illustrates one of the key points of the Madhyamaka school in the simplest and most effective way:

> For the Madhyamikas there is no proof that can establish the mind's true existence, nor are there any valid reasons that demonstrate the true existence of objects and knowledge. They state that the existence of something can be explained only in relation to something else, whereas if a phenomenon existed truly, intrinsically, it would not need any support. Object and subject (consciousness) exist on the basis of mutual dependence.[12]

55 *Of the Incurable*

We must differentiate between *positive nihilism*, spurred by Great Doubt, which eventually becomes great faith, great affirmation, and the fashionable deconstructionist theories of the later part of the 20th century.

We owe to Derrida the major philosophical insight that, as David Loy puts it,

> There is no transcendental signified that language can point to, because every signified is only a function of other signifiers; all we can ever have in language is a general circulation of signs.[13]

The downside of this stance is that, given that language cannot point outside itself, we are then trapped in a proliferation of signs. In Derrida's world, we are left with nothing else to do but endlessly disseminate myriad of perspectives, each of them intrinsically devoid of meaning. Having started off promisingly, with the dismantling of time and causality in a manner similar to Nagarjuna's line of attack, Derrida seems "on the verge of somewhere else, if not a something else". Deconstructionism falls short, in that *it fails to de-construct itself.*

> From the non-dualist perspective, the problem with Derrida's radical critique of Western philosophy is that it is not radical enough: his deconstruction is incomplete because it does not deconstruct itself and attain that clôture which . . . is the opening to something else. This is why Derrida remains in the halfway-house of proliferating "pure textuality", whereas deconstruction could lead to a transformed mode of experiencing the world.[14]

The problem of getting stuck in emptiness, as it were, was already thoroughly dealt with by Nagarjuna. He demonstrated the relativity, the inherent emptiness, or non-true existence of phenomena, but he warned against the danger of transforming sunyata, emptiness, into a theory.

> *Sunyata* is the exhaustion of all theories and views: those for whom *sunyata* is itself a theory are incurable.[15]

As Loy points out in his remarkable *Non-Duality*, Shakyamuni Buddha did not attempt to create a new theory of language with *sunyata* as its explanation. Instead, fully aware that "ordinary language is full of deluding ontological commitments", he accepted the fact and demolished it "from within".

Nirvana extends just as far as everyday life.
There is not the slightest difference between them.[16]

Both Nagarjuna and Derrida invalidate the main conjecture of meta-physics –"that we can mirror the whole terrain from some Archimedean point of pure, self-contained thought". They both demonstrate how this is an illusion. Neither *Sunyata* nor Derrida's *Differance* are points of reference. The former, as expounded by Nagarjuna, eventually developed into Zen, a practice that to this day repudiates any theory and opens up, through meditation, a "new mode of experience". With Derrida, the only solution left to the inability of language to mirror reality is endless dissemination, what Loy calls "bad infinity", a place where,

what is unsatisfactory about each strategy is disguised by alternatively having recourse to the other.[17]

Unlike Nietzsche and Nagarjuna, Derrida begins the process of deconstruction but does not complete it.

The consequences of his thought on modernity have been huge, and not always beneficial. The word "construct" has become fashionable; it is now a commonly-held conviction that long-cherished beliefs are nothing but "constructs". The modern trend is to de-construct everything and everyone, and that can be helpful in sharpening our capacity for investigation. While happily demolishing away mere constructs, we miss two important aspects. First, we miss the element of *connectedness* inherent in any construct: something is non-existing by itself, but positively *existing* as a facet of the great diamond. Second, we do not de-construct our own deconstruction, *we do not doubt our own doubt*.

The result, on an existential level, is "post-modern irony", and the superficial sophistication of the city dweller. A condition of lukewarm confusion, of quiet desperation, of desperate cheerfulness that in some cases finds a home in old-fashioned metaphysics, in time-honoured, if blurred, religious values, and in reactionary politics.

56   *The Dance of Damocles*

The philosopher's unbridled freedom is the most arduous state to dwell in. In Nietzsche's case, the nihilist formula *if nothing is true everything is permitted*, soon became *if nothing is true, nothing is permitted*.

"To live outside the law, you must be honest", sang Bob Dylan. The true outcast tiptoes on the threshold of asceticism. The anguish, the icy solitude, is unbearable. "Alas, grant me madness," Nietzsche cried out when dwelling in the midst of these cold flames.

Our eyes are protectively shut to "the time of the assassins", to a world truly devoid of God, of moral foundations, of meaning, of the very ground under our feet. Every true philosopher, every practitioner of the Way finds himself sooner or later navigating his way in the midst of the open sea. The unchained freedom he experiences there opens his life to Chaos. We respond by resorting to temporary relief from the Law and from the Goddess of Necessity, *Ananke*. During our package holiday away from mechanized life, we dream up a world of satisfied desire, slowly regressing into the womb. And if we move deeply enough within the whirlwind of Chaos, we will soon find a new form of slavery.

Caught between Necessity and Freedom, Law and Chance, the true person of no rank dances. Caught between two hungry tigers, the overman picks a blackberry by the side of the road.

A sword hangs over us, held by a fine thread. Camus was right: Damocles never danced better than when he found himself beneath the sword hanging by a fine thread.

57 I have seen the future, baby, and it's murder

The death of God is not a subject for theological disquisition. It is an existential state of agony so profound as to leave one bereft of any sense of meaning. Its consequences, felt by Nietzsche in the second half of the 19th century, are terrifying. He recognized that the fate of the coming generations, i.e. of the 20th and 21st century, was to live in a world devoid of any distinction between man and animal. In Nietzsche's words:

> If, on the other hand, the doctrines of sovereign Becoming, of fluidity of all concepts, types and species, of the lack of any cardinal distinction between man and animal — doctrines which I consider true but deadly — . . . are thrust upon the people for another generation with the rage for instruction that has become normal, no one should be surprised if the people perishes of petty egoism, ossification and greed, falls apart and ceases to be a people; in its place a system of individualist egoism, brotherhoods for the rapacious and the exploitation of the non-brothers, and similar creations of utilitarian vulgarity, will appear in the arena of the future.[18]

The death of God is both an "attempt at a diagnosis of contemporary civilization" and a metaphor for groundlessness; it is both a state of utter bondage, of stupefied and dull materialism, and a tremendous potential for setting new goals.

The latter is the one possibility opened up in Zen by the Great Doubt, by the willingness to pursue doubt to its bitter end. Approaching the Great Doubt without Nietzsche's light-hearted scepticism leads inevitably to the sour, ultimately fruitless pessimism that is so fashionable nowadays: an anglicized, anaesthetized version of good old Schopenhauer.

According to this view, which is currently all the rage, humanity is a doomed race, condemned to boredom and futility. People are at the most, as the title of a fashionable book has it, "straw dogs". Such paranoid outlook plunders and pillages from that great reservoir of elusive Daoist wisdom, without ever dreaming of coming anywhere near its depths. For how can one who is used to blabber understand singing? It is with great relish that nouveaux pessimists describe a world of failure and defeat. They do so with the satisfied detachment of the State-salaried, and with the studied radicalism of a graffiti artist whose work is commissioned by corporations.

This is Darwinism for the masses: man is an ape, life is a bitch, and then you die. Clad in anti-liberal, pseudo-radical jargon, 21st century pessimism can afford its hyperboles and sound bites of doom and gloom precisely because *it does not dwell long enough in the field of ground-lessness*. These are bored professors, who, having never tasted groundlessness, never saw it turning into the Great Field of Affirmation; at the most they have formulated the *possibility* of groundlessness through logical inference.

By dwelling in true nihilism long enough, one reaches a life-affirming stance. This is truly a strange place to be: it exudes profound affirmation of life, a deep sense of wisdom and compassion, yet it does not rest upon any belief, creed or ideology.

58 *Free Radicals*

The Madhyamikas are the most radical philosophers who ever lived; they made a lasting and inimitable contribution to both eastern and western philosophy. Before the publication of T. R. V. Murti's study *The Central Philosophy of Buddhism*, the predominant opinion in the first half of the 20th century (as expounded by Poussin and Jacobi, among others) was that Nagarjuna's philosophy was *pure nihilism*:

> According to Poussin, . . . the Madhyamikas' analysis ultimately destroys the notion of causality just as effectively as it destroys all ideas of experience and religion. Not only do the dharmas of Buddhist philosophy not exist substantially: they do not exist at all, either in reality or in appearance.[19]

Nihilism is here understood *not* in the Nietzschean sense of the Platonic denigration of becoming and the subsequent need to create an ideal, more "real" world beyond appearance, but instead in the prevailing meaning of the word as denial of substantial reality.

The "nihilistic interpretation" interprets Nagarjuna's view that all dharmas are empty (*sarva-dharma-sunyata*) as the natural continuation of early Buddhism's critique of the doctrine of the self. *All* dharmas (all phenomena, manifestations) are hallucinations, an "illusory city in the sky" (*gandharva-nagara*):

> Hindrances, actions, bodies, those who act, and the effects of their actions
> Are like a mirage or dream. They seem as unreal as the city of Ghandarva.[20]

59 The Dark Side of Socrates

Cynic thought surfaced in Greece during a time of decline. It is, as Giorgio Colli puts it, "the dark side of Socrates". *Cynicism always appears in times of crisis*. It manifests in individuals and in entire cultures, as the rotten fruit of a sick tree. In every epoch, its chief characteristics are easily detectable: "plebeian, run of the mill rationalism" as its tool; "shameless exhibitionism" as its style; "derision of the past, of myths, the break with tradition" as its main themes. Such a "pragmatic attitude" provides an "illusion of superiority" to frustrated people. To which we may add an overall denigration of life, which manifests profusely and in the most varied fashion, from gritty social realism to apocalyptic, pseudo science-fictional style.

We find it in Rousseau, grandly doing his dirty laundry in public, and in our contemporary John Gray, when he reminds us that man is a beast. The same fanaticism, the same *Schadenfreude*, the same infantile pleasure in destruction, or in giving an extra push to what is already on the verge of falling; the same unsavory appetite for ignominy, the same bitterness.

New cynics elect Schopenhauer as their mentor: without possessing his profundity of thought, they nevertheless share his pessimism. Some go as far as electing Nietzsche as their mentor. But that is unfair, for Nietzsche, was a "genius of the heart".

60 *Beyond Deconstructionism*

There is a danger of equating Buddhism solely with its deconstructionist faculty, with its painstaking dissection of both the self and of the illusory values which depend on it.

The scope and breadth of Zen exceeds analytical perspectivism, fashionable post-modernism, and any hip new trend expressed by buzz words followed by "ism". Zen surpasses those trends because it does not stop at dismantling revered systems of thought, but extends its critique to the farthest corners, until doubt doubts itself, until nihilism overcomes itself, until a new affirmation is born. This affirmation does not rest on anything, and yet it has tremendous power.

Deconstructionism is based on a misinterpretation of Nietzsche; it wilfully relies on Nietzsche's perspectivist phase, and it altogether misses his affirmative period, his own transition, from *The Joyful Science* onwards, from Great Doubt to Great Faith.

PART THREE

THE WILL TO POWER AS GENEROSITY

61 A Brief History of the Will

The history of the West is the history of the self, of its heroic exertion to affirm itself. Anything desperately craving to assert itself surely betrays one thing: profound self-doubt. In this case, the doubt is legitimate, given that, intrinsically, *the self does not exist*. Could it be that the history of the West is the history of a fiction?

The self asserts itself through the *will*, which came to light with the Judaeo-Christian tradition. The ancient Greek civilization that preceded it did not have a concept of the will as we understand it (individualized, monadic), but saw it instead as part and parcel of *Moira*, destiny. It was the Judaeo-Christian tradition to introduce the will of God and subsequently the so-called "free-will" of the individual. The infinite drive of the self towards happiness and self-realization is eternally doomed to failure, for neither happiness nor self-realization can happen without the self forfeiting itself (which is, paradoxically, the last thing the self intends to do).

Descartes reversed the perspective, from a God-centered to a human-centered mode, making things worse by stating that the cause of evil was the human will; and that although this will was infinite, human understanding was limited. Seventeenth-century rationalism pumped the human will further, until it reached the gigantic proportions it later assumed in our contemporary societies. Schelling – who went as far as saying that all primal being is will – probably reached the highest point in this climb. With Nietzsche, alongside Freud, Marx and Feuerbach, there is a shift and the will is no longer ruled by the "rational", but experienced instead as "a great freedom".

62 Beyond Heraclitus

Western secular thought is essentially *man-centred*. Whether existentialist, sceptical or scientific/materialistic, its concerns are with mankind and its struggle on this planet. Religious thought, on the other hand, is God-centred: its vision intensely express humankind's yearning for the sky. From the standpoint of Nietzsche's will to power, *both secular and religious thinking are optical illusions*; both anthropomorphic and God-centred views are discarded. The search begins for the matrix of forces that animate all sentient beings. The shift to will to power, to affirmation, comes about as the point of resurgence after the final débâcle, just prior to the discovery of the *innocence of becoming* (*Unschuld des Werdens*). Nietzsche did not merely re-work Heraclitean thought, but instead arrived at the same philosophical milestone in an original way. Seen from the standpoint of the will to power, this world of impermanence appears to be *transparently immanent*. Seen after a breakthrough, a genuine opening of one's perception, *the world appears entirely devoid of sin*. The *innocence of becoming* represents, and can be interpreted as, one of the modes of western thought to come closest to *sunyata*, or spaciousness.[1]

As with sunyata, we cannot ascribe a metaphysical quality to the notion of will to power. This has been Heidegger's mistake, alongside other thinkers who followed in his footsteps, including Nishitani himself. For this "principle of absolute becoming" is not represented as being, as separate, nor is it mistakenly identified with the human sphere only. Instead, it is a representation, a myth, holding metaphorical, *poetic truth*. It profoundly resonates with meaning, but it cannot be neither separate, nor one-with, and solely attributed to, human life. If the will to power were a separate principle, we would fall back into what Nietzsche abhorred the most: metaphysics. If it is to be identified with the heroic will of the ego, we would fall back into literalism and hubristic thinking.

The King of Samadhi has "eye horizontal, nose vertical". He is not a God, but neither is he a mere ego.

63   *Poetry Again*

Myth and mythical language might just be one of the best ways of avoiding a ruinous fall into both hubris and the triviality and glamorized gossip of "factual" history. Having shamelessly resorted to myth and to mythical language: this is the charge of various thinkers against Nietzsche, each of them motivated by a different agenda: some to re-establish his reputation firmly within the ranks of "serious" philosophers; some to simply deride his religiosity. Nishitani Keji's specific allegation is strongly influenced by Heidegger: namely that, by resorting to myth, Nietzsche lost what he calls *historicity* (Heidegger's *Geshichtlikheit*) and *actuality*. Actualization, it must nevertheless be said to Nishitani's credit, does not necessarily imply that man is all. The down-to-earth quality of Zen is also mixed with a wonderful poetic ambiguity, where demons, buddhas and bodhisattvas are spoken of in an *as if* mode, never conceding to either literal worship, or acerbic rationalism. And within this *middle realm* of supreme ambiguity, both aesthetic appreciation and artistic productivity are possible.

These same qualities one finds in Nietzsche's – of *mythos*, of archetypal, non-literal truths – confer extreme ambivalence to his writing. This is also the realm of humour: Nietzsche's wonderful puns are often lost in translation, whereas Hakuin Zenji was more fortunate: his irreverent sarcasm and invectives are wonderfully rendered by gifted translators such as Norman Waddell. Here is an extract from Hakuin's commentary on the Heart Sutra, at the point where he comments on the sanskrit word *paramita*:

> The Chinese for this means, "reach the other shore". But where is that? He [the Buddha] is digging himself into a hole to get at blue sky. Shrimps may wriggle and jump, but they can't escape the dipper. The place where the Treasure lies is near at hand. Take one more step! Master Hsieh sits in his boat wringing water from his fishing line. Even the clearest-eyed monk is secretly troubled.
>
> > Is there a soul on earth who belongs on "this
> >   shore"?
> > How sad to stand mistaken on a wave-lashed quay!
> > Pursued with the roots to life unsevered, practice
>
> Remains a useless struggle, however long it lasts.[2]

And here he comments on the word *practices*, from the passage in the Heart Sutra that says, "The Bodhisattva free and unrestricted *practices* the deep wisdom paramita":

> What's he prattling about now? Making waves. Stirring up trouble. It's sleepless at night. Moving around during the day. Pissing and passing excrement. Clouds moving, streams flowing, leaves falling, flowers scattering. But hesitate or stop to think and hell rears up in all its hellish forms. Yes, practice is like that all right, but until you penetrate by the cold sweat of your brow and see it for yourself, there's trouble in store for you, and plenty of it![3]

64   *Will to Power and Instinct of Freedom*

Will to Power is *not willpower*, nor the desire to acquire power over others as commonly understood. The wish to rule over others is based, as Goethe says in Faust, on one's failure in exercising self-mastery:

For each one who knows not how
To rule his own, his inborn self, is all too fain
To rule his neighbour's will, as prompts his own proud mind . . .[4]

how possible?

It is true that the formula Nietzsche chose is infelicitous, and always in danger of being misinterpreted, as indeed it was the case countless times.

He could have called it *instinct of freedom*, as the two sometimes seem to be one and the same.[5] According to Kaufman, he did so as to differentiate its formula from Darwinist ideas, but that would mean accepting a reductive interpretation of Will to Power, applied solely to the human realm. Moreover, it is not in Nietzsche's style to avoid dangers of misinterpretation, but to choose instead the most direct, uncompromising route. Within the human domain, the word *power* neutrally acknowledges the elements of aggression and desire, as well as its positive counterparts: self-mastery, compassion, courage and, ultimately, overflowing abundance that spills out into *dana*, or generosity.

Freud spoke unashamedly of the *sex* impulse, not of *love* and eroticism. He did not mince his words. However, he did not *endorse* the indiscriminate acting out of the sex impulse. In the same way, Nietzsche did not endorse or justify, in the name of "will to power" the aggression, the delusional hunger for power and domination of man over his fellows. At the level of the individual, will to power is above all *self-mastery (self-overcoming* in Nietzsche's language) and self-discipline. The truly virtuous person, the true person of no rank, is not merely pious; *he is passionate, but has learnt to sublimate his passions.* It is the weak that hate the constraint of style and fancy themselves as wild and unrestrained. They will quote and interpret Nietzsche and Zen randomly, in the attempt to justify their immoderation, their mediocrity, and their lack of self-mastery. On the other hand, both Nietzsche and Zen are far from the attitude of the Stoics and the ascetics (and from the Christian view as well), in as much as these advocate the *curbing* of the instincts, a method that kills away the essential humanity of the individual. In Christian iconography, the dragon is slain, whereas in Chinese representations of the Buddha he often sits on the back of the dragon.

Already for the young Nietzsche his hero Manfred, Lord Byron's creation, is an overman who rules over spirits. Mastery is fundamentally self-mastery, achieved by an individual capable of perceiving glimpses of the new world. But only "scholarly oxen", as Nietzsche calls them in *Ecce Homo*, could misunderstand his conception "Darwinistically". In other words, humanity does not gradually evolve towards higher spirituality; that would mean applying the flawed parameters of history and the delusional idea of progress to an occurrence that by its very nature is unquantifiable.

The radical shift known as religiosity happens *outside* history. Not because it is a marginal phenomenon, nor because it is "transcendent" or "eternal", but because the idea of history is itself a concept, and is surpassed by the experience of the overman.

All great things occur away from glory and the market-place: the inventors of new values have always lived away from glory and the market-place.[6]

65 *Zarathustra Bodhisattva and the Will to Give*

Schopenhauer's greatness was to stretch to extreme consequences the thought of his predecessors. By introducing ideas from Buddhism *as he understood it*, he opened up provincial Europe, at that time infatuated with Kant and Hegel, to the wisdom of the East. He identified in the will the very *essence* of things, and in music the supreme manifestation of that essence; in so doing, he ended up weighing the world up and downgrading it as illusion, appearance and representation. In spite of his aesthetically based, artistically satisfying intuitions, the consequences of his stance are calamitous, for they encourage *denigration* of the world rather than gratitude for the great mystery of becoming.

Nietzsche took off where his educator Schopenhauer had left – he spat out the bones, as it were, disposing of pessimism and metaphysical ambiguity, creating a philosophy of the will that replaced the crumbling metaphysics of old. The importance of this cannot be overlooked: Nietzsche's philosophy of will is not a form of metaphysics – it *replaces* metaphysics. He is the messenger of great news, of *glad tidings*. God is dead; *metaphysics are dead*. We can now *will*, which means we can *create*. And we can experience for the first time profound and true *joy*. Creation and Joy are the two great teachings of Zarathustra Bodhisattva.

All *feeling* suffers in me and is in prison: but my *willing* always comes to me as my liberator and bringer of joy.
Willing liberates: that is the true doctrine of will and freedom – thus Zarathustra teaches you.[7]

Will liberates; will is joyful. This is the *will* of the true person of no rank. Ordinary will craves mere toys, pastimes and virtual games in the waiting room of civilization's terminal diagnosis: it wants power, money and prestige. This is *confining* the will to the restrictions of the small self, whose only hope is to sheepishly and hypocritically obey fossilized values.

Will to power is *not anthropomorphic*, and this is what humanists of all creeds will always have trouble understanding: if it were man-centered, it would be translated as will, *desire for, power*. Its origin and meaning is *greater* than the human realm. Will to power is *non-human*.

> [Will to Power] must be understood in a completely different way: power is *the one that* wills in the will. Power is the genetic and differential element in the will. This is why the will is essentially creative . . .
>
> In this way the will to power is essentially creative and giving: it does not aspire, it does not seek, it does not desire, above all it does not desire power. It gives: power is something impossible in the will (something mobile, variable, plastic); power is in the will 'the bestowing virtue', through power the will itself bestows sense and value.[8]

Will to Power is above all will to give; at the level of Zen practice, it is no other than *dana*, generosity, the first of the ten *paramitas* or perfections.

> Lust for power: but who shall call it *lust*, when the height longs to stoop down after power! Truly, there is no sickness and lust in such a longing and descent!
>
> Oh who shall find the rightful baptismal and virtuous name for such a longing! 'Bestowing virtue' – that is the name Zarathustra gave the unnameable.[9]

Secondly, will to power is will to truth. The philosopher seeks the truth. And so does the seeker of the Way. Nietzsche turns the whole thing around, and so does Zen. What if the task of the Sphinx is to ask questions, and perhaps the right questions?

> Who really is it that here questions us? What really is it in us that wants 'the truth'?
>
> Granted we want truth: why not rather untruth? And uncertainty? Even ignorance? – The problem of the value of truth stepped before us – or was it we who stepped before this problem? Which of us is Oedipus here? Which of us sphinx? It is, it seems, a rendezvous of questions and question marks. – And, would you believe it, it has finally almost come to seem to us that this problem has never been posed – that we have been the first to see it, to fix our eye on it, to hazard it? For there is a hazard in it and perhaps there exists no greater hazard.[10]

Thirdly, will to power is will to *art*. Already in the 19th century, Nietzsche lamented the origins of that same phenomenon we today commonly refer to as "dumbing down", a phenomenon that has now reached its pitiful nadir. Back then he lamented the fact that Art was progressively judged more from the point of view of the spectator than from that of the artist, and that the spectator in question was less and less artistic. Art had became mere diversion, entertainment. We have now come full circle; a spectator is now the artist; an entertainer can call himself an "artist". Art as pastime and leisure belongs to the restrictive worldview embraced by *reactive* forces, to what D. H. Lawrence called "the dark river of dissolution", a disinterested, unengaged palliative to the pain of living, nothing more. In Nietzsche's view, Art is a *stimulant* of the will, it belongs to *active*, creative, to the luminous river of life.[11]

Art had also become fabrication and deceit, it had been used, and continues to be used, in order to consecrate the untruth, to bless the lie. Reactive forces bend the will into will to deceive. True artists seek after the knowledge of truth, they are the inheritors of new possibilities of life.

66 Phantom at the Opera

Unlike the true man of no rank, we are reluctant to undergo the necessary deaths and shedding of our skin, and instead project ideals outside ourselves. These ideals are a sign of weakness. What in Zen is continuous refinement, and in Nietzsche self-overcoming, does not constitute an ideal but is instead an "awakening from all aspirations with their delusions and unconscious self-deception. It is the return to the essential will of the self".[12] It is an ongoing discipline, an ongoing process of transformation.

There is no place of rest, no enlightenment "once and for all", no space of perfection and purity from where one can gaze down at life.

Every transient milestone *en route* is a renewed opportunity for a freshly painful death, for the recognition that the substantiality of the enquiring subject is fictitious, that the seeker himself is a *phantom*. He realizes this with horror and surprise, for he sees that he casts no shadow in the eternal noontide, and that in the continuous re-enacting of the last judgment, no reflection is seen in the mirror in front of him. This return to the essential will of the self is a return to the essential will of the cosmos, the flooding of boundaries, the second coming of one's double.

In this vertiginous space one recognizes delusions, ideals and aspirations as indirect manifestations of the will to power, of the will of the cosmos.

The *Will* is not the will exhibited in the logician's shop window alongside items such as time, history, eternity, and, above all, the "free will" of the "individual".

In conventional western thinking, the themes of historical and antihistorical are always mingled with the idea of will. Within a secular framework, this might be a defensive strategy used to counteract the perceived danger of our utter meaninglessness in a universe with no beginning and no end.

Other strategies include scientific versions of the creation myth, where the fantasy of a cosmic premature ejaculation – the *Big Bang* – universally accepted as Secular Genesis, substitutes God's laborious six-day endeavour, as well as various improvised cosmologies attempting to construct a genetic ground for a universe intuitively perceived as groundless.

With the Eastern idea of karma, and indeed with Nietzsche's will to power, a "meaning" is introduced. This is because in both cases the individual's "will" and the will of the whole (destiny) are one and the same thing. It is neither giving in to religious fatalism, nor to hubristic secularism.

The human self-will, rooted in the ego, is a "daemonic infinite drive" which "lies hidden even behind the man-centered reason of modern secularism". In the East, "this infinite drive arose to awareness already very early with the idea of karma". [13]

The essential difference is that Buddhism does not shy away from *sunyata*, the "bottomless point" *beyond* the standpoint of will. There is no urge to fill the gap, as it were, there is no growing sense of a frightening groundlessness that needs to be entertained by the weaving of religious or secular dramas and cosmologies, or by the inflation of the human realm, the glorification of the individual ego.

Nietzschean will to power has been misread to mean precisely that: the overriding desire for ego-dominance, whereas it is the *abdication* of the ego, the recognition that the self is not the ego, and also the complete identification with destiny.

Nietzsche's formulation of the Will to Power is beyond both determinism and metaphysics, for it is neither separated from, nor identified with, the notion of *force*.

> My proposition is: that the will of psychology hitherto is an unjustified generalization, that this will *does not exist at all*, that instead of grasping the idea of development of one definite will into many forms, one has eliminated the character of the will by subtracting it from its content, its 'whither?' – this is in the highest degree the case with Schopenhauer: what he calls 'will' is a mere empty word.[14]

67 As a Box and its Lid

Nietzsche experienced *sunyata*, relativity, the groundlessness of existence. He went there alone, with no map, no scriptures. He knew that "form is emptiness", that the self is not "truly" existent, but, in his parlance, a manifestation of the will to power.

He realized this fundamental point, and that was in itself a great achievement, for he did not *stumble* upon it, but reached such understanding by courageously *dismantling all beliefs*. The other side of the coin is that *emptiness is form*. We have gone from the relative to the absolute; now it's time to turn the coin. Perhaps Nietzsche did not complete the journey from the Absolute *back to the Relative*: this is Nishitani Keji's critique of Nietzsche, a critique which, as vital as it is, is nevertheless open to debate. Were we to agree with the objections Nishitani raises, then Nietzsche, unlike his number two Zarathustra, never descended the mountain.

The greatest difference between Nietzsche's path and the path of Zen is of degrees in the relation between self and not-self. Nietzsche's insights were unique in the West, for he recognized the insubstantiality of the self. Particularly unique was the recognition of various elements (*drives*) within the individual, often working against each other, and the precariousness of the ego's stability and unity. These fundamental insights will later be articulated and developed further by Jung in his research on *personifying*.

But perhaps even more important to us is Nietzsche's recognition that the *self is not ego*. Just how far Nietzsche stretched this point is the question here. According to Nishitani, he did not go far enough; "non-ego does not mean simply that self is not ego," he writes, in customary Heideggerian mode.

> It has also to mean at the same time that non-ego is the self. It must reach self-awareness as something come from the self's absolute negation of itself. It is not the case that the self is merely not the self . . . It must be the case rather that the self is the self because it is not the self. Were it simply a matter of the self not being the self, the way would still be open to follow Nietzsche in taking will to power as the true self, or the "selfness" of the self.[15]

There is one step further, which Nietzsche did not take: precisely the step taken by Zen. The step is that of *actualization*, manifestation. The point made by Nishitani is relevant, in spite of the fact that it eventually leads him to the charge of anti-historicity and to a negative appraisal of myth.

> Only by going a step further does the standpoint of true non-ego appears in the reversal, "self is not self (self is non-ego) therefore it is self". This reversal . . . is precisely that existential self-awareness wherein the self is realized . . . as an emergence into its nature from non-ego. It is *Existenz* as "body-and-mind" dropping off, dropped off body-and-mind.[16]

It is crucial to bear in mind that will to power is an experimental thought, another exegesis entertained in the theatre of world-knowledge, where no theory can rightly claim objective validity and universality.

68 *Basking Luxuriously in Trivia*

Will to power must not be understood quantitatively, for if this were the case, it would eventually aim at preservation and constancy. The most common misinterpretation of the will to power, what the formula itself seems to imply when pondered by a coarse intellect, is a thirst driven by a hungry-ghost mentality. The hungry-ghost perspective is the dominant view in our day and age, but it does not have to be accepted as a dogma. Nietzsche himself suggests that will to power cannot be understood as a frantic attempt at rummaging through everything and preserving every-thing, for that would suggest that life had withdrawn from the whole and was *basking luxuriously in trivia*: a possible definition of post-modernism?[17]

What is more crucial is the giving away, the generosity of the gambler who, with Zarathustra, is almost disappointed when he wins at the dice throw, for he can afford to lose. The greatest power is the power to give, and above all to give oneself. In Buddhism, generosity is the first and fore-most "transcendental perfection", or *paramita*. It is not an injunction, a commandment, nor a pious rule of conduct. It is what arises from the very core of one's being once inner strength and courage have taken roots. It is a natural overflowing of energy. It cannot be the domain of the mob, nor of those individuals who have interiorized the mob. It is not taught in our institutions, because it does not belong there. It is not driven by the dream of need, by a hungry-ghost, setting-sun mentality.

Only a shoddy individual will interpret will to power in his own terms, as desire for political aggrandizement and social prestige. Egoism is a misguided interpretation of will, much in the same way as atomism is a misguided interpretation of force. Only a dancer, a risk-talker, a true artist/philosopher, will recognize it as overflowing generosity, joyful desire to give, and give oneself.

The standard view of power is the Hegelian view, the slave's concep-tion of power. Hegel might be presenting the image of the master, but underneath it we always find the slave.

> The slave only conceives of power as the object of recognition, the content of a representation, the stake in a competition, and therefore makes it depend, at the end of the fight, on a simple attribution of established values.[18]

Similarly, in discussing vanity from the point of view of the "noble man", Nietzsche observed in 1886 how the vain individual is all too ready to accept every good opinion about himself, and conversely reject every bad opinion.

> It is "the slave" in the vain man's blood, the remains of the slave's craftiness . . . which seeks to seduce to good opinions of itself; it is the slave, too, who immediately afterwards falls prostrate himself before these opinions, as though he had not called them forth. – And to repeat it again: vanity is an atavism.[19]

In examining the striving for distinction already in 1881, an idea that precedes Adler's "striving for superiority", Nietzsche underlines its less sympathetic, less kind and laudable attributes. Our striving for distinction, he says, far from being a charitable need to contribute to common humanity, is instead driven by the slave's mentality of controlling and dominating the other. In an extraordinary passage in the Book II of Daybreak, Nietzsche writes:

> We want, rather, to perceive or divine how the next man outwardly or inwardly *suffers* from us, how he loses control over himself and surrenders to the impressions our hand or even merely the sight of us makes upon him; and even when he who strives after distinction makes and wants to make a joyful, elevating or cheering impression, he nonetheless enjoys this success not inasmuch as he has given joy to the next man or elevated or cheered him, but inasmuch as he has *impressed* himself on the soul of the other, changed its shape and ruled over it at his own sweet will. The striving for distinction is the striving for domination over the next man, though it be a very indirect domination and only felt or even dreamed. There is a long scale of degrees of this secretly desired domination, and a complete catalogue of them would be almost the same thing as a history of culture, from the earliest, still grotesque barbarism up to grotesqueries of over-refinement and morbid idealism. This striving for distinction brings with it *for the next man* – to name only a few steps on the ladder: torment, then blows, then terror, then fearful astonishment, then wonderment, then envy, then admiration, then elevation, then joy, then cheerfulness, then laughter, then derision, then mockery, then ridicule, then giving blows, then imposing torment: -here at the end of the ladder stands the ascetic and martyr, who feels the highest enjoyment by himself enduring, as a consequence of his drive for distinction, precisely that which, on the first step of the ladder, his counterpart the barbarian imposes on others on whom and before whom he wants to distinguish himself.[20]

The ascetic and the barbarian share the slave's view of power and distinction. Their prestige and status is highly dependent on social recognition, on the crowd's appraisal and awe. Their power is not the real and tangible strength of the overman, for whom no recognition is necessary, as he acts out of the spontaneity of his own nature, and whose contribution shines *sub specie aeternitatis*.

69 *Gift Economy and Dana*

A true gift goes against both our ideas of justice and our ethical ideas. Our idea of fairness is based on the economic principles of universal exchange: the moral obligation of equal settlements between individuals, and between individuals and the community.

It goes back to the primary relation between creditor and debtor. The transgressor is punished, and punishment is a debt to society. At the heart of our ideas of justice and ethics is the *jus talionis*, an eye for an eye. A true gift is the artefact of a nobler civilization, of a nobler economy: a gift economy, or an *economy of expenditure*. In giving, one delights in the joy of the receiver. That mutual joy is being now substituted by the universal market of gift-articles, true cemeteries of giving where one's own sentiments of generosity and gratitude are spelled out by the mechanized clichés of the global economy.

It might be that a nobler economy only survives in the arcadia drafted by radical poets and philosophers. Or that its fragments find expression in isolated acts of kindness unaccounted for.

On an individual basis, generosity is possible because of *plenitude*. We feel rooted in our being, overflowing with energy, and we cannot but give ourselves to others. It is more *abgeben* (to bestow) than *schenken* (to give).

This form of generosity is un-selfconscious, and far removed from the "altruistic" shadow of guilt, debt and bad conscience which characterizes many of our charitable, good-intentioned forms of giving.

A strong individual is able to give without holding anything back. And the same applies to strong communities: they generate a new notion of justice, allowing themselves, in Nietzsche's words,

> the most refined luxury there is – that of allowing those who do it harm to go unpunished.[21]

Strength is the ability to actively forget the debts owed, to bear minor hurt without reacting, to *hold back retribution*.

Dana, the Buddhist paramita, is the opposite of *ressentiment*. Any creation born out of ressentiment is a system of diseased values, because it is based on weakness. Moving out of the poisonous sphere of *ressentiment*, and into the plenitude of *Dana*, of true generosity, is, in Nietzsche's language, *deliverance from revenge*, the *bridge to the highest hope*.

An economy of expenditure will be reflected into an *aristocratic form of ethics*, a system that goes beyond our "shopkeepers' scales" method, and beyond our compulsive need to counterbalance guilt with punishment.

Aristocratic is not social status, breed or heritage, but the overcoming of the instinct for revenge on which our western idea of democracy is based. In a noble society, generosity replaces revenge, and the bestowal of gifts comes out of an excess of strength (*Uberfluss von Macht*).[22]

Giving is itself a high form of Art; as all great Art, giving is born out of necessity. The spiritual teacher is depicted in Indian traditions as a cloud full of rain who cannot but give. The cup is overflowing, the bee has too much honey. A noble individual practices *dana* constantly. Her very breathing is a form of generosity, for she has sidestepped the selfish perspective for a higher view.

A higher, noble community could be thus evaluated "according to how many parasites it can endure".[23]

70 Feminine Economy and the Empire of the Self-Same

We are forgetting how to give presents (Adorno).[24]

There are essentially two types of economies. One, based on the law of return, is rooted in Locke's definition of property in his *Second Treatise of Government*, according to which a person has the right to possess whatever "he removes out of the state that nature hath provided and left it in [and] he hath mixed his labour with". [25]

These notions of property and labour have so far constituted our official "History". The other type of economy too has a long history, but has rarely made the historical headlines, for it has been rarely voiced. It is rooted in more "feminine" practices, where giving is performed without expectation of return, where the de-propriation of oneself is done without self-interest. Feminine economy is based on the exchange of *gifts* and masculine economy on the exchange of *commodities*.

> Commodity exchange establishes a relationship between the objects exchanged, whereas gift exchange establishes a relationship between the subjects. In other words, commodity exchange is a price-forming process, a system of purchase and sale. Gift exchange is not.[26]

Our economic reality is, in the words of Hélène Cixous, "the Empire of the Self-Same", having its basis in Hegelian philosophy: the self (understood as a solid, separate entity) goes out into the other in order to come back to itself. The other is separate, different, a potential danger. The self must defeat it or make it its own. *Objectify and possess* is the motto of primitive economies. *Weak, coarse, revengeful* are the attributes Nietzsche used. Modern thinkers, post-Jungian and feminists among them, will instead use the term *masculine*. This model, whatever the label we might choose to define it with, can only conceive of commodities. This is why Adorno is still right when he says that in capitalist society *a true gift is impossible*.

The alternative model, what Nietzsche calls noble, *aristocratic* – what we would call *feminine* – does not divide self and other.

Mother and child do not relate as self/other. They do not experience competing interests of quantifiable exchange of commodities. According to Hélène Cixous, mothers naturally experience what she calls the "not me within me". In Vajrayana Buddhism, the mother/child model is used in meditation to overcome the separation of self and other. Every sentient being is visualized as having been our mother in a previous life. Whether we appreciate this teaching literally, its efficacy in meditation practice is undeniable. Try it and see for yourself.

Masculine–feminine polarities are modes of interpretation in the understanding of possible types of economy. A feminine economy would be able to contain, and provide a creative implementation for, masculine exuberance and strength.

On the other hand, the same strength inflates, in a coarse and self-aggrandizing male economy, to the point of self-destruction.

THE CROOKED PATH
OF ETERNITY

TIME AND THE ETERNAL RETURN

71   On Science as Temptation

The eternal return of the same has been subjected to all kind of misinterpretations, all stemming from an ambiguous fragment in the *Nachlass*, where Nietzsche states that it represents "the most scientific of all hypothesis". This has led many to see the eternal return as an attempt to build a cosmology. Nowhere in Nietzsche's writing approved for publication do we find any attempt to see it as such. And even what is stated in the *Nachlass* must be taken with a pinch of salt, for '"scientific" in the 19th century did not mean what is meant now by the term, that is, based on the natural sciences through verification and analysis. "Empirical" might be an adequate contemporary equivalent of the 19th century use of the word "scientific". Confronted with the idea of the eternal return, we are dealing with a psychological, "mythical" truth, an aesthetic rather than a scientific truth.

The eternal return is scientific (empirical) also in another sense: not in seeking the supposedly "objective" legitimacy of science – a peculiarly modern preoccupation shared even at the beginning of the twentieth century by Freud and Jung, but instead in the deconstructive function of science: the humbling possibility of being proven wrong by a new set of enquiries.

Every formulation in Nietzsche is at the same time *experiment*, *attempt*, and *temptation*.

72   A Round of Applause for our Next Commentator

The riddle of the eternal return has puzzled Nietzsche's readers for more than a century. The huge array of interpretations reveals something about each commentator and systematizer, including myself. In this respect Nietzsche has played the role of Prince Myskin: his presence and pronouncements, strangely neutral and detached, bring forth something essential from his interlocutors. It quietly reveals hidden aspects of their psyche. The revelation is modest, apolitical and pre-ideological. It does not lead to any external transformation.

Come forward, commentator, say your name, state your claim.

Detractors have right of way: for them, the notion of eternal return is an obscure, meaningless riddle. They do not comment on it directly, they succeed in ignoring it, and in consigning its creator to the intellectual Gulag labeled "irrationalism".

Others applaud it too readily, seeing in it, alongside the Will to Power, the key element of an imaginary system of metaphysics. The trouble with such an obliging explanation is that they refuse to see the obvious fact that Nietzsche did not create a system, nor did he postulate any metaphysics: both the creation of a system and metaphysics require a consistent lack of integrity. For that, one needs to be a "German philosopher" in the fashionable Hegelian – and later Heideggerian – mode. To create a system and join in the metaphysical chat-room, one needs to embrace the current orthodoxy – *any* orthodoxy will do – no matter how atrocious, idiotic and even murderous.

"There is no great philosopher without a great systematic work", thus states the crass, still popular, prejudice. Mrs. Foster-Nietzsche, Nietzsche's treacherous sister, certainly believed that particular prejudice to be the truth, and consequently embarked in the task of re-assembling her brother's frivolously "literary" posthumous notes into a "solid", "consistent" work. This later became that Frankenstein of philosophical literature known as *Will to Power*. She made sure that Nietzsche's work provided a ready-to-wear "philosophical" system for those whom her brother had repeatedly called *canaille* (scum): namely, the anti-Semites into whose fold she had married and whose "ideas" she promoted. Hers might be an extreme case, but many other examples suggest that the need for a system is inherently totalitarian.

An equally misguided interpretation, closely linked to the above, is represented by those who are somewhat disappointed by Nietzsche, from an altogether different angle, but at heart for the same reason: they see his early thought as iconoclastic, pessimistic; they praise in him a "positivist" who later turns to a form of religious transcendence, thus betraying atheists' and free-thinkers' treasured hamlet. They feel betrayed, and react hysterically to the word "eternal" whenever they read of the formula of the eternal return: they interpret it as nostalgia of paradise; they smell incense and feel dizzy in the damp, sumptuous interiors of suspended disbelief. They misread overman as Superman, they dress up Lao-Tzu as Conan the Barbarian, and misprint Will to Power as willpower. Their fear is the fear of the desert.

73   The Uncanny Guest at the Door

There is tremendous depth of meaning in the Nietzschean idea of the eternal return. Its implications are enormous. It is similar to Archimedes' *Eureka* in its manifestation, though Nietzsche himself was at first horrified, and not entirely sure, of this "heaviest burden" he had conceived for himself and for humanity. It was an experience, not a construct, that would allegedly have added metaphysical validation to his unsystematic thought. It carried within itself an element of "inspiration" and "revelation", two words closely related to romantic and religious experience, but in no way dissimilar from the breakthrough that takes place in scientific discovery. Art, science and religion all partake in the field of human endeavour, and every new creation, any new finding and experience is imbibed with inspiration and revelation. At the same time, all three endeavours are ultimately flawed: mankind pursues these lofty diversions in order to avoid having to face groundlessness, the absence of true existence, sunyata.

The thought of eternal return *occurred* to Nietzsche. It *invaded* him. It opened up a new dimension to the problem of finality, with which the West has wrestled unsuccessfully for centuries, often proposing a helpless infinity determined by the inability to realize certainty,[1] as the only alternative to religious fatalism. The eternal return transcends the dichotomy of recurrence and extinction.

Nietzsche attacked transcendence in any form. God is dead; there is no *Being* behind *Becoming*. No Spirit disguised within matter. No Ghost in the machine. There is not a One playing hide and seek among the many. There is no Self. There is no such thing as "the thing in itself". No such thing as "historical process". There is no Nirvana, at least not in the way Schopenhauer, and subsequently western culture, understood it.

Such forceful refutation of transcendence is not born out of pessimism and cynicism, but out of a profound acceptance of what is and out of a great passion for enquiry. Nietzsche understood that every form of transcendence, each carefully disguised mode of a "beyond", heralds what he calls "the uncanny guest at the door": nihilism. We create a beyond because we cannot fully appreciate, and be thankful for, this transient life.

To appreciate one's life is another term for the essence of Zen practice, and the implications of such appreciation are tremendous. The eternal return is the "mythological" counterpart of such great affirmation, the equivalent aesthetic manifestation of such wonderful appreciation of impermanence.

74 *An Enigma to Provoke Understanding*

The eternal return of the Same (*Die Ewige Wiederkehr des Gleichen*) is where most commentators falter, stutter, avert their gaze, or dismiss the idea altogether. As Maurice Blanchot pointed out that

> for a long time, nearly all the commentators . . . have been hindered by this doctrine which seemed arbitrary, useless, mystical, and furthermore, very anti-quated, since it already lay about in Heraclitus.[2]

When discussing the eternal return, Lou Salomé, who in 1894 published the first full-length work on Nietzsche, writes of how filled with horror he was by the idea, how he regarded it as a kind of terrifying, suspicious thought. Spurred by her advice, he went on to study natural science in an attempt to ground his idea according to the predominant belief system of his time.

He could not *prove* the eternal return, and Lou was surprised that, instead of feeling "freed from the task of being its harbinger, from a fate he anticipated with horror", he instead was seized by it, "hardened" by the "irrefutable conviction", almost "as though a magic spell".[3] Her own reaction to the thought itself, and to Nietzsche's subsequent obstinacy to stick with his initial intuition, is crucial to understanding the cultural and intellectual climate of the times: everything had to be proven "scientifi-cally". The art of psychoanalysis itself, whose ranks Salomé was to join, ambled its first tentative steps in the colourless hallways of science. Clinical language, case studies, all was directed towards the approval and validation of the intellectual elite of the time, whose points of reference were ruled by deterministic science. This in spite of the fact that both Freud and Jung moved in a territory more akin to mythology and the arts. Wittgenstein famously saw psychoanalysis as a powerful mythology, which one must see through.

That no one grasped at first the thought of eternal return, that it was simply regarded as an archaism, an incomprehensible riddle, is no surprise: it *is* ungraspable, unfathomable. It discourages both the belief in an otherworldly redemption (the religious fallacy) and the view that history is moving along nicely towards more and more progress (the historic fallacy). It sees through the illusions of the Enlightenment and its unreasonable faith in Reason. It sees through the wishful thinking, the dualistic rupture at the core of the entire Judaeo-Christian tradition.

The *eternal return is an enigma*, and so is a Zen *koan*. An 'enigma' is not a mere puzzle or a fanciful, hermetic image or obscure expression; it is not designed to prevent insight, but to incite it. It often carries a double meaning, or indeed several layers of meaning; it may open doors to the absolute realm, to the relative, and to any realm in between.[4]

Later in the 20th century the idea of the eternal return was taken on board as *existential* and *transformational*, a point made by Deleuze, Klossowski, and T. Strong among others. Am I willing to repeat eternally my present deed? Am I prepared to re-live eternally this very life? How far does my appreciation of life go? Am I prepared to say *Yes* wholeheartedly to both joy and pain, love and suffering, to the point that no variance subsists between me and my destiny? Would I be prepared to re-live my life for eternity, with all its joys and sorrows? If unable to do so, sooner or later I will find some consolation, a system of metaphysics, an addiction, and an elected pastime. Religion might be the opium of the people, but so is any form of transcendence, no matter how secular and scientific. It heralds nihilism, rooted in resentment and bad conscience.

Attributing an *existential* meaning to the idea of eternal return is of course only one of the interpretations available to us. *Plurality of views* is the bewildering and often unsettling trait of Nietzsche's thought. He does not only attack his adversaries but mercilessly *turns the weapon of critique and contradiction on to himself*. At times the thought of eternal return can be interpreted as cosmological truth, at other times as expression of an existential and moral choice; more often than not, it simply appears to be a bewildering enigma, a koan whose solution is impossible, whose meaning is impenetrable, but able nevertheless to bring about a radical transformation. It does not fail in uncovering the inherent *groundlessness* of existence, and it is this very groundlessness and meaninglessness which spurs one to *create ground and meaning*. Salomé was right on this point. And she was certainly right in believing his friend to be a "religious being". Where she is conceivably mistaken is in thinking that affirmation of life necessarily heralds what is commonly described by that devious word, *transcendence*.

75   *On the Sex Life of Angels*

Immanence versus transcendence is a dualistic conundrum brought about by theology. Outside the monotheistic traditions they happily co-exist. At first, one might conclude that the dichotomy is also found within the various schools of Buddhism, with Zen representing the immanent approach – with its emphasis on the everyday – and Vajrayana, with its emphasis on transcendent deities, at the other end of the spectrum.

These notions might be useful to the historian, or to any other embalmer of the living truth, but within the experience of Zen both immanence and transcendence are dualistic concepts. A Zen Master might employ those terms for didactic reasons. In order to teach, he must use (dualistic) language; but it would be misleading to ascribe ontological meaning onto the words used.

To be religious is to embrace life fully. The overman and the eternal return are not attempts to create a new metaphysics or a new path to transcendence, but instead poetic metaphors for *plenitude* and *gratefulness*. The religiosity inherited from metaphysics is, on the other hand, motivated by a sense of scarcity. It manufactures transcendence, and builds its systems around a primary delusion.

It is tempting to be unashamedly partial to a religiosity steeped in pure immanence. Historically, this has been the way of the "heretics", of adventurous religious thinkers and philosophers who fostered such vision and have often been dealt with in the most brutal fashion: burned at the stake, or, in modern times, exposed to ridicule and isolated.

However, the antithesis immanence/transcendence is a peculiarly western hang-up; its very formulation smells of Medieval theology, anecdotally preoccupied with dangerous inanities, and it colours our understanding of awakening, or enlightenment, which is rigidly conceived either solely as something inherent within us which nevertheless needs to be realized as our fundamental Buddha-nature (immanent view), or, at the other extreme, as an unreachable goal, something we must strive for through countless rebirths (transcendent view). As Stephen Batchelor points out, "there are dangers both ways".

> If we emphasize immanence, we run the risk of ignoring the vast difference between awakening and our current state of delusion. On the other hand, if we raise enlightenment into something almost humanly impossible, then we run the danger of denigrating our own capacity for really making any significant change at all. We have to recognize that our human experience is not reducible to either a gradualistic temporal paradigm . . . or reduced to a . . . paradigm in which enlightenment is already present..... Human existence is more complicated than that . . .
>
> The practice therefore is learning to live at the juncture between a vertical dimension of depth and immanence and a horizontal dimension of time and transcendence.[5]

76 Whether you have been happy, or full of sorrow

The eternal return is the highest metaphor for the appreciation of life. Nietzsche was so impressed by a poem Lou Salomé had written, 'Hymn to Friendship", that he set it to music. The poem says:

> Surely a friend by his friend is loved
> As I loved you, oh mysterious life
> Whether in you I have cried or rejoiced,
> Whether you have been happy, or full of sorrow.[6]

Lou's objection that the reconciliation in Nietzsche of "world, God and self" is pernicious is relevant, for it represents *in nuce* the hubristic approach of later philosophies such as existential humanism.

After the death of God (and the death of the Gods too, according to the existentialist stance), the only dimensions left are abstract metaphysics and the concrete physical world. Having rejected the former, we would be left, so Lou Salomé's argument goes, with human beings inflated to God-like proportions. It is questionable whether one can directly attribute such a standpoint to Nietzsche, but there have been schools of thought founded precisely on this misunderstanding.

To this day, one of the commonly held views of the Renaissance is of a deeply humanistic era that forfeited the soul in favour of the self, and elevated highly creative humans to the inhabitants of Olympus. What is forgotten is that the beauty and love celebrated by the Renaissance artists are imagined qualities belonging to the soul. Michelangelo wrote:

> Amore e' un concetto di bellezza
> Immaginata o vista dentro al core,
> Amica di virtute e gentilezza.

> (Love is a concept born of beauty
> Imagined or seen within the heart.
> Bosom friend of virtue and kindness).[7]

77 No-Self

Later developments in Nietzsche's thought do not justify Salomé's interpretation, for the self with whom both world and God (and fate itself) are identified, is not only made of many selves, but is ultimately unsubstantial.

Such misinterpretation is possible only if we assume that the self Nietzsche writes about is the same as the Cartesian ego, but this is not the case, for with the former we are very close to the Buddhist view of *anatta*, or no-self. His later insights, in spite of him not having had the chance to elaborate them further, testify this.

In the Nietzschean will to power, as we have seen, there is no such thing as an individual *will* driven by the ego, nor a *power* as we normally understand it.

78 *Trial and Error*

In an attempt to find scientific validation to his thought of the eternal return, Nietzsche immersed himself in the study of the natural sciences. In a letter to his friend Peter Gast from Sils Maria, dated 18 August 1883, he writes:

> At that time [1873] I was studying the atomic doctrine up to the works of the Jesuit Boscovich, the first to demonstrate mathematically that, for the exact science of mechanics, the premise of solid atomic points is an unusable hypothesis: a proposition that now has, for natural scientists trained in mathematics, canonical validity.[8]

Roger Boscovich, who had written a work titled *Philosophia Naturalis*, was an original physical theorist, and in studying his and other scientists' works, Nietzsche conscientiously apprehended the leading scientific theories of the day. He was not morally engaged in conjectures, but was instead preoccupied with giving philosophical diagnosis to scientific formulations.

Not satisfied with the atomistic, quantitative reduction of all phenomena, he was very intrigued by Boscovich's findings. In observing elasticity and its relation to impact, Boscovich had assumed that elasticity implies a displacement of the relative position of particles in the elastic body. This suggested that the atoms might be constituted of small particles, or "sub-atoms". Boscovich saw phenomena as "effects of force" or as originating from a theoretical center of force. His "elaborate conceptions of "force points" or "force centers" was "reclaimed in the nineteenth century because of its compatibility with the emerging trend towards a dynamic rather than a mechanistic theory of natural process".[10] He was in many ways a forerunner of quantum physics, a field of endeavour that in more recent years has contributed enormously to the understanding of energy and matter.

> Of what is the body made? It is made of emptiness and rhythm. At the ultimate heart of the body, at the heart of the world, there is no solidity. Once again, there is only the dance.
>   At the unimaginable heart of the atom, the compact nucleus, we have found no solid objects, but rather a dynamic pattern of tightly confined energy vibrating perhaps 1022 times a second: a dance [. . .] In the world of subatomic physics there are no objects, only processes.[9]

79   The Heaviest Burden

When we reach a point where freedom and necessity amount to the same thing, the most exhilarating sense of liberation is accompanied by a marked feeling of carrying the burden of a grave responsibility. The reverse in also true. We find this in Nietzsche, but also in Dogen Zenji. In the *Bendowa* fascicle (a "talk about pursuing the truth"), he tells of his journey back to Japan, having studied in China with his teacher. His determination to spread the Dharma to all living beings felt as if a heavy burden had been placed on his shoulders.

The path of liberation propounded by Dogen is literally termed in Japanese as *shutsuro*, "path to get out", and also as *shusshin no katsuro*, "the vigorous road of the body getting out". This "getting out" is what makes all phenomena in the universe suddenly real, tangible. Their profound weight is being experienced for the first time, alongside a great sense of liberative purpose.

80   Enigma Variations

It seems strange that a rigorous critic of metaphysics should salvage the word *eternal*. Traditionally, eternity relates to time, just as being relates to becoming, permanence to impermanence, infinite to finite. In this conventional view, time is the devourer, Chronos, and this elemental outlook is confirmed by the four key variations on the theme:

(1)   eternity conceived as "endless duration";
(2)   the mystical *nunc stans*, the ever-present which never becomes the past;

(3)   the simultaneity of all disparate parts of time;
(4)   timelessness.

The eternity of the eternal return is none of the above. Its "eternity" is not set as a backdrop against "time". For Nietzsche, there is no end. Becoming goes on and on, it happens again and again. Nothing is ever finished. Nothing is "once and for all". Becoming unfolds innocently, untainted. There is no equivalent view in the West. It bears a resemblance to the eastern wheel of life and samsara, with one crucial difference: for Nietzsche *desire for deliverance from the wheel is nihilistic*, it betrays a lack of appreciation for what is. Nirvana, in the understanding of 18th century western thinkers, is understood as taking place once and for all, and as distinctly separate from samsara. But is nirvana separate from samsara?

> Against the value of that which eternally remains the same (Spinoza's naïveté, Descartes' also), the value of the shortest and most transitory, the seductive flash of gold on the belly of the serpent vita.[10]

Detractors of the idea of the eternal return have been too many to mention. And those who have praised it unquestionably have perhaps been the worst detractors. One of the most eloquent misunderstandings of Nietzsche's thought comes from Buddhist social theorist and scholar David Loy, author, among others, of a formidable study titled *Lack and Transcendence*. His reflections are highly relevant and interesting, for they come from an existentialist as well as a Zen Buddhist perspective. This is why it is worthwhile to confute his ideas, in homage to a tradition of honourable combat.

Loy acknowledges that Nietzsche is "perhaps" the first known western thinker to realize that morality, search for truth and meaning of life are "constructs". He writes:

> Stripped of its will to power, Nietzschean perspectivism, which liberates all truths from the supervision of a dominant one, turns out to be similar to Nagarjuna's realization that "no truth has been taught by a Buddha to anyone, anywhere.[11]

The fact that Nietzsche's perspectivism needs to be "stripped", in Loy's view, of the will to power, in order to qualify for an analogy with Nagarjuna's philosophy, shows that Loy has understood the will to power literally, as an act of the heroic ego, rather than a supreme act of surrender and giving.

Let us read further:

> The need to ground the groundless sense-of-self cannot be denied. When we attempt to ignore it, by devoting ourselves to secular pursuits, we end up sacralizing them – and therefore demonize them.[12]

96 • • • • • • • • • •

For existentialist thinkers such as Loy, there are either abstract ideas or "secular pursuits". The middle realm of poetry and art, of music and metaphor, seems to escape their perception entirely. A great shame, because perhaps no other western school of thought has produced a more thorough investigation, nor has it looked at the human condition more unflinchingly than existentialism. Though conceding that, as a myth, the eternal return is "better than most", Loy concludes that it is

> not a good enough myth because it still seeks being: it attempts to make the here and now real by making it recur . . . eternally.[13]

Loy sees Nietzsche as the first "post-modernist" and, in a perverse role-reversal, attributes to him a stance on nihilism he never assumed in the first place, using against him an argument borrowed entirely from Nietzsche himself:

> Nihilism is not the débâcle of all meaning but our dread of that débâcle and what we do to avoid it, compulsively seizing on certain meanings as a bulwark against that form of lack.[14]

Loy has found an answer: *lack*. Lack, the boundless desires of the hungry ghosts, the invisible worm eating away at the heart of humankind, finds at last the recognition it deserves: it is being elevated by Loy to metaphysical proportions. One is surprised he does not write it with a capital *L*, thus perpetrating the existentialist tradition of substituting God with capitalized abstractions.

Giving *lack* centre-stage gives away reliance on a mythology of deprivation. No wonder Nietzsche is misread: Nietzsche's mythology speaks of the very opposite: overflowing abundance, the cornucopia of plenty, out of which *dana paramita* is made possible.

Loy puts Nietzsche "in the same camp as Plato" and misconstrues the eternal return as an attempt to *escape* the sense of lack. He reads the "eternal" dualistically, as opposed to perishable, and misses the point entirely, for "eternal" is instead the *measure* of how much one can sustain the meaninglessness, the groundlessness of existence. We must not forget that Nietzsche was at first horrified by the thought of eternal return, and that what he reproached Indian Buddhism for was the desire to escape suffering. But why refuse to escape suffering, given the chance? Was Nietzsche a masochist? No, he was not. His formula is the *non plus ultra* of life affirmation, *not born out of attachment to life, but as the supreme act of embracing one's destiny, one's karma*. It is not, admittedly, the view any small self can sustain. It is *the view of the Master*.

In Nietzsche's view, by proclaiming suffering to be an ontological reality, Buddhism (the Buddhism he knew of) *does not embrace suffering* as a major source of human endeavour. It is a view of Buddhism in tune with 19th century ambiguity on the subject, which regarded it either as an Epicurean doctrine of godless serenity, or as wistful escapism from the obligations and the hardships of life.

Literature of the time often referred to the "black melancholy" of Buddhism, and Schopenhauer's pessimism was evoked alongside the Buddha as both were seen as essentially gloomy characters aspiring to the extinction of hope and desire.

Creating a new metaphor, a new myth, out of acceptance of *the beautiful necessity*, courageously identifying necessity and freedom, does not entail a new metaphysics, nor does it mean going back to *being* and transcendence. What is it then? It is simply a *poetic act*. To *literalize* Nietzsche is to forget that he was first and foremost an artist, a musician, a prose-stylist of the first grade, *before* being a philosopher. More a *creative thinker*, we would say nowadays, than an academic; something to do not only with his unique, even peculiar nature, but also with a phenomenon traditionally rare in the Anglo-Saxon schools of thought (with some remarkable exceptions): an *intellectual* in "continental" Europe, and particularly in the Mediterranean, which Nietzsche was drawn to and largely influenced by, is not necessarily an academic, but can be instead an aesthetically minded, creative individual.

In attacking the idea of the eternal return, Loy says that it is a myth *born out of desire*. He reads the metaphor *literally*. Does a metaphor need to be read literally? Would one literally step out of a hundred-foot pole as required by a famous Zen koan? The eternal return is nothing less than a *koan*, an existential riddle to meditate upon, to be lived by, to be thoroughly transformed by. We can "crack it" the moment we are prepared to embrace our life fully, *as it is*. It is an "affirmation of the world" as "let-go", not as "grasped at".

The eternal return is not an egocentric whim devised in order to retain one's lost toys, dolls and knick-knacks, nor, as Loy says, one's "cherished musical moments". That would be ludicrous. Nor does it want to repeat *ad infinitum* a joy that would instead be "destroyed by the self-consciousness which reflexively distinguishes itself from the music in order to enjoy enjoying it". Loy's verdict on the metaphor of the eternal return does not spare blows below the belt. Having decided that it is motivated by attachment and childish desire to repeat pleasurable experiences, he censoriously concludes:

> Striving to find the past in the future is less a formula for joy than a psychoanalytic definition of neurosis.[15]

So there you are. We have heard it all before: Nietzsche was mad from the start, was he not? And how could it be otherwise? Such far-fetched, unsystematic ideas! But he was worst than mad; he apparently was (and in this Loy obliquely agrees with Heidegger) the "most unbridled Platonist in the history of western metaphysics".

8 | *"Everywhen" and Alien Cosmology*

The thought of the eternal return introduces a thoroughly alien perspective; it presents us with the *cosmology of the outsider*, for it does not subscribe to either the western idea of linear time, nor to the archaic perceptions of cyclical and circular time. After all, *cyclical time is but a special case of linear time.* We can only think of 'cyclical' as a line returning to itself and forming a circle. Contemplating the thought of the eternal return presupposes a suspension of our disbelief, an independence from our cherished ideas of *origin* and *creation*, whether derived from religious or secular cosmogonies.

In contemplating the idea of the eternal return, I found it useful to reflect on the Aboriginal perception of time. I cannot claim to have understood it, nor have I been able to outline definite associations between the Aboriginal view of time and the eternal return, but a glimpse of it helped me nevertheless de-centralize the overpowering western prejudices on the subject.

In the first chapter of his book *A Place for Strangers – Towards a History of Australian Aboriginal Being*, Tony Swain discusses the two crucial subjects of *time* and the *body*. "The two are one" from an Aboriginal perspective, he writes. *There is no such thing as ontological "time" out there.* He clears the way from the most common misconception that attributes a vague "timelessness" to the Aboriginal view of time and its appropriation not only by the New Age, but also by eminent anthropologists and scholars such as Eliade. A common mistake is to trap oneself between the interpretative cages of linear versus cyclical time:

> A people's view of time must not be forced to cast its vote in a two-candidate typology but should rather be left to be 'understood in their own terms'.[16]

Aboriginals speak neither of linear nor of cyclical time. Instead, their view of time comes close to what Tony Swain, echoing Paul Ricoeur, calls *rhythmic time*.

> Rhythmic time recognizes recurrent and distinct patterns, but without suggesting that the patterns loop back upon themselves to form circles. If we remove our presuppositions regarding Aboriginal statements about seasons, celestial activity, kinship and so on, we are left with the more faithful claim that these are presented as predictably patterned rhythms.[17]

Swain goes one step further, stating that Aborigines "operate from an understanding of *rhythmed events"*. In this way, he *disposes* not only of cycles, *but of time itself*.

From Plato onwards, Time "imitates Eternity and *circles around according to number"* (*Timaeus*). Numbers are an essential component in the conception of both linear and cyclical time. The rhythms in Aboriginal life, however, are *unnumbered*: "Aborigines traditionally used no counting at all" (that does not mean that they could not *quantify* things).

> In the popular Western view, time still, so to speak, ticks on even if nothing occurs; its emancipation from events is ensured by its own subjugation of an ongoing numbered measure. But in Aboriginal thought there is nothing beyond events themselves. This is entirely apparent in their cosmologies, which lack any reference to ultimate pre-event origins. For Aborigines, there is nothing more fundamental than the statement: events occur.[18]

"Aboriginal appreciation of events" is "subtle as well as aesthetically and philosophically well developed". In the following Aranda reading of natural patterns outlining "time points of night and day" we do find poetic descriptions, but we do not find *time*:

> The Milky Way is stretched out across the centre of the sky.
> The bandicoots back into their barrows.
> Light glimmers.
> The outline of trees and objects are clearly defined.
> The sun is burning down.
> The sun is low in the sky.
> The shadows are variegated.
> The sun is sinking.
> The sky is aflame with red and yellow.[19]

Rhythmic, predictable patterns are described, but there is no evidence of an interpretation being employed.

82   *Invitation to Drowning*

Affirmation of life is not *attachment*. Twenty-first century lifestyle among the privileged in developed countries represents a sophisticated and urbane form of misery, combining raw desire with the more rarefied seeking of the Way: designer clothes and smart drugs paired with spiritual weekends in search of enlightenment. Squeezing life as a lemon, burning the candle at both ends; many such cozy platitudes might describe our attachment to life, and still it would come nowhere near the

Nietzschean formula of *living dangerously*, for this implies embracing life in its totality, including suffering and death.

The hedonist surfs on the vast ocean without ever drowning. And only the drowned come to know the ocean intimately. We can only be attached to life by objectifying it, by turning it into a commodity. We want to hold on to our cherished moments, to the fleeting joy experienced in instants of self-forgetting, But we do not yearn for the recurrence of anguish and pain. If I want joy to return, I have to accept its counterpart too. If I am not able to do that, I am still attached to life, not affirming it. The wonderful holidays whose memory I still relish were also made up of moments of irritation and discomfort, and were I to repeat the experience I would experience those unpleasant moments too.

In *Zarathustra*, it is the ugliest man who affirms the eternal return. Not the happy lover, the radiant sage, the beautiful princess, the pampered celebrity. Not the self-satisfied leader of men, nor the successful artist, but *the ugliest man*: an unfortunate, unhappy creature.

Nietzsche's life was not a bed of roses. He was seized by horror when contemplating the implications of this heaviest of thoughts (*das schwerste Gewicht*), and the joy he envisioned would recur eternally was a *joy born out of the deepest agony*.

Imbibed in the atmosphere of late Romanticism, the austerity of solitude and pain injects a sobering, caustic effect to rapture, simultaneously embracing past, present, and future. Not a "mystical revelation", but the way things unfold in *the music of becoming*.

Denigration of life seems to have been one of mankind's main occupations, and obsessive attachment the only consistent way of relating to life. It is a miracle to find such a thorough affirmation of life within western thought, and it should be celebrated.

83 Healthy Repetition and Miserable Circularity

Psychologically, the recognition of the eternal return of the same is an *affirmation*, the manifestation of *active* forces at work. It tells us that the organism feels strong enough, healthy enough to face up to life's challenges and unpredictability. Conversely, metaphysical ideas of heaven, eternity – as well as secular beliefs in evolution and progress – offer by and large abstract consolations, means to appease the natural hum of perilously floating into the ocean of life-and-death. Those b belief, for that matter – betray the presence of *reactive*. They are motivated by fear and contempt. Heaven offe.

delight, and progress bestows on us the bogus certainty that goodness is triumphantly advancing at all times. They both present us with a surrogate answer to an inevitable *impasse*, and in the process reveal a deep-seated, neurotic need for *narcotic happiness*, for some arcadia, for the assurance that there *is* after all a rationale to human misfortune and anxiety.

Fritz Perls, a psychoanalyst turned founder of *Gestalt* therapy, differentiates between "neurotic compulsion to repeat" and "healthy repetition". In his view, the former is a sign that an incomplete situation in the past is still incomplete in the present:

> Every time enough tension accumulates in the organism to make the task dominant, there is another try at a solution.[20]

This is no different from any other repeated accumulated tension; the "neurotic repetition" is "energized". Perls calls this state of affairs *miserable circularity*.

With healthy repetition, on the other hand, the task is completed and "equilibrium is restored", once "the organism has maintained itself or grown by assimilating something new".

> It is only by assimilation, completion, that one learns anything and is prepared for a new situation; but what has failed of completion is ignorant and out of touch and therefore becomes more and more incomplete.[21]

It is only through *assimilation* that an *event* is transformed into an *experience*. There has been incorporation; the experience has been woven into one's soul.

Two things remain to be seen: first, whether the whirlwind of becoming can ever truly manufacture an entirely *new situation*; but it would be contemptuous to pounce on a belief justified within the nineteensixties' universal buoyancy, a temptation that I will resist. Secondly, it is legitimate to ask whether Perls' *miserable circularity* might itself transmute into awareness of the eternal return of the same, in an alchemical process from within, as it were, and without the need of a stabilizing therapeutic intervention.

This would imply that poison *is* medicine, neurosis health, and delusion enlightenment. I might want to remain eternally in hell, out of compassion for others (the Bodhisattva's way); or I might find some kind of redemption in the refusal to sell out to transcendental hope and secular, therapeutic salvation.

The vision of the eternal return is in itself a rare occurrence in human life, a breakthrough akin in its destabilizing effect to what Zen calls *satori*, or "seeing into one's true nature". That miserable circularity might in itself be experienced as liberation is of course the *absolute* view, and does not preclude the need of "working on oneself" in the *relative* realm, of addressing specific ways (problems, neurosis, compulsions) in which the self protects itself from an imaginary external threat.

84 When a Philosopher Sings

"Eternal" is the only word that survives both the wreckage of great doubt and the turmoil of polytheism. It is an attribute of poetry and art. It is not eternity as we know it, but a poetic and paradoxical recall of fate and freedom, a clear and present danger to both Enlightenment's ideas of freedom and progress, and to the crude determinism of orthodox religious belief.

Thus the logician will attack the thought of eternal return as inveterate transcendentalism, or indeed madness, whereas the believer will see it as extreme nihilism.

We know that analytical thought and aesthetic sensibility can work wonders when sufficiently developed in a mature individual. Normally the two qualities are kept separate by the human need for specialization. It is not proper for a philosopher to break into song, nor is it for a dancer to philosophize. And so the first becomes too dry, the second too far gone. Both arts become more specialized, and made into items we consume, or narratives we attend to in our spare time.

85 Angels, Daemons and Ghosts

The eternal return is a daemonic annunciation. We know from Rilke that a meeting with an Angel is a numinous, terrifying occurrence. No matter how benevolently depicted by religious iconography, every Angel is terrifying, every Angel is a monstrous creature, an almost deadly bird of the soul, inspiring awe, terror and bewilderment. An Angel's presence upsets our everyday reality, shatters our illusion of consistency and solidity. An Angel comes to deliver a fatal message, whose significance is charged with a sense of destiny. Hamlet experiences a similar bewilderment when confronted with the ghost of his dead father. Angels and ghosts might inspire awe, even terror, yet their messages are forever spurring one to conversion, positive action, and the reinstatement of justice and equilibrium. Yeats wrote:

> I feel in Hamlet as so often in Shakespeare, that I am in the presence of a soul lingering on the storm-beaten threshold of sanctity. Has not that threshold always been terrible and crime-haunted?[22]

But what if we are faced with a daemon? What could his message be? What heavy thought is going to possess our mind and weigh us down? A daemon will almost certainly be perceived as a *demon*, and will feel repulsive, because, to our mind, he lives and breathes the slavery of the hellish realms. His mind will feel repulsive, even if his ways might be charming and seductive.

What could his message be? He will not offer redemption, nor proclaim and rejoice in our innocence. He won't send us on a mission to avenge wrong doings. Instead, he will burden us with the heaviest thought.

What is the heaviest thought? That there cannot be redemption, that there is no other world, no promised land, and no enlightenment either. That what you see is what you get. Are you able to appreciate it and be grateful, so much so that you would be willing to experience your present condition eternally?

If angels dwell in heaven, and ghosts in Hades, daemons belong to the earth. And why are we after all so ready to betray the earth? Why is the thought of eternal return so horrifying?

I do not know if angels, ghosts and daemons exist factually. But the daemon heralding the truth of the eternal return produced in his first interlocutor, and to countless others after that day in August 1881, the need to will suspension of disbelief. Our ordinary thoughts and beliefs stop in their track when faced with the doctrine of the eternal return. That is a rare moment, for thoughts and beliefs have us rather than we them.

Most readers will exorcise the daemon and the daemonic thought of eternal return. It is all too easy to dismiss it as a re-hashed archaism, or as an attempt to rebuild a form of metaphysics in the place vacated by God. Its existential impact is however fully retained:

> How well disposed would you have be to yourself and to life to desire nothing but this ultimate eternal affirmation and seal?[23]

86 *God's Vicious Circle*

Nietzsche's experience moves beyond the limitations posed by theological notions. Lou Salomé had known Nietzsche well. They had been close friends and *almost lovers*. Her misunderstanding of his thought is poignant as it is unfortunate, for it anticipated and encouraged later misinterpretations. In the first serious critical work on Nietzsche ever published, she sees him as Columbus, who set off on his journey with the purpose to find new land, and found instead the old. She wrote:

> Because of the lack of a metaphysical belief there was, after all, nothing other than the suffering and sorrowful life itself that could be glorified and idolized.[24]

"Nothing other than life" already testifies of the profound need, even in a highly intelligent individual such as Lou Salomé, of justifying life through some metaphysical representation. The task of reedeming life from the denigration subjected to it by religion and philosophy was going to be a mighty task indeed:

> He who prompted by some enigmatic desire, has, like me, long endeavoured to think pessimism through to the bottom and to redeem it from the half-Christian, half-German simplicity and narrowness with which it finally presented itself to this century, namely in the form of the Schopenhaueran philosophy; he who has really gazed with an Asiatic and more than Asiatic eye down into the most world-denying of all possible modes of thought – beyond good and evil and no longer, like Buddha and Schopenhauer, under the spell and illusion of morality – perhaps by that very act, and without really intending to, may have had his eyes opened to the opposite ideal: to the ideal of the most exuberant, most living and most world-affirming man, who has not only learned to get on and treat with all that was and is, but who wants to have it again as it was and is to all eternity, insatiably calling da capo not only to himself but to the whole piece and play, and not only to a play but fundamentally to him who needs precisely this play- and who makes it necessary: because he needs himself again and again – and makes himself necessary – What? And would this not be – *circulus vitiousus deus?*[25]

87 *Power as Representation and Display*

The way in which mainstream western thought has understood and defined *power* is a sorry tale told by an idiot, by an inferior, reactive being who sees *power* as an object of representation.

In Hobbes, the so-called powerful man is able to rejoice only when seeing his "power" *recognized* by others. In Hegel, consciousness needs the recognition and representation of another (non-self) in order to affirm itself as self-consciousness. Even in Adler the notion of power is still subject to the need for *recognition*, in this case as representation of superiority compensating for organ inferiority, although his descriptions of "failures" include those who are on a quest for relief on the "useless side of life", i.e., *for the semblance of superiority* rather than for the overcoming of difficulties.

Semblance of superiority is what we have historically associated with power, both on a grand scale and on a microcosmic one.

For Nietzsche such *reactive*, sub-standard views constitute a *slave* morality and the vanity behind them a form of atavism.

The chief mode here is that of *representation*. In Deleuze's words,

> The mania for representing, for being represented, for getting oneself represented; for having representations and represented; this is the mania that is common to all slaves.[26]

88 *Redemption from Revenge*

The passage from independence to affirmation also marks redemption from revenge. One who has seen through the stupidity of one's upbringing, who has rebelled against cultural conditioning and the many gradations and nuances of self-imprisonment, eventually sees through his own rebellion. There is only so much blaming one can do, even when blaming takes the inward route of guilt and self-deprecation. Having really seen through one's own iconoclastic tendencies, one reaches the other shore.

The other shore is this shore, as we are reminded in Zen. It is the innocence of becoming. It is this very same world, no longer endured as a valley of tears against the Platonic backdrop of *being*.

We are then ready to play with the same absorption and seriousness of a child. *Play* here is *not* understood as the *opposite* of work, as it is perceived in most Northern Presbyterian cultures. It is not the drunken or "dirty" weekend offsetting and confirming the undisputed domain of productive labour. Instead, it is work/play, the reconciliation of a fragmented view, the overcoming of a dualistic misconception.

It is no longer form versus chaos, duty versus pleasure, Apollo vs. Dionysus, death vs. life, time vs. eternity, immanence vs. transcendence, fate vs. free will, samsara vs. nirvana, delusion vs. enlightenment, blindness vs. clarity. No longer knowing or not knowing.

Outside the polarity of acquisition/expenditure, the innocence of becoming (the perspective of the other-shore-that-is-this-shore) no longer regards power in the hungry-ghost fashion, as envisioned in a world where chronic insecurity reigns, paired alongside politics, money, prestige and status.

Seen from the innocence of becoming, that world is not dissimilar from what D. H. Lawrence calls, through the voice of Birkin in *Women in Love*, "synthetic creation", "the silver river of life, rolling on and quickening all the world to a brightness". [27]

True power lies elsewhere. It is often a quality present in gentle people. "I have found force – Nietzsche wrote – where no one looks for it: in simple, mild men who have not the least desire to rule." True power is a sign of abundant life, a life that cannot but give, not out of a calculation – (in order to earn a good reputation, merit for future lives, or escape punishment on Judgment Day) – but out of the sheer inner *necessity to give*.

Will to power, akin to will to give, is free of the venom of *Wunschbarkeit*, the wishful thinking adorned with *should* and *should have*, the subtle and not-so-subtle denigration of life founded on the lack of appreciation for the way things are.

Knowledge and power are re-written by Zarathustra for his Western readers, and in learning the lesson we may come to Buddhism afresh.

From this redefined notion of power comes *Joy*.

> *What* does joy not want! It is thirstier, warmer, hungrier, more fearful, more secret than all woe; it wants *itself*, it bites into *itself*, the will of the ring wrestles within it,
>
> it wants love, it wants hatred, it is superabundant, it gives, throws away, begs for someone to take it, thanks him who take it, it would like to be hated;
>
> so rich is joy that it thirsts for woe, for Hell, for hatred, for shame, for the lame, for the *world* . . . Higher Men, learn this, joy wants the eternity of all things, wants deep, deep, deep deep eternity![28]

89 The Discipline of Freedom

Having stumbled upon the heaviest of thoughts, Nietzsche proceeds to formulate his own interpretations. It has been suggested that at some point the fluid intuition of the eternal return coagulates into a doctrine, even into a dogma. If so, the full scale of its meaning still remains ambiguous, for even within Nietzsche's own formulations, the ambivalence is there from the start. One thing is certain: the all-too-easy interpretation is rejected outright, alongside "solutions" of the *wisdom-while-u-wait* variety. Zarathustra mocks the ready-made answers given by the dwarf – who embodies the spirit of gravity – on the enigma of time:

> 'Everything straight lies', murmured the dwarf disdainfully. 'All truth is crooked. time itself is a circle'.
> 'Spirit of Gravity!' I said angrily, 'do not treat this too lightly! Or I sha
> you squatting where you are! . . . ' [29]

This heaviest of thoughts is a curse, but it turns eventually into a blessing. Once this thought has entered Zarathustra – as a living being, as a snake's head – he is "as dead for seven days", but in his convalescence he enjoys hearing his animals chatter, utter words as "rainbow and seeming bridges between the eternally separated".

Having been cursed with this terrifying thought, Nietzsche went on to expound it, at first by trying to demonstrate that it belonged to Physics rather than Myth.

90 Force and Power

We need to distinguish between *force* and *power*: force is primitive, restricted; power is ever increasing. Nietzsche uses the word *force* when speaking of the universe without specific reference to humans. The word *power* is more fundamental; it includes the totality of the world with specific reference to humankind. Whether or not the eternal return can be demonstrated "scientifically", or understood mythologically, is beside the point. It is a sign of the times that Nietzsche tried hard to ground his visionary, enigmatic thought into the natural sciences. Freud will do the same years later, and try to found psychoanalysis on so-called "objective", or "scientific" grounds.

As we know at this juncture, thanks to Nietzsche's "perspectivism" being absorbed by deconstructionism and post-modernism, the scientific view is an ideal like any other. It is not a matter of choosing between Mechanism and Platonism; *as ideals, the highly objective and the highly subjective are eventually reconciled.* They are also factually reconciled in the Nietzschean formula *ego fatum*, where *determinism and free will become one and the same.*

When I breathe, the whole universe breathes with me. When I sit, the whole universe sits. The dualism between objectivity and subjectivity has been seen through, and enlightened action is equal to "doing the next thing".

The eternal return is also impossibility. It simply cannot be sustained in our ordinary, deluded state. Its atmosphere is a hundred times as rarefied as mountain air; prolonged exposure to it would kill us.

> To endure the idea of recurrence one needs: freedom from morality; new means against the fact of pain [. . .]; the enjoyment of all kinds of uncertainty; experi-mentalism, as a counterweight to this extreme fatalism; abolition of the concept of necessity; abolition of the "will"; abolition of "knowledge in itself".[30]

In order to be able to endure such extreme form of determinism, one needs boundless freedom and an unparalleled talent for playing. Do we possess enough discipline to be free?   *So fully...*

If we interpret the eternal return one-sidedly, from a mechanistic point of view, living becomes impossible. If I am merely a clog in the cosmic wheel, if character both determines and is determined by fate, how can I make my unique contribution to existence?

If, on the other hand, we are prepared to remove necessity, will and knowledge, our eternal prison turns into boundless space.

This is no other than saying "I am fate". I am already the fate at whose feet I prostrate myself. And as I bow to the Buddhas and Bodhisattvas of the past, present and future, they bow back to me. Bowing is a wonderful *(frame)* act: at once heartfelt, amusing and profound.

The eternal return is the most extreme fatalism, but is none other than the game of chance.

In prostrating oneself, in dropping off body and mind, one becomes a true gambler.

I cannot settle with being an undignified, calculative and resentful player. I cannot resort to probability: once the dice are thrown, I will face the music of chance, I will play and dance, in the arms of sorrow, joy, or within the deeper joy that comes from accepting sorrow. This is highest fatalism colluding with chance.   *w/ Heidegger*

9 | *History of a Lie*

"Is seeing itself not – seeing abysses?"[31]

The *Self*, which until Hume had been perceived *not* as a substance, a "soul", receives a fatal blow with Nietzsche: the shift is radical and complete. It is as far as western thought has been able to go: the self is no longer considered as substance, but linked to time itself.

Nietzsche treads on the bumpy trail undertaken throughout western thinking from Descartes to Hegel, but uses it as a springboard, or as a grindstone to sharpen his talons.

That seemingly narrow and straight path, polished by Descartes' ingenious *cogito ergo sum*, is still a route many prefer to take, for it steers clear of the nastiness of un-sedated reality and its treacherous complicity with chaos and groundlessness.

The path was later "ploughed and dispersed" by Hume, transcendentally recouped by Kant, with whom the cogito is "an *a priori* condition of all knowledge (but no ergo is permissible), and then made a royal, world-historical throughway for the Absolute Spirit by Hegel.

With Kant and Hegel, almost in spite of themselves, self relates more and more to time, and as a consequence, its substance is being increasingly denied. The meaning of the world is thus less and less abstracted and separated from the Self, and from this standpoint conceiving a relation between Self and the world is pointless.

The denial of substance of the Self, its unity with time and the world, has progressively – and in various, often-opposing forms – been stated by western thinkers after Descartes. Any mode of thought advocating Descartes' formula as valid would be a regression, for it would entirely bypass the evolution of western thought itself. But it is precisely on Descartes' formula that current mainstream western thinking rests.

On the one hand, Nietzsche's ideas on time and the self certainly revolutionize western thinking. They pose a Sphinx-like riddle on the whole wobbly edifice of western knowledge. And yet, they can be experienced as the very culmination of that knowledge, anticipating – and to some extent overcoming – the crisis represented by later development: existentialism, deconstructionism.

92 The Crooked Path of Eternity

Very few have taken the idea of the eternal return seriously. It is the crucial point of Nietzsche's enquiry, and it can neither be avoided, nor turned into a formula. At the existential level, there are interesting points in common with Zen Buddhism. If everything recurs eternally, a natural selection is necessary of thoughts and deeds that I am prepared to repeat eternally, and those that I am not. I must live so that I "wish to live again". This is not mere "positive resolution" nor passive resignation, but instead great affirmation of past, present and future. Normally, there is a sense of passivity, of resignation in accepting one's past, what can no longer be changed. The past is redeemed when I am able to face it squarely and say, "I willed it that way". The statement is not wishful, positive thinking, or pseudo-religious attempt at patching up loose ends and constructing a homespun redemption. The person who declares, "I willed my entire past" has realized both meaninglessness and groundlessness; he has contemplated nothingness stretching out for the whole of eternity.

The despairing negation of existence has turned into the most complete affirmation: *To live that I must wish to live again.*

From that moment on, one lives, thinks, and acts "eternally". It is, in

Nietzsche's words, "the religion of the freest, most serene, and most sublime souls – a lonely meadow-land between glide-ice and pure sky".

Eternal return is total absorption. No beginning, no end, always at the beginning, always ending. All is redeemed . . .

Karma is just as *unfathomable*. As in the doctrine of eternal return, within the law of causation *freedom and necessity are one and the same thing*. In receiving the Buddhist precepts, and by practicing the Bodhisattva Way, one embraces one's own past, and the past of the ancestors. And by embracing it, the past is redeemed. Redemption here does not entail a change from evil to good in the dualistic sense. It involves, however, understanding, gratitude and appreciation. *I willed it that way*, and even the slightest change (wishing that something painful would have not occurred) would mean altering the entire picture. Freedom and necessity are one and the same.

93 A Taste of Eternity

Eternity is a static idea born out of the dualistic division of essence and matter. The eternity glimpsed by Nietzsche near the rock on the lake of Silvaplana is pure occurrence, not static persistence.

To penetrate this vision and enigma, to penetrate this *koan*, we have to move beyond the dualistic delusion, beyond Descartes and Hegel, beyond Marx and existentialism.

Downgrading Nietzsche's eternal return to the archaic idea of cyclic time is equal to reading nirvana as a permanent state *outside* living-and-dying. *The eternal return is taking place this very moment.* We might begin to have a glimpse of it if we remove the *moment* from ideas of *purpose* and *process*.

Not moving toward religious epiphany, or secular progress, this very moment manifests the innocence of becoming. Nagarjuna wrote:

> If you think that 'things' really exist, then you must believe in [the duality of] eternalism . . . and nihilism. For a 'thing' must be either permanent or transient.
>
> [On the other hand] to think that 'things' really exist means there can be neither nihilism nor eternalism. For coming into existence itself is a succession of rising and passing away of cause and effect.[32]

94 The Blessing and the Curse

Suspension of disbelief is necessary when confronted with the paradox of eternal return. More than any other, this particular thought took posses- sion of Nietzsche and breathed its demonic life into him. It set out as a horrific curse, but in the end became a magnificent blessing. It generated, and continues to generate for us, the possibility echoed by W. B. Yeats in a poem titled *Vacillation*:

> While on the shop and street I gazed
> My body of a sudden blazed;
> And twenty minutes more or less
> It seemed, so great my happiness,
> That I was blessed, and could bless.[33]

95 An Annunciation from Hell

Annunciation of the Virgin Birth is made by an Angel, an emissary from Heaven. A terrifying apparition, nevertheless, for "every Angel is terri- fying", according to Rilke. The rustle of wings on a kitchen floor, as he sits, compassionate and strangely aloof, in the modest abode.

The *insinuation* of the eternal return is whispered in Nietzsche's ear by a demon. It is an annunciation from Hades. It is earth-shattering, intro- duced by the enticing question *What if?* What if the ideas of linear time and linear history were comfy fabrications?

What if that which we value most – art, science and religion – were illusions, at best "stimulants" to make life bearable? What if the idea of progress, growth, love and development are also illusions? What if progress is another word for hi-tech barbarism?

What if God does not exist? What if the self does not exist and it is a mere combination of drives, energy patterns devoid of intrinsic existence? What if the self is a puppet playing the hero in the drama of the psyche? What if the self is a shameless lie? What if morality is founded upon barbarism and utilitarian aims? What if the need for "change" and "trans- formation" is an all-too-human, modern form of neurosis? What if true enquiry into the nature of reality and the human condition is to be found conspicuously absent from academia and institutions? What if the enlightenment, awakening, self-actualization are all blatant lies? What if the philosophy of the "Enlightenment" is a dogmatic religion devoted to the God of Cold Reasoning? What if there is no Promised Land, no Liberation, no heaven or hell?

The experience is vertiginous, unsettling. The radical questions it poses upset our sleepwalking regime of denial and oblivion.

Challenged with the riddle, we relive Hamlet's dilemma when confronted by his father's ghost. His initial bewilderment rattles the cage of the familiar world, insinuates a new dimension of invisibility and retribution, diametrically opposite to what until then we believed to be good, divine, trusted, desirable and familiar. The seductiveness of the thought provokes us to undertake a dangerous journey.

> What strange, wicked, problematic questions! It is already a long story – yet does it not seem as if it has only just begun? Is it any wonder we should at last grow distrustful, lose our patience, turn impatiently away? That this sphinx should also teach us to ask questions? Who really is it that here questions us? What really is it in us that wants 'the truth'? – [. . .] We asked after the value of this will. Granted we wanted truth: why not rather untruth? And uncertainty? Even ignorance? – The problem of the value of truth stepped before us – or was it we who stepped before this problem? Which of us is Oedipus here? Which of us sphinx? [34]

We are invited to awake our *negative capability*, to face the enigma and the contradiction without resorting to Socratic logic, scientific faith, religious dogma. Also, without resorting to our current dependency on *feelings* and on the *child archetype*. Having cleansed our thoughts from vague, timorous metaphysics, having helped us leave behind those meagre ideals of redemption through art, morality or religion, we are still provoked into a poetic rejoinder to life.

Vain is the attempt to find a cosmology in eternal return: this divine comedy is not overburdened by theology. ~~a thought~~ or reason

That does not mean, as Wallace Stevens malevolently suggested (echoing Aristotle, echoing Plato, echoing Jung, and the entire High Court of *Logos*), that Nietzsche's work is "just poetry". The eternal return is not an attempt to describe "the way things really are". That is the task of coarse cosmologies founded on one of the greatest human fallacies: *literalism*. In the words of Norman O. Brown:

> Literalism makes the world of abstract materialism; of dead matter; of the human body as dead matter. Literalism kills everything, including the human body. It is the spirit Blake called Ulro, which sees nothing but rock and sand, jostling together in the void; Whitehead's Misplaced Concreteness: "Nature a dull affair, soundless, scentless, colourless; merely the hurrying of material, endlessly,

meaninglessly". Literalism makes a universe of stone, and men astonished, petrified. Literalism is the ministration of death, written and engraved in stones; tables of stones and stony heart.[35]

96 Time is a Child

The thought of eternal return is a *metaphor* and a source of *inspiration*. The meaning of *inspiration* has been reduced to caricature: we picture the poet sitting at her desk, gazing at the oak tree in the garden, holding her pen, or with fingers on her keyboard, waiting for inspiration to arise.

The real meaning of the word is equivalent to *dancing*; it is a complete *surrender to life's autonomous self-affirmation*. It is in this context that *the entire world is affirmed as a work of art*.

The thought of eternal return is also a *metaphor*, or dis-placement: by embracing it, we move from one perspective (the one that dominated the West for two thousand years) to an altogether different view. This view is, in a sense, *no view*. It is immanence, a place from where, by definition, no view is possible. In harmony with Heraclitus, everything impermanent and perishable becomes valuable, worthy of affirmation.

Nietzsche's great effort was to have dressed this radically new point of view in a language that is both poetic and positivist.

He was all too aware of the curse that befalls humankind: the inability to see, with Augustine, transient life as other than, simultaneously, the result, proof and manifestation of its own fall from grace. According to this view, *transient life is evil*: whether shadowed by religious thinking, decorated by Romantic pseudo-appreciation, or coated in secular or decadent worship of ephemera, our Judaeo-Christian culture positively believes this. Socratic and Platonic thought created the foundation for such belief.

Heraclitus alone suggested that seeing some things as evil is a partial, all too human judgment. He also sees time non-teleologically, *without aim or goal outside its own activity*.

97 Losing the Plot

Time is non-linear, circular and perpetual; it is self-contained and self-sufficient, for it does not seek redemption and justification outside itself.

The greatest difficulty in contemplating the thought of eternal return is the fact that it debunks the subject, the "I". The self is no longer the main actor of the individual's life, but life itself is, in its playful, terrifying, wondrous ways. Such reversal is precisely what Aristotle conceived as *tragedy*: a situation where *life is larger than the hero*, a mystery to which he is at the most a witness, in Chapelle's words, "a plot for which he is the cast, the medium for its enactment and unfolding".

98   *A Twice-Told Tale*

There is no escaping the Nietzschean demon. The hour-glass of our existence is being turned upside down, over and over again, and we are faced with the thousand facets of our destiny. No promised land awaits us; no gates lead to heaven. Shakespeare writes in *King John*:

> There is nothing in this world can make me joy. Life is as tedious as a twice-told tale, vexing the dull ear of a drowsy man.[36]

We are being fooled, echoes Nietzsche. What's more, we *understand* that we are being fooled, and yet lack the power *not* to be fooled. We labour and toil, we struggle aimlessly. The psycho-analytical experience confronts us with the Nietzschean demon, and with the struggle of Sisyphus. We are forced to confront timelessness itself: no longer an abstraction, a theological hypothesis, but the reality revealed by unconscious mental processes, a reality tearing apart our idea of linear time. In Freud's words,

> Unconscious mental processes are in themselves 'timeless'. This means in the first place that they are not ordered temporally, that time does not change them in any way, and that the idea of time cannot be applied to them.[37]

BEYOND THE DREAM
OF CHANGE
Towards a Zen Psychology

99 The First Psychologist

According to Nietzsche, both philosophy and religion had failed to understand the deeper aspects of the self, and this is why he regards his task as that of a psychologist, all the while being fully aware – against the unbridled optimism of the age of reason – that the hardest thing for a man is to know his own self.

Thus, there are two powerful archetypal voices to whom Nietzsche opposes his own life-affirmative philosophy. The first one represents the denigration of life perpetrated in all ages by religion. Whether it manifests as asceticism, as a system of ethics, or as plain bad conscience, the basic message is that life is not worth living. According to this pious, priestly voice (Silenus'), existence is shadowed by error and sin. To its credit, religion acknowledges the reality of suffering, recognizes the long shadows cast by illness and death. One cannot accuse Silenus of indulging in denial, but a closer look reveals religion's vested interests: winning new adepts to its propaganda of life-denigration. His is a commanding voice, gnawing at the heart of humankind, summoning blemishes, trepidation and decay in the service of its embittered, frenetic proselytizing.

An equally authoritative voice is Socrates'. He represents philosophy in its debased form, as the *subordination of all drives to reason*. This voice is beneficial in helping the self cope with events in the bright light of day, in controlling its anxieties and fears, in narrowing down the domain of suffering, mental anguish and pain. It does not manage as well, however, in negotiating the night and its shadows.

Neither religion nor reason provide ways in which humans can satisfactorily confront suffering. At best, they provide *consolation*. Hence, a new science is called for, a science that will make use of art and good humour. Nietzsche calls this new science *psychology*. Not only did he probe into the labyrinth of his own psyche, subjecting himself to a high standard of self-discipline in an unbroken questioning of his own opinions and beliefs; he also shed light into the darkest corners of the collective psyche, discovering that those moral beliefs humans have taken for granted for centuries, such as *retributive justice* and *asceticism*, were the product of a deep-seated *hatred*.

Before coming to recognize the need for psychology, he attempted the aesthetic route. He enquired whether there could be an aesthetic justification for existence, and a redemption through art. At first he believed that the aesthetic solution could provide a valid alternative to the consolatory answers of religion. Disillusioned by aestheticism and Wagnerian histrionics, he journeyed to the farthest corners of positivist doubt and reasoning. From that wasteland he emerged once again in a newfound role, wearing a new mask: he became a psychologist.

It needs to be stated again: *Nietzsche is the founder of depth psychology*. In him we find the whole of the Freudian, Jungian and Adlerian ideas in the acorn state. Many of his insights were later utilized and developed, often without acknowledgment. In that respect, he shared a destiny similar to Alfred Adler's, a great pioneer of psychology whose tremendous contribution went largely unacknowledged.

100 *Dream-thinking*

Depth Psychology did not start with Freud. His ancient predecessor was Heraclitus, and his true founder in modern times was Nietzsche.

Of the three eminent psychologists who laid the officially recognized foundations of depth psychology, Freud and Adler openly acknowledged Nietzsche's pivotal influence, but Jung did not. He wrote of the crucial "autonomous activity of the psyche" which is a "continually creative act", that activity of the psyche that "creates reality every day". He chose to call this *active fantasy*. Fantasy for Jung is the

> mother of all possibilities, where . . . the inner and outer worlds are joined together in living union.[1]

He wrote of the "great difficulty" born out of the fact that "fantasy is for the most part a product of the unconscious . . . essentially involuntary", sharing the same quality as the dream.

Several years before, Nietzsche had written:

> When we close our eyes the brain produces a host of light-impressions and colours . . . . Now the understanding, in concert with fantasy, immediately works this in itself formless play of colours into definite figures, shapes, landscapes, lively groups . . . . Here, then, fantasy continuously presents images [to the mind], depending on the visual impressions of the day for their production, and dream-fantasy operates in just the same way.[2]

Nietzsche did not formulate an *id*, nor a *collective unconscious*, but was well aware that

> ancient humanity and animality, in fact the entire primeval period and past of all sentient beings, continues in me to meditate, create poetry, love, hate, speculate.[3]

In being *here now*, as the great Nietzschean scholar Graham Parkes puts it, we are always potentially *there then* too. If we engage with History *existentially*, we draw a far better understanding of our own age.

> There are great advantages to estranging oneself from one's time to a great extent and being driven away from its shores, as it were, back onto the ocean of past worldviews. (HAH, 616)

Jung dismissed Nietzsche's understanding as a form of late-Romantic aestheticism. He unceremoniously referred to him as an "educated philistine" (an epithet coined by Nietzsche himself) who apparently

> had discovered his Number 2 past middle-age and let it loose on upon a world that knew and understood nothing about such things.[4]

He complained that Nietzsche was

> a blank page whirling about in the winds of the spirit.... [He] had lost the ground under his feet because he possessed nothing more than the inner world of his thoughts – which incidentally possessed him more than he it.
> He was uprooted and hovered above the earth . . . succumbed to exaggeration and irreality. For me, such irreality was the quintessence of horror, for I aimed, after all, at this world and this life . . . Thus my family and my profession always remained a joyful reality and a guarantee that I also had a normal existence.[5]

The charges are bitter and unfair. Nietzsche was painfully aware of his own isolation, a condition due to his illness. He was well aware that his books would not be appreciated until decades later, and that his monumental effort would finish him off.

Nevertheless, his contribution is immeasurable. As Adler teaches us, an individual's contribution to the vast community takes many forms, including that of the solitary work of a man of talent.

Compared to Jung's burgeois, parochial life-style, Nietzsche was certainly an uprooted individual. But he did possess a deep love and connectedness with each place he lived in.

Jung's misconstruction of Nietzsche reflects the same misunderstanding that the first half of the 20th century had towards him. A misunderstanding born out of patchy reading, rooted in a prejudice that sees philosophy as a logical endeavour. Jung considers Nietzsche a poet, in the Platonic and Aristotelian sense of a lesser individual than a philosopher. This crucial misunderstanding of philosophy, as an enterprise devoid of psychological insights and aesthetic sense, continues undisturbed into the 21st century.

Graham Parkes' insights on Jung's ambivalent appraisal of Nietzsche are truly illuminating. At one point Jung admits that Nietzsche is "one of the greatest psychologist that ever lived". Nevertheless, he paradoxically refuses to acknowledge Nietzsche's insights into psychology because at the time when those insights were voiced (1883) "there was no psychology". The psychoanalytical Church had not been founded yet; how could a single individual come up with *any* significant psychological insight?

The specific insight Jung was concerned about was that very same which later was to make his own work stand out: *personification.*

Personification means giving *autonomous voices to various drives*, an insight which was to have vital implications in modern psychology.

Personification was precisely the method used by Nietzsche in writing his most popular work, *Zarathustra. Zarathustra himself is an autonomous voice.* Nietzsche wears the voice as a mask, but (mostly) does not identify with it.

How much he identifies with Zarathustra, (the voice of the Master), is open to debate. My sense is that he was too identified with it, and that this fact created serious hindrances in his more intimate relationships, particularly with Lou Salomé.

Nietzsche states firmly that the *I* is a *restrictive fiction.* Jung wrongly *assumed* that Nietzsche *stumbled* into the crucial insight of personification, without being able to either understand it or master it. It is an error that strangely echoes those of Christianity, which relegated all sages of antiquity into Limbo, simply because, according to this biased logic, no one can be considered a saint who was born before Christ.

Jung significantly misunderstood the character of the dwarf in *Zarathustra:* he sees him as Zarathustra's higher mind, whereas he represents the *spirit of gravity,* the rationalist and Christian thought from Plato to Schopenhauer. He also misreads Nietzsche's will to power as "instinct of preservation", in the same line of those who misconstrue the eternal return as attachment.

Jung reads Nietzsche's position as *aestheticism,* an appraisal which is correct only with regard to his early work, before he broke away from Wagner.

101 Hello Stranger

Attempting to refute the thought of eternal return, trying to interpret it as a cosmology, a system, a scientific theory, is Horatio's approach, as portrayed by Shakespeare in Hamlet.

Horatio   O day and night, but this is wondrous strange.
Hamlet   And therefore as a stranger give it welcome.

There are more things in heaven and earth, Horatio,
Than are dreamt in your philosophy.[6]

Hamlet's profound ambiguity, his puns and evocations, "create the ghost", as Patricia Berry points out:

By poisoning what is said, he creates a space within which words *because* of their duplicity (multiplicity) have meaning. To serve the ghost, to make something of it, to remember it, there must be a further poisoning. Reality *is* equivocal, so the mode is not to go along naively (Ophelia) or with empty words (Osric) or custom (Polonius) but to craft the space between meanings.[7]

We are here in the presence of *Dionysian logic*; oblique, metaphorical, deeply ambivalent. Seen in its light, cosmology, science, religion and philosophy appear as timid attempts at exorcism.

Demons, ghosts and apparitions may not be real, but the impact of what they communicate to us is tremendously meaningful.

In the case of the demon heralding the eternal return, how well inclined would one have to become to oneself and to existence to desire nothing more than this eternal seal? We are faced with a few probing questions regarding the nature of our thoughts, motives and deeds: are we prepared to live as if our life will be recurring eternally? Within this existential paradigm, there is one more level where this enigmatic thought becomes factual: the psychoanalytical framework.

According to Daniel Chapelle,

the individual in psychoanalysis is invariably compelled to relive fixed experience patterns. They recur and keep recurring as if in psychoanalysis life leads nowhere but in circles, eternally back to itself.[8]

Psychoanalysis is a way of dealing with, and responding to, our human resentment over impermanence. Not unlike the idea of the eternal return, it aims at re-interpreting the past, understood "as the process of *passing* rather than as *content passed*" (my emphasis).[9]

More specifically, there would be instances in which, according to this view, *the actuality of eternal return is being enacted within the psychoanalytical practice*, the "alpha and the omega" of it being "the repetition compulsion in its manifestation as transference".

Chapelle starts by analyzing Freud's definition of what he called "the uncanny" (*Das Unheimliche*), "a seemingly novel event" which would in effect represent "a recurrence of an old and familiar but forgotten event". [10]

102 *The Compulsion of Destiny*

We see an enactment of eternal return in compulsion. In Zarathustra's case, his own compulsion derives from what he perceives as an autonomous force (a sub-personality? a voice in the psyche?) that compels him to experience the same thing again and again.

In psychoanalytical exploration, the individual finds himself continually obliged to re-experience "fixed experience patterns".

> They recur and keep recurring as if in psychoanalysis life leads nowhere but in circles, eternally back to itself.[11]

Nietzsche, whose thought and experience had an enormous influence on psychoanalysis, wrote:

> If one has character, one also has one's typical experience, which recurs again and again.[12]

Beyond the Pleasure Principle, which is his major book on the subject of the compulsion to repeat, Freud describes it as

> an essential character-trait which always remains the same and which is compelled to find expression in a repetition of the same experience.[13]

He also calls it "the compulsion of destiny". We do not need to prove the thought of eternal return "scientifically", or to build new-age cosmologies on its foundations. It is manifest in everyday life, particularly in the compulsion to repeat.

Some of its other manifestations are *projection* and *transference*, which do not apply solely to psychoanalytic therapy, or to psychotherapy, but to our everyday interactions, to the domains of work, love and community.

In the specific case of analyst and analysand, what takes place is, in the words of Paul Ricoeur, a relationship

> in the course of which the patient repeats, in the artificial situation of analysis, important and meaningful episodes of his affective life.[14]

Such is "the Sisyphean fate" of the analysand, a paradoxical situation of endless, repetitious, and (from the absolute perspective) futile labour: the whole being . . . exerting towards achieving nothing at all.[15]

103 *No Such Things as Health*

One of the fundamental differences between depth psychology and self-help psycho-babble is that the former does not endorse any delusional idea of normality, but states instead that pathology is part and parcel of the human condition. There is no such a thing as a normal, so-called "objective" outlook on life. Life is "always lived in perspective, from within the distorting viewpoint of a pathological prejudice". In fact, "without the perspective of one form of pathology or another, there could be no life". In the words of John Donne,

> Yet because outward storms the strongest break,
> And strength itself by confidence grows weak,
> This new world may be safer, being told
> The dangers and diseases of the old:
> For with due temper men do then forgo,
> Or covet things, when they their true worth know
> There is no health; Physicians say that we,
> At best, enjoy a neutrality.[16]

Health seems to be a word, an abstraction found only in medicine textbooks.

> The notion of health we are accustomed to from medicine defines health in a negative manner, as life minus its headaches, its stomach ulcers, its high blood pressures, its anxieties, its compulsions, its suffocating family situations, its frustrations at the job, and its conflicts in erotic relations. This kind of health is defined as life minus everything that makes it what it is.[17]

For Nietzsche, health is polymorphous, with sickness constituting the essential element at its core. Freud states something similar in both *The Psychopathology of Everyday Life* and *Jokes and their Relation to the Unconscious*, where he demonstrates the existence of a polymorphous psychological health in everyday life.

In depth psychology, from Freud to Hillman, pathology is seen as an inherent condition of human life. Hillman introduces the idea of "pathologizing", according to which life autonomously creates "illness, morbidity, disorder, abnormality, and suffering in any aspect of its behaviour".

104 *Dionysus and the New Puritans*

New Puritanism, post-modern and post-Darwinian, is the complementary aspect of new Libertinism. In a world devoid of meaning, given to the excesses of logic and rationalism, sex is an anaesthetized, demystified commodity, a fetish and a diversion to be enjoyed alongside designer clothes, interior design and nouvelle cuisine.

Dionysus, god of revelry, is interpreted one-sidedly, as the primordial chaos of the instincts which rational humans attempts to suppress; he is the beast ritually and surreptitiously let out of the cage in part-time, duplicitously respectful lives, or *dictating* the existence of the *addicted*, of the possessed, of full-time rogues. The latter eventually achieve status and even prestige through the homage paid to them by literature and the media.

Dionysus, or at least his modern effigy, was single-handedly created by Nietzsche. Before him, we thought of the Gods of ancient Greece as curious, capricious characters inhabiting perfectly sculpted bodies in an Arcadian Olympus. In spite of his widespread nominal popularity, Dionysus is still largely absent in the modern world. Only his raw, undeveloped, un-sublimated manifestation is known to us, but we know very little of his mature state. Our "terrible love of war" and cruelty is expression of this. And so is our inability to understand, and deal with, our passions and emotions.

New Puritanism is a sign of sickness: it is engendered by an interesting but inherently superficial phenomenon, the so-called sexual liberation and desublimation of the nineteen sixties. Indulging an emotion is to be overwhelmed by it. Repressing it is equally a way to capitulate to its power. A moral code fails as much as a libertarian one does. In both cases we are shadowboxing in the mist, and we end up wounding ourselves as a result.

105 *A Tale of Two Centuries*

Nietzschean psychology has yet to be explored fully. Like Zen, it is alien to the Western mind-set, which has been tyrannized for too long by irrational logic, immoderate reason, and by religious and scientific superstitions. Accepting the existential implications of Nietzsche's psychology means undermining the very foundations of western culture and reveal the lies on which our civilized world has been built.

106 On the Four Forms of Conduct

The four forms of conduct are, according to Dogen Zenji, "walking, standing, sitting, and lying down". Sitting in the meditation posture of zazen seems to be by far the privileged form of conduct in Zen practice, although this practice is not restricted to sitting alone.

"To disport oneself freely in this samadhi," wrote Dogen in *Bendowa* ("Negotiating the Way"), "the right entrance is proper sitting in zazen".[19]

> The Dharma is amply present in every person, but without practice, it is not manifested; without realization, it is not attained. It is not a question of one or many; let loose of it and it fills your hands. It is not bounded vertically or horizontally; speak it and it fills your mouth.[20]

Zazen is the whole truth of the Buddha Dharma; nothing can be compared with it.

Nietzsche's breakthrough, on the other hand, came through *walking*. His entire philosophy is based on the agile, exultant movements of limbs in motion. He often cautioned his readers against the dreary consequences of the sedentary life.

Standing and lying down surely have also been the gates of significant breakthroughs, the latter being for example the essential condition for dreaming, which is at the centre of psychoanalytical discoveries.

107 Pleased to Meet You

A fundamental point must be reiterated here: philosophy is an *art*, and a philosopher an *artist*. An artist is one who specializes in the gifts of *experimentation* and *temptation*. The first is an act of creation: less self-existing gesture than timely dance step. The second is daring oneself and one's fellow human to re-vision the world, life, and one's place in it. Nothing less.

108   *Flowers in Space*

The idea of the eternal return is the most thorough and heartfelt appreciation of living-and-dying. Living-and-dying (*shoji* in Japanese) is itself *nirvana*, liberation. Mainstream "spiritualist" views in western philosophy are akin to those of the non-Buddhist Senika, whose views Shakyamuni Buddha refutes in the *Garland Sutra*. According to this view, things perish, but "mind" is eternal.

> A great many students of Buddhism, when they hear the word Buddhanature, mistake it for the self expounded by the Senika heresy. That is because they have not encountered a [true] man, they have not encountered their [true] self, they have not encountered an [authentic] teacher. They unwittingly mistake the wind and fire movements of their conscious mind for the enlightenment and awakening of the Buddha nature.[21]

If we learn the spiritualist or transcendentalist view as the teachings of the Buddha, we are even more foolish than the person who gets hold of a pebble and thinks it is made of gold. 'Nirvana' is not outside living-and-dying.

At the other end of the spectrum we find the materialist view, also popular in western thinking, equating matter with atoms, the *body* with mere *flesh*. This is *complementary* to the spiritualist view in that it denies life-and-death of its intrinsic dignity and grandeur. One view *needs* the other, for they both maintain the dualistic delusion at the heart of western mainstream thought, reflected in the arbitrary division between body and mind. Dogen said:

> You must know that the Buddha Dharma preaches as a matter of course that body and mind are one and the same, that the essence and the form are not two.[22]

For Nietzsche, the mere conception of a beyond – in *any* form – is a sign of life-denigration. For Dogen, it is dismissal of the Buddha Dharma:

> In thinking that birth-and-death is something we should turn from, you make the mistake of rejecting the Buddha Dharma itself. You must guard against such thinking.[23]

In both Nietzsche and Dogen's vision, *we become who we are*, we affirm what continually becomes. We are, in the words of Master Seiho, "the children of fire" who, paradoxically, "come looking for fire".

Great effort is needed in pursuing what is already given. Absurd and

128 • • • • • • • • • •

paradoxical as this might sound, it is nevertheless the only sane task worth pursuing. The rest – spiritualism, materialism, dialectics, positivism and many other pursuits – are equal to what Dogen called *kuge*, or "flowers in space": mere abstractions, chasing phantoms, building castles in the sand.

109 *One Bright Pearl*

Zen – not unlike Nietzsche's philosophy – is a strategy for naturalizing humans and *de-humanizing* nature. They both present us with a thoroughly *anti-humanist insight*, in that they shift the focus from man, his self, his ego, and his overrated importance in the general order of things, to the "ten thousand things". Dogen Zenji says it in such a wonderful way:

Practice that confirms things by taking the self to them is illusion: of things to come forward and practice and confirm the self is enlightenment.[24]

He calls realization "the state of ambiguity itself". Not the self-conscious attainment of some knowledge, beliefs and expertise, but instead an unfathomable state where *we are lived* by the entire universe, a state of complete abandon and, paradoxically, of razor-sharp wakefulness.

"The whole universe in all directions is but a splendid bright pearl", Master Gensa (835–907, a successor of Master Seppo) had said. Dogen comments:

the entire universe is not vast and large, not minute and small, or square, or round; not the mean, nor right, not the 'lively vigor of leaping fish', not 'unbared and distinct all around'. Moreover, because it is not birth-and-death, and it is not coming and going, it is birth-and-death, and it is coming and going.[25]

No human measurement and perspective can inscribe it or describe it, *no philosophical system can comprehend becoming.*

All the universe is an unceasing process, pursuing things and making them the self, pursuing the self and making it things. [. . .] Because of pursuing things and making them the self, the universe in its entirety is unceasing. Because its own nature is prior to such activity, it is ungraspable even in the essence of the activity.
One bright pearl is able to express Reality without naming it, and we can recognize this pearl as its name.[26]

The one pearl goes directly through 10,000 years: the eternal past has not ended, but the eternal present has arrived. The body exists now, and the mind exists now. Even so, [the whole universe] is a bright pearl. It is not grass and trees here and there, it is not mountains and rivers at all points of the compass; it is a bright pearl.[25]

No matter what the "circumstances" might be which humans find themselves in, the universe does not cease to be a bright pearl. What a human being can do is perceive and positively *affirm* the existence of the bright pearl: this is what Nietzsche called *amor fati*, love of destiny.

Just at the moment of the present, whether suspended in space or hanging inside a garment, whether kept under a [dragon's] chin or kept in topknot, [the one bright pearl] in all cases, is one bright pearl throughout the whole universe in ten directions.[26]

110 *I Willed My Past*

Training in Zen Buddhism is long and arduous, and what seems hardest is accepting who I am. This is due to the *neurosis of perfection*, the wild weed of self-blame and guilt, the accessories the self perceives as inadequacies. There is a basic human drive of longing and displacement, a gnawing feeling that *there must be something else*: if not heaven, then the fully integrated human being, safely located on a hypothetically unassailable ground of health, normalcy, even "enlightenment". And if perfect health and enlightenment escape us, then there is material happiness, sexual satisfaction, and perfect union through love. Life *as it is* does not seem to be enough. It is transient, imperfect. The "imperfect" tense in grammar denotes an action that is *continuous*, subject to constant change. Imperfection denotes *becoming* itself, an act forever on the verge of being perfected.

We like to imagine *being* hiding behind the vestige of becoming. There must be a soul, hiding within, or hovering above, our mortal body. And there must be a God, benevolent or irate, sizing up the horrific chaos, natural cataclysms, injustice and inequality, the brutality of our species. How can one say Yes to all this? The doctrine of eternal return is dangerous in its ambiguity and amorality: two attributes which apply to life itself. The eternal return of the same also means that a serial killer is condemned to the repetition of his nightmare and to eternally inflict agony on his victims. The eternal return means the eternal return of Hitler and also, as Nietzsche wrote with perverse humour, the eternal return of his own sister . . .

There is a sense of impasse and fatality that borders on superstitious fatalism, with one important difference: I willed it so.

I I I *Mission: Impossible*

In Mahayana Buddhism, Bodhisattvas are willing to remain eternally in samsara in order to help others. Perhaps by voluntarily dwelling within cyclic existence, they end up discovering that this very life of suffering and pain *is* nirvana; that our mechanized beehive, garnished by bright lights, surrounded by crematories, plagued by Guernicas and blessed by a strange joy, *is* the promised land.

There are four Bodhisattva vows:

Sentient beings are numberless: I vow to save them.
Desires are inexhaustible, I vow to put an end to them.
The dharmas are boundless, I vow to master them.
The Buddha Way is unsurpassable, I vow to attain it.

We might as well call them Mission Impossible, a lost cause, a fight against windmills. What makes their utterance possible is our human capacity to give, our surplus of energy which manifests itself in all forms of giving.

Some people are like candles: they burn slow; others are thunderbolts. Both partake in one aspiration, both are willing to burn. Nietzsche wrote:

You grape-vine! Why do you praise me? For I cut you! I am cruel, you bleed: what means your praise of my intoxicated cruelty?
'What has become perfect, everything ripe – wants to die!' thus you speak. Blessed, blessed be the vine-knife! But everything unripe wants to live: alas!
Woe says: 'Fade, Be gone, woe!' But everything that suffers wants to live, that it may grow ripe and merry and passionate,
Passionate for remoter, higher, brighter things.[27]

I I 2 *A Crime Not Committed*

Zen practice is an art, as everyday living is an art. Zen practice and everyday living are one and the same. Some people are professional artists: through their creations, they often succeed in intensifying our experience of being in the world. In generating their work, they often have little time left for the art of living. An artist invites demons and chaos, and his creations are born out of precarious encounters with the darkness. The winds of dissatisfaction move the pendulum of impetuous mood swings, and many a neurosis is temporarily diverted into artistic conception: another crime not committed. By cultivating oneself, by being the *creator* as well as the *creature*, one sculpts one's destiny from the acceptance of *necessary freedom*. It is rare to find in the same person both a creator and an artist of living. In Nietzsche's view, Goethe accomplished that rare feat, for he projected onto him his ideal of a great human being. It's not unlikely that Goethe *was* a great human being, despite his marriage of convenience with German Idealism. Perhaps he was, after all, both a poet of living and an exquisitely gifted artist. This most rare of phenomena can take place. Taoist sages and Zen masters have also been great poets, painters and calligraphers. They expressed *dana*, or generosity, in many different ways. Both artistic expression and the art of living thrive on the absence of the subject, in the denouement of the dualistic separation between subject and object. In the case of the professional artist, such development is involuntary and temporary, and thus enshrined into a peak experience: artists are notorious for making a big fuss over their celebrated *petite mort*.

The poet of life no longer attaches importance to ultimate wisdom. This individual is a tightrope walker, a dancer poised between the absolute and the mundane, between God and conventional wisdom. He or she has made their life into a work of art; their motivation is the joy to burn, because it is in the imprint of every star to do so. That is also the meaning of offering incense: offering my very life to each and everyone. How can I possibly offer what is not mine in the first place?

I fulfill the legacy by moulding an erratic silhouette in the shifting landscape, by carving a statue able to break into dance, and whose resting place is dust.

113   *Never Betray the Earth*

Metaphysicians are well versed in the curious skill of growing roots in heaven, in the cultivation of what I once overheard a priest call "celestial nostalgia". The earth is for some synonymous with dirt, with murky entrails and entanglements.

Zarathustra reverses the equation: a tall, strong tree, whose branches are open to the sun, rain and storms, has its roots deep in the soil. The higher the branches, the deeper the roots. There are fascinating similarities here with Japanese folklore. The tallest tree, the Japanese say, is also the one most exposed to the storms.

By reversing the metaphysical vision, one reinstates the *dignity* of the earth. The soil might be murky, but its dark entrails are essential to growth. The artist/philosopher invites demons, and willingly encounters hardship. Through dealing with such difficulties, at times precariously, at other times successfully, his art and philosophy grow strong, an art and philosophy with feet on the ground, a tree with roots reaching far into the soil. "Never betray the earth", Zarathustra's dictum, is the very heart of appreciation and gratefulness, the core of true religiosity. Without embracing the earth (imperfection, "evil", becoming, transience), religion is a blank gaze into a sky of made-up purity (perfection, "good", being, eternity).

114 *Break On Through to the Other Side*

If philosophy is chiefly a *yang* activity, since it endeavours to discern, dissect, analyze, cut through and unmask – in other words using much wisdom and little compassion – it nevertheless uses, in so doing, the *yin* qualities of openness, receptivity, insight, intuition. There are two poles to wisdom, as there are to any specific human faculty, or, if we apply religious configurations, to any deity: the *yin* and the *yang* aspects.

Generally, the *yang*, or masculine side of wisdom, is more widely recognized and acknowledged than its *yin,* or female counterpart. Through the centuries, the sword of Manjushri has symbolized the thoroughgoing approach of Zen. We need discernment and clarity if we are to unmask delusions and ignorance.

At the same time, we also need, as my teacher says, to "nurture the life of the true self", and avoid many dangers in the process, not least sacrificial burn out, an ever present possibility for the artist/philosopher, especially if he is not rid of Romantic influences.

Groundlessness is a terrifying experience. A person can die from too much knowledge, from breaking through to the other side. It is the destiny awaiting many artists, an unsolicited honour precluded to mere entertainers. It brings with it a visitation from the void, a face-to-face meeting with chaos, an initiation into the mysteries of Dionysus.

Holderlin burnt out like a falling star, and so did Nietzsche. The former's intensely *yang* wisdom welcomed the beautiful dark mother too eagerly, and was destroyed in the process. In his versions of Holderlin, Jeremy Reed writes:

Flames stand pressure above the vineyard

which turns black
at autumn's arrival.
Everywhere a pulse drummed up by the sun
twitches in shadows of the vine.
It's beautiful when the leaf falls
to evaluate life, and how it dies in the cells.[28]

115 Before Jung

Feminine (considerate, perceptive, highly sensitive and caring) in his private dealings with people, in his writing Nietzsche used instead an unambiguously *masculine* wisdom, applying the psychological scalpel to the body of western man. He "sounded out" human ideas, and found them worn, inadequate, and out of tune.

A forerunner of depth psychology and an oblivious inheritor of the great Indian philosopher Nagarjuna, he surveyed the "self" and found it devoid of true existence.

The "I" that speaks in Nietzsche is constantly shape shifting and often collective; at times this "I" is a grammatical construct for that which observes the occurrences in the undergrowth of the shared psyche. And when he talks of woman (*das Weib*), he refers to the female aspect of the androgynous psyche, what Jung was later to call *anima*.

116 Magnificent Monsters

When discussing the human passions and emotions, and the need to achieve mastery over them as opposed to mere suppression, Nietzsche refers to them as "magnificent monsters".

> The 'great man' is great owing to the free play and scope of his desires and to the yet greater power that knows how to press these magnificent monsters into service.[29]

Likewise, in many of the statues of the Buddha, we see him seated on a lion.

117 *A Deeper Season than Reason*

The fable of objectivity is not new. A favourite banner of late pseudo-scientific terminology, its roots are to be found in metaphysics, in the Platonic idea of the *pure perceiver*. Such an "objective" viewer must no doubt under the anesthetic: how else can he avoid being misled by desires and passions – above all by love. Sadly, a knowledge thus acquired is sterile, cold-blooded, and lifeless.

The "conscientious man of the spirit", whose dictum is "better to know nothing than half-know many things", the so-called unbiased, "scientific" seeker of truth is to Zarathustra "a man with leeches". He never realizes that the *truth* he is chasing after is a mere *perspective*.

Still, he is a "higher man", for undoubtedly a great deal of dignity and courage is found in the "objective" pursuit of scientific knowledge. The man of science despises careless work, prejudice and superstition, but his unshakable belief in the objectivity of truth ultimately sucks his life-blood like leeches, and undermines his search. For all the love of empiricism and experimentation, he still relies on dualistic metaphysics.

For the contemplative thinker in the mainstream western tradition initiated by Plato, *to see objectively*, purely, immaculately *is to know*. A similar hazardous view is often found among some western Buddhists, who enthusiastically refer to a reified "reality" that is magically going to be revealed to the adept once he is purged of delusions, attachments and defilements.

In the Platonic view, the pure seer regains lost innocence – the innocence that was misplaced in the quagmire of human drives and instincts – through the liberating act of seeing. The height of knowledge is thus achieved by bypassing all other senses in favour of *sight* – sharp, eagle-eyed view, closer to the zenith, in the proximity of God himself. This has led philosophers to be *de-sensitized*. Whether coated in a thick layer of theology or by a shiny veneer of science and hyper-modern technology, religious thinkers of the Middle Ages and self-appointed Cyber-Gurus of the 21st century have bought into the fable of objectivity and reason, have bowed to the supremacy of seeing, of the intellect over the rest of our human faculties. Techno-wizardry might aspire to be cutting-edge, but in fact it is blandly mainstream.

With Nietzsche, as with Heraclitus, Eckart, Bruno and other great western heretics, more importance is given to immanence, passionate involvement of the knower with the known, of the lover with the beloved.

In order to know we must love, let the object of our love be moved by our praise, and ourselves be moved. Only multiplicities of loves and involvements would give the knower a taste of what the wider picture might encompass: through many angles of vision, rather than through the abstraction of the "objective" view. Multiplicity is a Dionysian approach to knowledge, where boundaries between knower and known, dancer and dance, are blurred, and eventually dissolved. Objectivity is Apollonian, in its attempt to "understand" and ascribe a formal finitude to the object of study, in the attempt to preserve the illusory finitude of solidity of the knower. The Dionysian philosopher cannot avoid being an artist as well, as he recreates the meaning of communication as a process of essential loss, as *will to give*, to spend oneself out of overflowing abundance.

The Platonic philosopher resembles the ascetic. His chief concern is personal liberation, "knowledge", wisdom; he sacrifices, in his journey to freedom, the very life that sustains him. He despises life, as does any closet metaphysician whose denial of transience is expressed in modern, scientific jargon. A similar outlook is to be found in some Buddhist teachers when they refer to the body as a bag of filth, and encourage their students to visualize their entrails, or contemplate in their mind the slow process of decomposing. A sobering thought, and a magnificent form of *upaya*, aimed to aid the awakening of their students, especially when compared to our cult of youth and eternal beauty, to our colossal denial of death. It is only when the point is brought home too eagerly and with hammering persistence that one wonders whether it might conceal a deep-seated contempt for life and the body.

The body is a vehicle for practice, but that does not justify contempt towards it. If the body is a *mere* vehicle, it is nevertheless through this imperfect medium that we are able to dance.

The body is a conduit for the electric current of individual spirit to pass through, for knowledge and tradition to be incorporated, or at times discarded and re-created out of its ashes.

118 *The Rainmaker*

The feminine side of wisdom invites one to stop, replete one's energies, assess the distance already covered, and contemplate what lies ahead. It makes use of clear perception with no waste of vitality, while still exercising discernment, discriminative thought, and carefully weighed evaluation.

The Chinese story of the Rainmaker is an exemplary expression of the *yin* side of wisdom. There was a village stricken with drought, with potential severe consequences for the harvest and the very survival of the people. All prayers from the villagers had been to no avail. At last the residents decided to call in a rainmaker. He came, and agreed to help them, on one condition: he wanted a small room where to be alone. The first day went by, then another. The villagers were impatient, but on the third day, it finally rained. What did the rainmaker do? He allowed things to happen. He yielded to feminine wisdom. He waited. The rainmaker's art is *wu-wei*, the infinitely subtle and arduous art of *non-doing*.

119 *Such a Perfect Day*

Nietzsche never allowed himself to court and seduce (and be seduced by) feminine wisdom. Except in 1888, at the brink of mental collapse: *Ecce Homo* is his testament to this moment of sovereign repose and contemplation:

> On this perfect day, when everything is ripening and not only the grape turn brown, a ray of sun just fell upon my life: I looked back, I looked far ahead of me, and never saw so many and such good things at once.[30]

120 *Shelter from the Storm*

The wanderer – whose very ground has been swept from under his feet – needs a place where to rest, if he is to continue on his journey joyfully and with the same courage and enthusiasm as before. The exclusive use of *yang* wisdom, of the slaying powers of the samurai, of the double-edged sword of Manjushri, is a dangerous method. When not balanced by the life-giving attributes of its counterpart, the wanderer will self-destruct.

A person who has reached a one-sided development of *yang* wisdom is unable to distinguish between the primordial feminine expressed by the *Great Mother* and feminine consciousness as such.

While within the former there are no differentiations, no individual identities, the latter emerges as the need to reconnect, integrate, and harmonize parts made separate by masculine consciousness. Some may argue that there is a more balanced manifestation of wisdom at work in

Daoism and *Ch'an* than in Japanese Zen with its association with martial arts, repressive disciplines and a rigid outlook. It is a wide generalization, and as such inaccurate. Furthermore, as "Japanese" Zen slowly but surely takes roots in the West, it progressively looses its rigidity: there are many women practitioners in its sanghas; the machismo and samurai-style abnegation has been tempered by a more holistic, humane look at the human condition, with an acceptance of its inherent weakness and imperfection. The teacher, still by and large an inspirational figure-head and a living, breathing manifestation of the teachings, is less a feudal lord to whom surrender unconditionally than a more experienced spiritual friend to whom one turns for encouragement and inspiration.

As Buddhism grows roots in the West, its feminine attributes of yielding, of love and compassion, of letting go, of concern for all sentient beings, of wisdom that perceives emptiness, come to the fore.

Not last among these is *social engagement*, a natural consequence of the bodhisattva vows to liberate all beings from suffering. In spite of the danger of reducing Buddhism to an exotic brand of humanism, socially engaged Buddhism is wide reaching and generous in its output and contribution to the modern development of the Dharma. In Ken Jones's vision, awareness of the social dimension is equal to the opening of the fourth eye:

> Traditionally *the opening of the third eye* refers to a spiritual awakening. But such an awakening cannot afford to be culture-blind and socially illiterate. Thus, to open the fourth eye is to be aware and knowledgeable of the social and cultural contexts of the Dharma – and particularly the ethical implications of those contexts.[31]

A school of thought, a religion – if it is to remain alive and not merely collect old scriptures – changes with the times, contributing vision and insight but also learning from the lessons of everyday living.

It is less likely for an individual to go astray if he operates within a community of fellow practitioners. The solitary flight of the hero is part of the Romantic psychological make-up of anyone born in the 1840s as Nietzsche was. It is still a testimonial to his great courage and strength that he attempted it in spite of tremendous difficulties and the near impossibility to succeed.

121   *Dionysus' Arrested Development*

It is trivial is to advocate passion versus reason, irrationality versus rationality, as the Surrealist church did, and so is to prefer madness to sanity, the mind expanded by drugs to the prosaic mind, a misapprehension typical of the nineteen sixties counterculture, a misinterpretation of the Dionysian: Dionysus caught in arrested development. This is unwillingness, perhaps inability, to acknowledge the Dionysian full circle, for doing so would encompass the need to "spiritualize", i.e. *sublimate*, the passions.

Failing to understand the difference between castration and spiritualization of the instincts has been the blind spot of an entire generation, a mistake fatally echoed by the Derrida of *Esperons* for whom spiritualization *implies* castration.

True, we are no longer in awe of the primitive surgery as expounded in the Sermon of the Mount: "If thy eye offend thee, pluck it out." However, we have indulged the passions long enough to know that they lead into blind alleys and ultimately produce tedium and addiction.

The pseudo-transgression of modern, permissive art breeds a unique form of philistinism, the stolid invulnerability of the modern consumers of art, fostered within the invisible network of neo-Bayeruth middle-brow misdemeanour, of post-post modern mediocrity. A new, opulent and drugged-out crowd out for a good time.

To extirpate the passions is as detrimental as to indulge them. Rapture and intoxication, peak experiences, have as necessary counterparts valleys, world-weariness, unease and discontent. An individual (and a culture) is ailing if their survival depends on peak experiences. To misread Nietzsche's call to the open sea as an invitation to regress to the primitive elements of the psyche is a fatal mistake. New horizons imply *spiritualization of passions* and *sublimation of instincts*.

122 *Open Sesame of the Night*

Dionysus is life and death. If Dionysus were not also representing Hades, he would be merely the Roman Bacchus, the idol of a philistine crowd in search of entertainment. Heraclitus reminds us that Hades and Dionysus are the same.

During the time of *Lenaia*, the festival of Dionysus, revelers would march in procession and chant hymns to the phallus. Heraclitus' comment is that if it were not for Dionysus, their actions would be most shameless.

The peak of sexual passion opens for lovers the abyss of non-being, the contemplation of an absence made real by the small death of sexual orgasm.

123 *In Praise of Sublimation*

What is then *sublimation*? Popularized by Freud, the word already existed in medieval Germany as adaptation of the Latin *sublimare*, and later was used, with various meanings, by Novalis, Goethe, and Schopenhauer. It was Nietzsche, however, who first gave it its current meaning.

Goethe wrote of the need to refrain from enacting human feelings in their naturalness, and of their need "to be wrought, prepared, sublimated". Novalis pointed out that "the coarse Philistine imagines the joys of heaven as a fair", whereas "the sublimated one turns heaven into a magnificent Church". Schopenhauer spoke of "representation" as "sublimated into abstract concepts".

The above notions still reflect the two-worlds mentality: Goethe assumed the existence of an original naturalness, Novalis juxtaposed a church to a fair, the sacred to the mundane, and Schopenhauer imagined an ontological reality behind "representation".

These perspectives are all valid, however, as they prepare the ground for the *first modern formulation of sublimation*, which appears in Nietzsche's *Human, all too Human*, at the end of a paragraph titled *Chemistry of concepts and sensations*:

> All we require . . . is a *chemistry* of the moral, religious, aesthetic conceptions and sensations, likewise of all the agitations we experience within ourselves in cultural and social intercourse, and indeed even when we are alone. What if this chemistry would end up by revealing that in this domain too the most glorious colours are derived from base, indeed from despised materials? Will there be many who will desire to pursue such researches? Mankind likes to put the questions of origins and beginnings out of its mind: must one not be almost inhuman to detect in oneself the contrary inclination?[32]

Sublimation is no longer seen in dualistic fashion. It is not *ascetic self-mortification*, nor athletic *self-exhaustion*. Instead, it is an *alchemical process more akin to gardening*:

> One can dispose of one's drives like a gardener and, though few know it, cultivate the shoots of anger, pity, curiosity, vanity as productively and profitably as a beautiful fruit tree on a trellis; one can do it with the good or bad taste of a gardener and, as it were, in the French or English or Dutch or Chinese fashion; one can also let nature rule and only attend to a little embellishment and tidying up here and there; one can, finally, without paying any attention to them all, let the plants grow up and fight their fight out among themselves – indeed, one can

take delight in such a wilderness, and desire precisely this delight, though it gives one some trouble, too. All this we are at liberty to do: but how many know we are at liberty to do it? Do the majority not believe in themselves as in complete fully developed facts? Have the great philosophers not put their seal on this prejudice with the doctrine of the exchangeability of character?[33]

In sublimation, passions are acknowledged, upheld, felt in their full power, texture, density and colour. If to be a "good person" means overcoming one's primitive, self-centered impulses, then one who does not have such impulses or has killed them is *not* a good person! There might be more potential for development for the person with strong impulses than for the person with no impulses at all.

One needs to employ one's impulses, not weaken or kill them. Being too feeble, too cowardly, is not in itself a sign of virtue. Inherent in the German translation of the word sublimation is *lifting up* (*auf heben*): less a suppression of "basic" nature than its alchemical transformation into gold. The other word Nietzsche uses is *spiritualization*: even reason, which is known to tyrannize the human psyche, can be used as an aid in spiritualizing instincts for the purpose of self-mastery.

Similarly, Zen does not favour the suppression of emotions and passions, but provides means to transform them. In Zen it is said that the passions themselves are enlightenment. The ability to turn and face one's impulses squarely is called *the lion's roar*. A pious, sheepish attitude will not do. The practitioner must acknowledge the murderer, the rapist, the hungry ghost within him, uphold these frightening, demonic energies, feel them within himself, recognize them, familiarize with them, even be thankful of their existence as part of the rich assembly within his psyche.

Having ruinously cooked up Freudian psychology in the same cauldron as utopian ideologies, humanity in the second half of the 20th century has largely assumed that sexuality is the foundation of everything. To sublimate means most of the time to sublimate sexuality. We have not ventured beyond that, to see whether something else may lie underneath. Nietzsche suggested that this something is what he ambiguously named Will to Power, the elemental feeling of potency, strength, and the perpetual aspiration towards plenitude.

Interestingly enough, to both Nietzsche and Zen has been attributed a freewheeling, anything-goes, amoral approach to life. Both have been adopted by artists and bohemians at various points in history to justify licentiousness. And both have attracted the unwanted interest of warmongers and fascists who plundered quotes, tales and aphorisms at will. One of the reasons why such misguided notions are possible is precisely because there is a lack of understanding on the crucial point of sublimation.

It is a one-sided, essentially Romantic view to see Zen solely as an iconoclastic, absurdist Chinese and then Japanese cult. And it is equally erroneous to see in Nietzsche the "hammer of the Gods". First of all the "hammer" in question is not meant to destroy, but to sound out – not a sledgehammer, but a means to know if they resonate at all. The image of Nietzsche as iconoclast is also an interpretation stuck at the first stage of the Dionysian. The early Dionysus is opposed, in the *Birth of Tragedy*, to Apollo: it is the Dionysus we know, the reveler, the God of the theatre, of madness and intoxication, of orgy and the dissolution of boundaries. The later Dionysus, still wild, still vibrant, is opposed, in *Ecce Homo*, to the Crucifix. He is *the God of passion sublimated*, as opposed to passion repressed. He is both Dionysus *and* Apollo. The power of the "wild torrents of the soul" has been harnessed, "economized" and put "into service".

Nietzsche warns us against the fatal error of destroying the vital power within; it would be dangerous, he says, if those "great sources of energy" would "dry up". Overcoming the passions is not the same as obliterating them.

> The man who has overcome his passions has entered into possession of the most fertile ground; like the colonist who has mastered the forests and swamps. To *sow* the seeds of good spiritual works in the soil of the subdued passions is then the immediate urgent task. The overcoming itself is only a *means*, not a goal; if it is not so viewed, all kinds of weeds and devilish nonsense will quickly spring up in this rich soil now unoccupied, and soon there will be more rank confusion than there was before.[34]

The passionate philosopher, the practitioner of the Way "flows out"; he is "a person of great streaming", he is like a river. Compared to him, the mere scholar or the pious priest simply plods along, his eye "like a reluctant smooth lake whose surface is disturbed by no ripple of delight or sympathy"[35]. The mere scholar is not very dissimilar from the quietist meditator, the Buddhist-as-we-know-him.

Master Hakuin painted a captivating picture of these fellows:

> It was only because the direction of their practice was bad, because they liked only places of solitude and quiet, knew nothing of the dignity of the bodhisattva . . . that the Tathagata compared them to pus-oozing wild foxes and that Vimalkirti heaped scorn on them as men who would scorch buds and cause seeds not to rot.[36]

The closest kindred spirits to Nietzsche that I have found in the Zen Caravanserai are Master Dogen and Master Hakuin. Particularly Hakuin Zenji:

> [Hakuin] placed such intense demands on his body and mind . . . that he suffered a series of breakdowns which brought him to the verge of complete despair and physical collapse.[37]

Both of them, after their breakthrough, expressed themselves in thunderous, often arrogant, statements. Both have been audacious navigators through the perilous seas of Great Doubt. In Nietzsche's words:

And only now finally does the great terror, the great prospect, the great sickness, the great disgust, the great sea-sickness come to it.[38]

And in Hakuin Zenji's:

When you call forth this great doubt before you in its pure and uninvolved form, you may undergo an unpleasant and strange reaction. However, you must accept the fact that the realization of so felicitous a thing on the Great Matter . . . must involve a certain amount of suffering.[39]

124 *Passion and Sublimation*

The popular nineteen-sixties view of Zen was of a godless, free-wheeling, wild practice where individual freedom is all, where anything goes, where one's incongruence, deep-seated contradictions and neurosis could be somewhat justified and blessed.

It is remarkable that Nietzsche's philosophy underwent the same type of misunderstanding: here was a godless, proud man who had declared the death of God and the end of spineless morality, whose aphorisms and invectives spurred one to unbridled enjoyment of the senses! Both interpretations are immature. Both are, nevertheless, less harmful than previous interpretations which, amazingly, read both Nietzsche and Zen in a militaristic, fascistic fashion.

Enough has been written on this later mode of misreading, and of the way in which both philosophies invite misunderstanding, through the inherent ambiguity of their text.

Such ambiguity is essential to any non-systematic philosophy, and is a sign of intellectual integrity, as well as a very fine quality that makes of philosophy an Art, rather than a system of logic.

Kierkeegard famously remarked that Hegel's system was a great accomplishment, as long as one saw it as an experiment; but since he intended it as a system of absolute knowledge, it was merely ludicrous.

The later misunderstanding of both Nietzsche and Zen in the second half of the 20th century had to do with the fact that neither "doctrine" rejects the passions, but values instead their great power in the service of the alchemical process of sublimation.

Our Judaeo-Christian world is dualistic, and cannot understand sublimation fully. Even the best minds within our own culture rarely move outside the dualistic framework.

Sublimation in Freud is not very different from repression of the instincts, in his view a painful but necessary surgical intervention performed for the sake of civilization. And even in the last of Shakespeare's plays, *The Tempest*, we sense a Manichean antithesis between Ariel, a light, mercurial spirit, and Caliban, the earth spirit.

The very word sublimation evokes to a westerner the saintly endeavour of the pious man, the discipline of the athlete, the spiritualization of instincts in the pure aesthete.

Both in Nietzsche and in Zen, *sublimation is the very opposite of repression*. The religious western world cannot grasp it, nor can our secular societies. Sublimation is nothing less than *Alchemy*, and this forgotten Art has been banned by the western psyche alongside *demonology*, introspection and meditation. The latter is being re-integrated as "relaxation", but its deeper implications have only just begun to be explored in the western world. When explored in depth, meditation undermines the very foundation of the world as we know it.

It is easy to read Nietzsche's polemics against morality as an incitement to unrestrained pleasure or a return to the innocence of a mythical dawn of history. From Kirchner's beautiful bathing nudes to Georges Bataille's underworld ecstasies, Nietzsche's thought has aroused great minds to genial but flawed adaptations.

Without the passions, Apollo's art would be sophistry, empty play of lifeless forms, whether embalmed in a respectfully dead sonnet or in a tediously "controversial", embalmed shark.

But the new creature, Apollo/Dionysus, has learned sublimation: he has outgrown the triviality of hedonism, *and* has also rejected crude repression.

Have I been understood? Dionysus versus the Crucifix.[40]

Has he been understood? *Appreciation versus denigration of life.* Reverence for the sacredness of life versus contempt for this mortal coil. Tragic affirmation versus inane pessimism.

In the life of Shakyamuni Buddha too, we find an early appreciation of Dionysian pleasures, followed by ascetic renunciation and eventually by the integration of Apollonian and Dionysian energies. Contrary to popular belief, *Buddhism is not an ascetic path*, but instead a way of radical affirmation.

Dionysus versus the Crucifix is also Dionysus versus Wagner and Schopenhauer. Both aestheticism (represented by Wagner) and pessimism (as embodied by Schopenhauer) are forms of renunciation and decadence, in the sense of fathoming a superior, richer life and disdaining the unassuming magnificence of the everyday; both are seductive fallacies.

Dionysus also opposes the shallow optimism of Hegelians and Darwinists, for they both elevate *evolution* (respectively *historical* and *biological*) to metaphysical status. The thorough-going approach of Nietzsche's philosophy proves that it is possible to resist the shallow optimism of much western thought without freezing into a cynical stance of repudiation of life. *It is possible to appreciate life even in the midst of misfortune and pain*; in Nietzsche's case, a defiant creativity against all odds, as a response to the challenge of ill-health.

Nietzsche devised a strange task for himself. He was to be a gadfly on the neck of man, a philosopher/physician who attempted to cure humanity from the hypertrophy of the historical sense in our time.

1 25 *All you need is love (love is all you need)*

The new, de-sublimated morality of the nineteen sixties implemented, inflating it to an extreme, Augustine's dictum: *Love and do what thou wilt.* Augustine knew, of course, for he was the first certified recovering sex-addict in recorded history.

Desublimation did not deliver the promised liberation. On the contrary, it lulled people into accepting the *status quo* and in hindering further the flowering of their potential.

> One realizes with horror that earlier, opposing one's parents because they represented the world, one was often secretly the mouthpiece, against a bad world, of one even worse.[41]

In the specific case of sexuality, we know from experience that it is both a wonderful gift and a dark force of considerable power.

But the development of Eros is not favored by acting out. Acting out is one side of the coin; the other is repression. The third way, the way of *development* of Eros, is internalization, symbolization, spiritualization; in other words, *sublimation*. Unlike repression, which is inflicted from the outside by a moral code whose motives are suspect, the seeds of symbolization are not forced by will, reason or any external locus of evaluation, but are instead the product of self-regulation.

Sublimation produces a wonderful display of colours. It weaves the dance and poetry of courtly love. It displays gifts and blessings that never cease to enthuse and inspire. Desublimation, on the other hand, reduces the mystery of the *body* to prosaic fascination with the *flesh*; it dampens our instinct for personal and social renewal.

Far from being an act of liberative consciousness, "desublimation", as expressed by Herbert Marcuse, is a "truly conformist function". In *One Dimensional Man* he writes:

> Loss of conscience due to the satisfactory liberties granted by an unfree society makes for a happy consciousness which facilitates acceptance of the misdeeds of this society. It is the token of declining autonomy and comprehension. Sublimation demands a high degree of autonomy and comprehension; it is mediation between the conscious and the unconscious, between intellect and instinct, renunciation and rebellion. In its most accomplished modes, such as in the artistic *oeuvre*, sublimation becomes the cognitive power which defeats suppression while bowing to it.[42]

Among the irreparable damages of desublimation is the accentuated opposition of *Eros* and *Thanatos*, artificially disjointed in contemporary culture to catastrophic results. As an example of this, Marcuse draws attention to the representation of sexuality in classical and romantic literature, where it is depicted

> in a highly sublimated, "mediated", reflective form – but in this form, it is absolute, uncompromising, unconditional. The dominion of Eros is, from the beginning, also that of Thanatos. Fulfilment is destruction, not in a moral or sociological, but in an ontological sense. It is beyond good and evil, beyond social morality, and there it remains beyond the reaches of the established Reality Principle, which this Eros refuses and explodes [. . .].
>
> In contrast, desublimated sexuality is rampant in O'Neill's alcoholics and Faulkner's savages, in the *Streetcar Named Desire* and *The Hot Tin Roof*, in *Lolita* [. . .]
>
> It is infinitely more realistic, daring, uninhibited. It is part and parcel of the society in which it happens, but nowhere its negation. What happens is surely wild and obscene . . . quite immoral – and, precisely because of that, perfectly harmless.
>
> Freed from the sublimated form which was the very token of its irreconcilable dreams – a form which is the style, the language in which the story is told – sexuality turns into a vehicle for the bestsellers of oppression.[43]

126 *Three Phases of Erotic Sublimation*

James Hillman describes three phases by which he calls the "internalization of Eros" is cultivated.

> At first, it is an attitude of consciousness to accept what comes, yet not to act this out.[44]

This widens the space of psyche: much flows in, nothing flows out. Not an easy task, as fantasies present themselves as urges to act, but a task that "inhibits the ego as *doer*". The first phase in the internalization of eros is therefore the inhibition of ego activity.

The second phase is

to give energy back to the fantasies, to activate them, to endow them with enough libido, interest, attention, and love, so that they take on a vivid, spontaneous life of their own.[45]

In so doing, we use the vigour and agility of the sexual instinct in the service of consciousness, providing the necessary energy for significant change.

Through living-in, rather than only acting-out, immense instinctual energy is given to inner life. The lust and covetousness give the impetus to discover inner space . . . [46]

Because of the magnitude of energy generated, *fantasy* is transmuted into *imagination*. Daydreams and fantasies are changed into "scenic inscapes" populated by "vivid figures with whom one can converse and feel and touch their presence". The transformation of fantasy into imagination is at the basis of the arts, but is also the foundation of what Adler called the "creative self", our latent or manifest ability to sculpt our paths and destinies with the material at our disposal, our capacity to constructively turn fantasies into our future.

Through this difficult phase, one learns self-forgiveness and self-acceptance, and how to develop that crucial psychological quality, *attention*.

In the third phase, imagination manifests freely, spontaneously, creatively. The "inner" world (what we percieve as inner, interiorized) seems to act "unattended by ego-consciousness". Rather than having imagination, one is *lived* by it.

127 *The Triumph of Sublimation*

Nietzsche is full of admiration for Goethe. He praises his "impetuous naturalism which gradually becomes severe dignity". He talks of him as a "stylised human being" who had achieved "a higher level than any other German ever did". He admired him as a classical triumph over Romanticism. Goethe represents the manifestation of a mature Dionysian spirit, a successful example of the triumph of sublimation. Yet, Goethe also possessed a more matter-of-fact, Confucian aspect to his soul. He was also an accomplished courtier.

True *culture* can only be accessed through *breaking free from institutionalized mediocrity*. That does not necessarily mean embracing an antipodean's "return to nature", nor being unduly fascinated with all things primitive and uncontaminated. It is, instead, an invitation to a *higher form of cultivation*. It is a highly paradoxical undertaking: *becoming what one is.*

> To become what one is, it is assumed that one must not have the remotest idea of what one is.[47]

What one is, is in a constant state of becoming; we live and breathe within the innocence of becoming.

The goal of one's life is dimly envisaged; it is, at best, the psychologist's working hypothesis. The *unknown* part of the goal is precisely what constitutes for Adler the "unconscious", seen as one aspect of a unified relational system and *not* as a different entity.

On the one hand, Nietzsche accepted Darwin's general doctrine that there is no essential difference between humanity and the animal kingdom. He accepted the empirical fact inherent in that statement. Nevertheless, he was all too aware of the deadly outcome of a *literal* interpretation of Darwinism.

Man must *counteract* through sublimation. No animal is capable of laughter, nor can it produce religion, art and philosophy. The human kingdom as such is the realm of culture, of *education*. In the 21st century, *training* has taken the place of education. Former attempts at education (i.e. the encouragement and development of critical and creative faculties within the great stream of human endeavour) are slowly but surely substituted by *training* in increasingly specialized skills: the final graduation of all this training is the *multi-tasking super-ape*. In Adler's words:

> Whatever part of the drives becomes conscious, be it as an idea, desire, or volition, as well as whatever part becomes manifest to the environment through words or action, may derive either directly from one or from more drives and can have undergone cultural changes, refinements, and specialization (sublimation of Nietzsche, Freud).[48]

128 Who is Kinky?

In one scene of Euripides' *The Bacchae*, the king of Thebe, Pentheus, who had refused to pay due tribute to the God Dionysus and his cortege of revellers, finds himself eagerly watching the maenads and satyrs' ecstatic dances and rituals from up a tree. What he is doing is not dissimilar from surfing the Internet in search of porn. Patricia Berry impertinently asks:

And besides, who's kinky really — the many who are dancing or the one high up in the tree?[49]

Further discussing ways in which we deal with, or refuse to deal with, wild passions, emotions and affects, she adds:

But just to *be* these primal forces, the maenads, is not the point either, because self-indulgence is precisely what sends Pentheus up a tree — call him superego, parents, authorities, society, legislation. Wild expression and upper repression need and seem to constellate each other. The moment we lose ourselves in one, the other is going to occur. So it is crucial to step aside from this maenad-versus-Pentheus structure, identifying neither with the fantasy of full, wild expression, nor the fantasy of safe superiority.[50]

Interestingly, an acknowledgment of our inbuilt sense of modesty in relation to the body and its erotic possibilities keeps us from crossing the boundary and from being crushed by these powerful energies. Our unease and anxiety about erogenous zones, for example, might be a way of granting due respect to their numinous power.

Fortunately there is a built-in safeguard to keep us from this polarized situation, a safeguard belonging to the primal zone itself. We are protected from within it by a sense of weakness, the inferiority as accompanying the experience of the primal level. So long as we feel sensitive about hungry mouths, anus, clitoris, penis, about bowels and masturbation, they will not appear as overwhelming powers. When we are in touch with them, we will also be in touch with a sense of inferiority. Where there is primal sexuality, there is at the same time inhibiting humility.[51]

129 *Holy Enough*

A metaphor for life itself, Dionysus also represents the *essence of the tragic.*

Dionysus affirms all that appears, "even the most bitter suffering", and appears in all that is affirmed. Multiple and pluralist affirmation — this is the essence of the tragic.[52]

The tragic life rectifies our culture's outlook on suffering. For such a life is lived fully: it is a life of giving, a life which is both fully human and already inviting the Rilkean, overhuman Open Space inhabited by Angels. It is a life of suffering, but this suffering stems from the over-abundance of life, from the recognition of its sheer magnificence. It is the distress of a bee burdened with honey. It is the pain of experiencing the full impact of living without the usual anaesthetics provided by delusional thinking. It is the pain of suffering-with-others, for others are none other than me.

A *restricted* existence, lived comfortably among the confinements of greed, hatred and ignorance, does not graduate into the *radiant abyss* of tragic life. An *impoverished* life lived exclusively in order to satisfy the demands of the ego, the needs of the nearest and dearest (those with whom the ego readily identifies), the dictates of one's own particular brand of conditioning (political, cultural and religious beliefs) can only experience the solace of feeble consolations.

Among post-modern, "secular" societies and worshippers of the Goddess Reason, a life fully spent is a life well spent, a glorious, vacuous ride on the fast lane, a chimerical hunt for wealth, prestige and progress. To more traditional, "religious" societies, this "unworthy" life is on the other end experienced as a bridge to a greater, holier mode of existence in heaven.

From a Dionysian point of view, both secular and religious societies are essentially *primitive*. They cannot cope with the primal pain of living. They shun the magnificence of becoming. They endeavour to isolate and protect humanity from meaning, depth and intensity. Such view might be thought of as non-human, and in embracing it, we would *dehumanize* our world: but that is precisely where the hope lies. We need a radical anti-anthropocentrism, a radical anti-humanism, capable of redressing the equilibrium, of re-instating the relation between our species and the totality of existence.

> The word Dionysian means: an urge to unity, a reaching out beyond personality, the everyday, society, reality, across the abyss of transitoriness; a passionate-painful overflowing into darker, fuller, more floating states; an ecstatic affirmation of the total character of life as that which remains the same, just as powerful, just as blissful, through all change; the great pantheistic sharing of joy and sorrow that sanctifies and calls good even the most terrible and questionable qualities of life; the eternal will to procreation, to fruitfulness, to recurrence; the feeling of the necessary unity of creation and destruction.[53]

130 *Still on the Tragic*

To this day we misunderstand the tragic as *catharsis*, a notion entirely dependent on Aristotelian thinking. It was Aristotle who defined tragedy as catharsis: a moral, psychological, remedial purging. Such *reactive* view fails to honour the "magnificent monsters", those passions and emotions normally deemed as negative. Catharsis is an attempt to get rid of them, when in fact they represent our very life and soul.

We cannot expect to anesthetize the tragic by translating it into serene, aesthetic elation overseeing the abyss of suffering with equanimity and detachment. *Joy itself is tragic*. It encompasses both pain and ecstasy. It is "deeper than agony". No hope for us to even come close to it on merely aesthetic or literary level, unless we are able to be receptive enough to be transformed by the aesthetic experience, to partake of the "theatre of cruelty":

> So with the rebirth of tragedy the *aesthetic listener* is also reborn, whose place in the stalls has up until now usually been occupied by a strange *quid pro quo* with half moral and half scholarly pretensions – the 'critic'.[54]

To graduate into that joy, an audience needs to raise itself to the intrepid heights of the hero. *Joy* is the hero's foremost attribute.

131 *Salvation à la Mode and a Cup of Tea*

There is salvation and salvation. What is commonly meant by it is a receptacle for the anxiety of living, a vague hope that our psycho-physical frame, or its hologram, will be somehow preserved in the whirlwind of becoming: the immortal soul of man, conceived as a monad preserved for judgment day.

In Buddhist terms, this becomes the purification of all negative karma, the attainment of enlightenment for the benefit of all sentient beings. Another aspect of salvation involves plenitude of meaning, which occurs when any of the classic human preoccupations are invested by the live current of the individual spirit. We are "saved" when we fully embody within our own life the great tragedy and divine farce of recurring. These universal themes constitute the very essence of human experience.

This type of salvation is not *from* impermanence and samsara, but occurs *within* this "valley of tears": tears of transformation, tears of a deeper joy.

132 Hold No Grudges

Unconsciousness animates life: images reflected in mirrors, multiplied by screens, made absurd or fantastical or mythical in dreams. Dismissing this phantasmagoric dream – the pathology of the everyday – is to dismiss our very foundations.

The *eternal return of the same*, its wild possibility whispered in the philosopher's ear by a daemon, is the annunciation of a worldview and a mode of existence where images of doubles and of doubling become the norm. This is a worldview where the conventional narratives and mythical scripts – linear history, Gnostic tales of damnation, exile and redemption – are undermined. It coaxes us into a deep acceptance of the polyvalent, ambiguous aspects of the psyche, an exploratory mode that moves beyond the depiction of the double as cautionary tale.

Conversely, Wilde's Dorian Gray is motivated by *grudge against time*: he embodies the will to eternal youth, which is the core of religious and metaphysical delusion, the basis of humankind's bitterness at transience. Time as a hideous portrait hidden away from our gaze, its reality too imperfect, too troublesome for our acknowledgment.

The appearance of the double in literature, art and religion is initially based on what Freud in *Beyond the Pleasure Principle* calls the uncanny (*das Unheimliche*), "an insurance against the destruction of the ego"[55] and Otto Rank an "energetic denial of the power of death".[56]

133 Shared Blindness

Sangha, the Buddhist community, is the gathering of practitioners of the Way, the assembly of pilgrims without progress, whose humanity and imperfections are laid bare on the altar of impermanence.

In such *temenos*, or Buddha-field, our potential for true communication is realized. What makes communication at all possible are our wounds and imperfections, the courage to admit one's inherent sense of inferiority. *Inherent* because, as Adler reminds us, vulnerability, helplessness and inferiority are part and parcel of the human condition from the moment we enter this world.

What we may discover is that at the core of our inherent vulnerability there is a sense of not knowing. A sangha may provide at first a refuge where vulnerability, not-knowing and innate hopelessness can be openly admitted; where the non-true existence of the self can be safely verified. Facing up to the inherent groundlessness of existence is a terrifying experience for which a practitioner needs support and encouragement. Going alone is hazardous, as we know from many great and troubled minds.

Nietzsche himself in November 1884, cultivated the idea of creating a community: in his vision it was to be in the style of Pythagoras and the Knight Templars. He conceived it as a society of *shared blindness*, ruled by open-minded experimentation, meditation and reflection. He dreamt up places where thinkers, seekers and artists could contemplate and work and reflect. In his mind he saw non-denominational playgrounds for fostering the life of the spirit, for carrying both soul and spirit back into neglected "life".

In a letter of that period he writes:

> I want to create a new class: a league of superior human beings, at whose presence afflicted minds and spirits may find counsel; who, like me, not only are capable of living beyond political and religious beliefs, but who have also overcome morality . . .
>
> In considering the world as divine play, beyond good and evil, my predecessors are Vedanta Philosophy and Heraclitus.[57]

By the summer of the following year, the idea was abandoned altogether. His aspiration for community, a place of shared blindness and shared experience, was crushed by the conviction that his was a solitary fate.

134 *Communal Feeling*

Alfred Adler, the most neglected of psychology's great ancestors, was later to develop creatively some of Nietzsche's ideas, helping to redefine Nietzsche's idea of superiority, removing it from the predominant ego-driven interpretations, and reconciling it to his *Gemeinschaftgefuhl*, often translated as *communal feeling* or *social interest*. "A man of genius," he wrote, "is primarily a man of supreme usefulness":

> Mankind only calls those individuals geniuses who have contributed much to the common welfare. We cannot imagine a genius who has left no advantage to mankind behind him.[58]

Ways in which a genius, or, for that matter, an ordinary person contributes to the common welfare are manifold. Whether engaged in the helping or healing professions, or endeavouring to add beauty and clarity to the world, the ways of contributing are endless.

One thing that Adler's psychology does is to question the old cliché of the genius as having to be a person apart, ahead of their time, a social outcast.

Communication is possible when there is an exposed wound, a laceration, a show of imperfection. There is no possibility of communication between any number of solid, self-sufficient beings.

On one level, we are completely alone. On another level, we are completely inter-dependent. This is not the co-dependence of mechanized modern living, where a certain degree of satisfaction and even a perverse, quiet joy is gained in absolving specialized, highly automated tasks: the gray, saturnine contentment of being another brick in the wall of society. In this case the task, and the intrinsic function of the individual, is merely functional.

Communication is altogether different. There we find the potential for friendship and love, when these noble words are not tainted with mutual self-gratification and game playing in the chessboard of serviceable living. In communication we share our *discontinuity*, we feel courageous enough to admit our ignorance, our utter blindness.

A sangha is a community where one can be oneself, where one can safely admit one's powerlessness, inner darkness, not-knowing; one's smallness when placed in front of the vast mystery of the universe. On a wider level, the Indra's net of interdependence connects one to everyone and everything.

A sangha, a community of practitioners of the Dharma, is indispensable. I don't know, you don't know, and together we practice our precious ignorance. Elsewhere one can build and build, pile up knowledge as a bulwark against the elements, against the menace of incumbent death. Sangha could be a place of solace. So many great and troubled spirits will find kindred hearts and burning embers. Great plants growing together in utter aloneness, yet in subtle, mutually nourishing communion.

Great solace comes from the acceptance that it is absolutely fine to reveal one's ignorance and hopelessness. Then communication flows, friendship is possible, both the *star friendship* Nietzsche writes about in the *Joyful Science*, the cold river of love running in the stars' trajectory, *and* the warm-heartedness that flows between those who have gained enough strength and independence to afford *dana*, generosity.

One might come to a sangha at first with wanting something – quenching one's thirst, finding a temporary fix to a problem. Sooner or later the question is reversed, it becomes: "How can I *give* something?"

That something is then realized as one's life.

In this context, the Romantic idea of the person of genius is re-valued and re-written in Adlerian key. The person of genius, whether or not a solitary hermit, is a human being who is *supremely useful*, no longer in a mechanical, utilitarian mode, subservient to the logic of the machine, but one who contributes to the wider domain of culture, within and without the human sphere. The artist needs the response of a public, as much as the public, and culture in general, need the artist for he serves humanity *sub specie aeternitatis*.

Sangha is a *feminine* phenomenon, and she is not a matter of mere linguistics. In fact, "mere" linguistics always betrays unsuspected depths of meaning. One of the most remarkable elements in the development of the Buddhist Sangha in the West has been the the wider participation of women. This is not only in tune with the times and with issues of gender, but also with the need to acknowledge the feminine side of the psyche as an essential aspect.

The feminine is conspicuous for its absence in Nietzsche's philosophy. The lack of experience in interaction with, and of understanding of, the female psyche had considerable repercussions in his entire thinking.

> What I needed most . . . in order to heal . . . myself . . . was the belief that I was not the only one to be thus, to see thus – I needed the enchanting feeling of kinship and equality in the eye and in desire, I needed to rest in the trust of friendship; I needed a shared blindness [*eine Blindheit zu Zweien*] with no suspicion or question marks . . . [59]

135   *The True Person of No Rank and the Dentist*

Nietzsche's overman (*Ubermensch*), erroneously translated as "superman", is not to be associated with the ludicrous cartoon characters *Superman* or *Conan the Barbarian*, the eponymous hero in a film whose opening credits included the Nietzschean aphorism "What does not kill me makes me stronger".

The overman does not belong to the hero fantasy; it is not an image for the human ego who is to substitute God after His death. He is not an Hercules, nor a knight in shiny armor. The hero fantasy is a fantasy of *conquest*, born out of inferiority complex: out on a mission to make the unknown known, to go into pitch-black darkness with our shining headlights. We travel out there in the universe facing aliens, translating their ambiguous mutterings into Oxonian English, or into whichever language happens to be dominant at the time on planet Earth's poor crust.

When faced with a strange dream at night, we drag its characters onto the dissecting table of interpretation. We bomb countries or send troops there in Manichean "wars on evil" just so that we can place them on the map and learn a bit of geography in the process. The modern-day hero is an omnivorous creature, using *anything* at its disposal to reach its goals: liberal humanism, social and spiritual Darwinism, cybernetics and modern technology, even old-fashioned, quaint theosophical spiritualism dressed up as New Age.

The *overman* conjured up by Nietzsche is instead very close to what Zen calls a "true man of no rank" (*mui shinnin*).

The hero battles with an imagined, outer evil; similarly, the saint is successful in extirpating passions (*Leidenschafthen*) and emotions (*Affekte*), but in doing so he *eradicates his humanity*. The true man of no rank, although superior to ordinary people in spirit, *shares* with them passions and emotions.

In *Twilight of the Idols*, at the beginning of the chapter titled *Morality as anti-Nature*, Nietzsche writes:

> All passions have a period in which they are merely fateful, in which they draw their victims down by weight of stupidity – and a later, very much later one, in which they marry the spirit, 'spiritualise' themselves. In former times, because of the stupidity of passion, people waged war on passion itself: they plotted to destroy it – all the old moral monsters are in complete agreement that 'il faut tuer les passions'. The most famous formula for this can be found in the New Testament, in that Sermon on the Mount where, incidentally, things are by no means viewed from on high. Here it is said, for example, with reference to sexuality, 'if thine eye offend thee, pluck it out': fortunately no Christian acts according to this precept. Destroying the passions and desires merely in order to avoid their stupidity and the disagreeable consequences of their stupidity seems to us nowadays to be itself simply an acute form of stupidity. We no longer marvel at the dentists who pull out teeth to stop them hurting . . . [60]

The wise person is not enthralled by the passions: if he were to do that, he would fail to realize his true humanity. On the other hand, to become devoid of emotion is not to be fully human either, and this has been one of the problems with our western tradition. As Graham Parkes points out:

> The role and function of the emotions and passions in the overall economy of the psyche have been largely neglected, or else simply denigrated, in the Western philosophical tradition. The general disparagement of the affective side of life with which Nietzsche is faced has its roots in the ascetic aspects of the Platonic tradition, proponents of which are perturbed by the way emotion tends to work counter to the proper exercise of reason. [61]

A sage is closer to Odysseus than Hercules. He is, in Nietzsche's own words, "deaf to the siren song of old metaphysical bird-catchers" who have been adulating him, convincing him of his divine nature above common human emotions and passions. The overman is "translated back into nature". From *homo Sapiens* he develops into *homo Natura*.

He is like a lion at heart, whom society unsuccessfully tries to tame. Pre-dating Freud, Nietzsche refers to the fact that civilization tries to domesticate man into a pet. However, it would be a dangerous mistake to identify the overman with the "wild man". That would mean repeating Callicles' error. Callicles makes his famous claim against Socrates in Plato's *Gorgias*, and his case is bound at first to convince anyone endowed with a rebellious spirit. He attacks those who "praise self-control and justice because of their own lack of manhood" (492a). His argument is powerful:

> We seize the best and the most resilient among us when they are still young, in order to shape them and tame like lions; we lure them and trick them, and thus we make them subservient, teaching them fairness because it is beautiful and just. If then a man is born, I say, of strong nature, who shrugs away all these prejudices, breaks free of them . . . – trampling over our scriptures, our charms and spells, and all laws against nature [. . .] then natural justice will shine through.[62]

According to Callicles, the pious are so not out of choice, but because they lack the courage of indulging the strong passions.

> He who wants to live rightly must let his passions get as strong as ever, and not repress them; through valor and intelligence he must be able to give in to such desires, no matter how intense they might be, and gratify each of them whenever it arises.
>
> But this, I say, will not be possible for most people; and that is why, out of shame, they accuse those who can, in order to cover up their own weakness; and they claim . . . that immoderation is dishonorable; they say so in order to enchain, as I said before, those who are better endowed by nature. And themselves – incapable to procure full gratification for their desires – they praise moderation and justice because of their own lack of manhood.[63]

What he fails to see is something that a rebel who has truly revolted against conformity finds out sooner or later: *indulging the passions is not freedom, but a form of slavery.* Socrates himself, though complimenting Callicles for his frankness, explains that "happiness" consists in freedom *from* the tyranny of desire. Running after desires, he says, is akin to continually carrying water in a sieve and pouring it into a leaking jar.

In Zen there is disengagement from passions, but at the same time the merely rational, contrived objectivity of reason is deemed as inadequate. Zarathustra's answer to life is Yes, and Buddha calls this Yes *tathata*, suchness. In order to become what one is, mastery is needed. Today's term for that kind of mastery is none other than *sublimation*.

136 *Sun-faced Buddha*

For Masao Abe, the Nietzschean overman is *not* the true man of no rank, for he lacks a "thorough realization of death". In his view, Nietzsche did not see that the core of religion is *death,* not morality. He did not deal with death squarely, but viewed it "from the side of life alone . . . An existential self-realization of death is essential to a great affirmation of life". This, he argues, is present both in Zen and in St. Paul, who said: "We are always carrying in the body the death of Jesus, so that the life of Jesus may also be manifested in our bodies" (II Corinthians 4-10)

However, the result of St. Paul's message has crystallized into a millennial denigration of life, paired to a powerful denial of death through the flight into eternality.

With Nietzsche, the death of God turns instead into the Field of Great Affirmation. He does not deny death; it's just that his style does not allow for the luxury of melancholy, for the elegiac tone that we associate with mournful religiosity; his style is lyrical, his pace warrior-like and sun-drenched. Yet, many deaths occur within his life and work, a continual painful renewal. Quite the opposite than the timid hope of "eternal life".

137 *Beyond the Dream of Change*

The weakness of religion is that it tends to belittle life and the earth. Philosophy – as commonly understood – also fails, for it wants to dethrone life and worship only reason. Both religion and philosophy are blind to what is, and obsessed by what it could be. They are obsessed by the dream of change.

A great hope arose at the dawn of modern psychology. Here was an art that could have looked at human and non-human life in a new, unprejudiced way, without buying into the fable of change. A slim chance: psychology followed too sheepishly on the trodden path; it joined the brotherhood of life-denigrators. A paralyzing value judgment holds that the world as it is is simply *not good enough*. It is so despicably imperfect, so messy. It needs intervention, it needs redemption.

Of the three disciplines – religion, philosophy and psychology – the latter ended up being caught up the most into the dream of change, fluently reproducing the Judaeo-Christian illusion. The dream of change originates from a negative value judgment. We must dream up a heaven, into which we project our ideas of perfection, of permanence, of "being". Psychotherapy's militant activism geared towards the improvement of humankind is based on a profound disapproval of it. It is nothing but a lucid form of slander. As with religion and philosophy, the effort to *promote discontent* and change keeps the psychotherapy industry going.

Wanting to change: the pre-requisite is a lack of appreciation, paired with bad conscience, guilt and resentment. Psychotherapy, like religion and philosophy before it, needs an analogous process of re-thinking and re-visioning. It needs to move away from Judaeo-Christian prejudices and step into a new territory. The tools for this necessary transfiguration are present both in Nietzsche's enigmatic idea of the eternal return, as well as in Zen teachings and practice.

Affirmation of life, Yea-saying, is the medicine that will cure humankind from the weakness of its philosophies, religions and misguided psychologies. This means affirming existence *on its own terms and on its own terms only*. There is no room for so-called redemption, nor for the escape route of all therapies: "transcendence" of some form or other. *Unless we define redemption as complete affirmation of what is; unless we define transcendence as inclusive immanence*. According to the Nietzsche of *Twilight of the Idols*, "we have invented the concept 'goal' – in reality there is no goal".

Love of destiny turns necessity into *beautiful necessity*. Nietzschean *amor fati* and the eternal return of the same can be used as points of reference for new psychological work. That entails a momentous shift from the compulsion to change to the appreciation of beauty within necessity.

138 Why Nietzsche is Essential to Western Buddhists

Some contemporary Buddhists question the validity of the blood lineage, the uninterrupted transmission of the Dharma from the Buddha to Mahakashyapa to present-day teachers and Masters. Some of them are self-proclaimed agnostics: instead of the Buddha, they worship a new deity, the Question Mark. Others even initiated their own religion, sporting Buddhist phraseology and shiny new robes. The grudge against blood lineage and face-to-face transmission of the Dharma is made in the name of a thoroughly modern fable, *historicity*: the blood lineage, these people are saying, is not a historical *fact*. All the same, this non-fact shines through many generations in all its splendour, originated by an equally non-factual occurrence, an image nevertheless charged with extraordinary poetry and unfathomable significance: one day, instead of delivering his daily sermon, Shakyamuni Buddha silently held up a flower for a while. The honorable assembly of monks was puzzled and perplexed, so the story goes, with the exception of one bright fellow: Mahakashyapa, who must have recognized something, because he smiled at the Buddha. The Buddha smiled back and gave him a flower. Thus began the Zen tradition. Or so the (non-factual, non-historical) story goes.

The story speaks volumes on the *experiential* nature of Zen, on its approach based on transcendent immanence, of seeing into one's nature instantly, completely, without holding back. And so is with each remarkable non-factual story in the Zen tradition.

We do not know if Bodhidharma was a historical person. We cannot prove that dialogue ensued between him and Emperor Wu, nor whether Bodhidharma really faced a wall for nine years, or whether his first disciple cut off his hand to show his unwavering dedication and willingness to receive the most precious teachings. Likewise, we do not really know what transpires in the transmission of the teachings from Master to disciple.

We hear the tales, we have the images: of wine being poured from one container to the next; of the importance of form as container; of a deep intimacy that grows between teacher and student. None of this can be proven historically, dissected and explained scientifically, or made to fit within a particular framework.

History, science, evolutionism are interesting, valuable fictions, useful in many ways, but ineffective in understanding narratives outside their field of operation. It would be both tasteless and fruitless to poke one's Darwinian nose in the boudoir. It certainly has been done, with catastrophic results: pornography, the general obsessive fascination with the flesh (as opposed to an understanding of the body) are some of its more extreme, developments; generally, a narrow-minded reduction of sexuality to another "health & hygiene" concern is the most accepted form of the same malaise.

Approaching Zen and Buddhism while still holding on tight to western prejudices and creeds such as the belief in History, is a dubious practice. This is where knowledge and assimilation of Nietzsche's thought is crucial. There are two main reasons why this is an urgent task. The first is that Nietzsche re-orientates western thought, by *invalidating both Socratic and Hegelian dialectics* (the latter being the shaky ground on which all worshippers of History establish their notions), and by re-evaluating the most important thinker of ancient Greece, Heraclitus.

The second is *that Nietzsche is the unacknowledged forerunner of depth psychology*, a field of enquiry which helped re-define, among others, the notions of individual and collective memory, and thus of History itself.

Believing in History entails believing in linear time, progress and evolution. Hanna Arendt teaches us that Progress and Doom are two sides of the same coin: both articles of superstition. [64]

All of the above are only *hypotheses* that have solidified into unchallenged doctrines. By approaching Buddhism from such a prejudicial standpoint, and thus leaving the western edifice of knowledge intact, we end up with a questionable hybrid, and risk to evade profound, unsettling questions.

These questions have been boldly asked by Nietzsche, whose life and work represent the culmination and the point of no-return in western thinking: by taking on board his experience, and by making it our own, we might avoid major pitfalls. Nietzsche's views on time, the self, identity, morality, religion, living-and-dying chip away at the very foundation of western dogmas. It is ideal groundwork for the study of the Dharma.

We cannot apprehend Buddhism as an exotic appendix to fundamentally unchallenged Judeo-Christian themes.

Buddhist meditation techniques have been assimilated into the practice of the omnivorous global village dweller as a complement to relaxation, health, positive thinking and prayer, or as part of a rather fuzzy pursuit of enlightenment and well being. Meditation has in many ways become an aspect of *ego-therapy*. Thus the delusional foundations of our personal and societal constructions have been given a fresh, more oriental makeover, that's all. They are not disputed in the least. They are largely based on a paradigm, the ego, whose substantiality has yet to be demonstrated. Ego-therapy, ego-science, ego-technology, ego-politics, ego-religion have shaped the self-aggrandizing History, or *story* of the West.

Zen is a danger to the West. It is a danger to our ego-centered, delusional world. It presents us with the prospect of more and more people practicing wisdom and compassion in their lives, thus seeing through the games of aggression, deception and corruption that constitute our blood-spattered History.

Seeing, with Nietzsche's help, a mode of existence which honours the process of becoming, of transparent impermanence, eliminates in one blow the notion of the ideal, the eternality that generates materialism, dialectics and the dogma of History. We will be then more prepared to receive the paradoxical teachings of Zen. We won't need the prosaic confirmation of the journalistic lie – History – to validate our vibrant experience of the transmission, for we would have acknowledged the profound meaning of myth, its power to move the psyche into new discoveries, within or without the literalistic confinements of History.

For Rilke, destiny is what is packed into childhood. Less a place we move towards than a heightened symbol of what is there at any moment in one's life. The circumstances of the hero's death unravel what was there in a nutshell. Samson's death at Gaza was present all along during his life.

139 The Koan of Therapy

The repetition compulsion of transference is both "the alpha and the omega" of psychoanalytic treatment and the greatest hindrance on the path of healing. There is a profound ambivalence: on the one hand, we have the conscious mind stating "a desire for freedom from neurotic symptoms"; on the other, "an unstated but enacted desire to maintain symptoms at all costs". The latter is unconscious, manifesting itself through *resistance*.

According to Freud, symptoms enacted unconsciously through transference phenomena do the "inestimable service of making the patient's hidden and forgotten . . . impulses immediate and manifest". And he carries on by stating something of great import:

> When all is said and done, it is impossible to destroy anyone in *absentia* or in *effigie*.[65]

The phantom from the buried past, the ghost gnawing at the core of our being, are not merely evoked, remembered, spoken of. They become manifest, they *incarnate* through the neurotic symptom.

A demonic ritual is being re-enacted. The therapist, the spiritual teacher, or the psychoanalyst, who normally deal with an *effigie*, a *metaphor*, are able to come face to face, and deal with the repressed.

We are faced with obsessive, ritualistic actions. These give the patient the impression, says Freud,

> of being all-powerful guests of an alien world, immortal beings intruding into the turmoil of everyday life.[67]

140 Homo metaphoricus

There is an *internal necessity in compulsion*: the goddess of necessity, Ananke, overshadows the repetitive acts. For Aquinas, she is *quod non potest non esse*, "that which cannot not be". For Aristotle, she is "that because of which cannot be otherwise".

The compulsion to repeat is closely linked to ritual. One of the differences between the two is that the former is a personalized metaphor that needs to be re-enacted *ad infinitum*, whereas in the ritual the subject is emptied out of his narcissistic contents and becomes a conduit for the spiritual dimension to manifest.

It is simplistic to *oppose* the compulsion to repeat, seen as a manifestation of energies ensnared within the wheel of birth and death, to the realm of ritual as one speculatively offering a transcendent, liberative perspective. Such assumption is dualistic: it takes for granted that a life lived under the pressure of compulsion to repeat is intrinsically different from liberated life. According to Freud, in fact, *the compulsion to repeat is the one route into personal destiny*.

Having abandoned instinctual life in favour of culture, the only metaphorical key to paradise lost is through symptoms, the so-called "neurotic" symptoms. For Freud, as for Nietzsche, *Homo sapiens* is *homo metaphoricus*.

The archetypal image of our compulsion to live in a world of meaning is of course Don Quixote. "What is abnormal in him," wrote Ortega, "has been and will continue to be normal in humanity."

In the same paper where he presents the ideas of the compulsion to repeat and of transference, Freud also discusses the hypotheses of *protection against stimuli*. "Being in the world" means for him "in the first place being guarded against it". The protector also guards us against overstimulation from the "inside", e.g. by suppressing painful memories. This is in fact the origin of "projection":

> A particular way is adopted of dealing with any internal excitations which produce too great an increase of unpleasure: there is a tendency to treat them as though they were acting, not from the inside, but from the outside, so that it may be possible to bring the shield against stimuli into operation as a means of defense against them. This is the origin of projection.[67]

141 *Love and Death*

Freud introduced an unsettling notion in human consciousness: the *death instinct*. Like the thought of eternal return, it challenges well-cherished values. It also testifies of Freud's willingness – not unlike Nietzsche's – to challenge his own assumptions. He moved beyond what until then (1920) had been considered the undisputed principle of psychoanalysis: the pleasure principle, Eros.

Unlike Nietzsche (and Heraclitus), Freud failed to recognize the indissoluble bond between Eros and Thanatos, between love and death. His study was rigorous enough in discerning that the dual rule of love and necessity did not make man happy. However, in introducing the death instinct, he saw it as *antagonistic* to Eros, the two forces engaged, in his own words, in a "battle of the giants":

> And now, I think, the meaning of the development of civilization is no longer obscure to us. This development must show us the struggle between Eros and death, between the life drive and the drive for destruction, as it is played out in the human race. This struggle is the essential content of all life; hence, the development of civilization may be described simply as humanity's struggle for existence. And this battle of the giants is what nurse-maids seek to mitigate with their lullaby about heaven.[68]

142 *In Love with Necessity*

Psychoanalysis opened a new frontier, but its founding father, Freud, never moved beyond dualism. *He opposed Eros to Thanatos. He opposed Eros to Ananke.* He conceived love and death, as well as love and necessity, as opposing forces, a misinterpretation whose first outcome was a reinforcement of the denial of death.

Freud opposed love, beauty, pleasure and bliss, the whole gilded domain of Eros and Aphrodite, to Necessity, Ananke, portrayed as grey, mechanical, as time's dusty hand itself.

We are paying dearly for this metaphysical error, for we have designed for ourselves a more ominous life than our ancestors amid the "dark Satanic mills" ever could dream of. With renewed vigour, we skip and shuffle from car to plane, from train to crowded bus, joining the rat-race to nowhere, marching along on our pilgrimage to no-man's land.

The Freudian division between Eros and Ananke has poisoned both love and work. In the Presbyterean North of the human world, drunken labourers of hands and mind stagger out of crowded bars and pubs on a Friday night. In smoky rooms we grope for forbidden pleasures, living out a dream suppressed during the working week. *Work*, the one meaningful way humans can contribute to the world and their fellowmen, has been *reduced* to the Judaeo-Christian imperative of *duty*. Work has become a *curse*, an activity devoid of meaning, a memento of our disastrous fall from grace, of our inglorious, slippery path out of the Garden of Eden.

And love has been poisoned in the process: objectified, relegated to the hungry ghost realm of *commodity*. Each lover bent on what he or she can "get out of a relationship". And the time supposedly spent outside the realm of necessity has poisoned the sacred too: no more festivals, no more rituals but the zombified dance of oblivion.

It is an error to think of necessity as existing somewhere outside, independently. It is a mistake to fathom a total consciousness of becoming and to call it God, strangling in the process the countless Gods of becoming. On this false certainty religion has built its foundations.

It is equally an error to think of necessity as a principle existing "objectively", within History. The so-called "facts", the superstitious belief in causality to which rational and scientific thought have become so addicted, have become our new objects of worship.

The deterministic interpretation of the law of causation (karma) must also be dealt with, for it rests on the unsavoury habit of separating the doer from the deed, thus perpetrating what Nietzsche trivialized as "ancient mythology". The mechanical belief in cause and effect is, in his view, a result of the "metaphysics of language":

> We become involved in a crude fetishism when we make ourselves conscious of the basic premises of the metaphysics of language, in plain words: of *reason*. This is what sees doer and deed everywhere; it believes in will as cause in general; it believes in the 'I', in the 'I' as Being, in the 'I' as substance, and projects the belief in the I-substance onto all things.[69]

We must reject both causality and mechanistic determinism. We must also reject so-called *free will*. This position is non-dualistic, *beyond volition and necessity*. The way out of the dualistic prison is *amor fati*: falling in love with necessity, bridging the imaginary gap between destiny and free will in the sphere of the absolute, and between work and love in the sphere of the relative.

143 *Learn to Forget*

Our only hope is forgetting. "Forgive and forget" is the maxim that heals us from the poison of resentment and bad conscience. The ability to forget is an essential characteristic of the noble spirit. Of course, what we "forget" also becomes repressed and is acted out, according to Freud, no longer "as a memory but as an action". The action is repeated, and the person *does not know that he is repeating*.

> . . . the patient does not *remember* anything of what he has forgotten and

repressed but *acts* it out. He reproduces it not as a memory but as an action; he repeats it, without, of course, knowing that he is repeating it . . . As long as the patient is in the treatment he cannot escape from this compulsion to repeat; and in the end we understand that this is his way of remembering.[70]

Memory itself is not as clearly definable as we might think. We interpret the images of our past, and, according to Adler, early recollections need not be *factual*: the creative imagination has produced them from the storehouse of memory. *Memory itself is a faculty of the imagination.*

144 *Circular Time and Individuality*

In both the compulsion to repeat and in rituals, time is experienced as a process without beginning or end. In obsessive, addictive behaviour, as well as in highly ritualized space, we step out of the Judaeo-Christian world; we no longer relate to a beginning (Creation, or Big Bang), a middle (History), and an end (apocalypse, judgment day, ecological disaster).

We get a glimpse of how pre-Socratic, "archaic" man felt and sensed the world around him. The main characteristic in the archaic world is the absence of an "autonomous, intrinsic value".

Objects or acts acquire a value, and in so doing become real, because they participate, after one fashion or another, in a reality that transcends them.[71]

Modern-day utilitarianism is for archaic man synonymous with utter meaninglessness. *Meaning* is acquired only through *participation* and *identification* – of man with life itself, of man with a God, a deity, or a spirit. The way this is accomplished is through *repetition*.

The gesture acquires meaning, reality, solely to the extent to which it repeats a primordial act.[72]

Through repetition, an act becomes sacred and ritualized. The self is absent, and the deity inhabits the space. There is *no such thing as a profane activity*. This perspective does not belong to linear time, and does not accept the value of what is autonomous and individual. *The subject* (the self) *is no longer unique, but acquires meaning solely as a contributor to the species and to life* in general.

Thus we have an emphasis not on what is "individual", but on what is *exemplary*. As cultural – or often sub-cultural – expressions of these two opposite modes of perception, we have on the one hand so-called reality-TV, with its obsessional, voyeuristic look at the individual, conceived in our post-modern world as a bundle of whimsical drives run amok, as the flawlessly interiorized mob within a crooked monad; and on the other, Renaissance art, with its emphasis on the exemplary as a mirror allowing us access to the paradox of the human condition.

According to this persuasive belief, everything reminds us of the basic truth of circular time: moon cycles, all the great myths of birth and renewal; fertility and initiation rites.

The shift from circular to linear time *is* the archetypal fall from grace, the painful exile; it is paradise lost. It is echoed in a change of style: from poetry to prose; from myth to chronology; from dance to labour.

What is born then is a well-articulated denigration of life. Unsustained by the affirmative pathos informing the cosmology of eternal return, *suffering ceases to be meaningful: consequently, it can no longer be tolerated.*

The only medicine in the fallen realm of linear time are the vapid consolations offered by religion and science, and by the "art of the setting sun".

An affirmative cosmology is no longer possible, perhaps not even desirable. *Existence cannot be brought back to its original mythic dimension.* Ours is the world described by Rilke in his Duino Elegies, a world of "once, and no more": based on hope, and often ending in despair; a deeply wounded world, where man and his God are separated by the abyss opened up by Abraham's attempted sacrifice.

The geological shift into linear time did not happen suddenly: splinters of the old world survived through the centuries, making the Renaissance possible, as well as manifesting in the works of Dante, Bacon, Gioacchino da Fiore, Kepler, Giordano Bruno, Campanella, among many others.

If a cosmology of eternal return is unthinkable and archaic, its existential interpretation can be beneficial in restoring an affirmative mode of existence. It manifests in the pathology of everyday life, in our ordinary existence which consists of *nothing but* pathology, and through the enacting of meaningful rituals.

145   *You've Got to Serve Somebody*

As we have seen, there are two kinds of rituals: they are not exactly separate, for one can flip, or evolve into, the other. But there are, however, two recognizable perspectives from which ritual is generated.

The first one is orchestrated by the ego, in the attempt to ensure some solidity in what the ego perceives as the chaos of becoming and impermanence. The compulsion to repeat, any form of addiction and neurosis, they all belong to this form of ego-ritual. The ego attempts to reassert control over the totality of the psyche by bringing to the foreground a particular compulsion, an addiction, a neurotic pattern (whether or not acknowledged by the conscious self), thus robbing the individual of a healthier, more meaningful participation to the life of the whole. What is asserted here is a forceful denial of the painful reality of death through the creation of a parallel world opened up by ritualistic compulsion, where his Majesty the Ego can at last act out its dream of omnipotence. Unfortunately, this is done to the expense of a person's well-being and of *homeostasis*, or balance (not the *static*, abstract idea of health and normality, but instead a *dynamic* equilibrium, actively generated in the cross-fire of living). Such *unbalanced* mode of existence is given full support by the predominant values of post-modern society: it constitutes the *norm*.

If we understand ritual only within this pathological context, our interpretation of the eternal return will be limited. We will understand the circularity of time in wish-fulfilling terms, as half-hearted yearning for eternity, as fortification against an intrinsically imperfect existence.

This is by far the most common understanding of the problem of time and eternity, popularized by Oscar Wilde's tale of *Dorian Gray*, a *puer aeternus* motivated by ill-will against impermanence. We all understand the dandy's grudge against old age and death: it is the bedrock of our Judaeo-Christian culture. Thus we are all conditioned to interpret the koan of eternal return precisely in *Dorian Gray*'s terms, as a desire born out of attachment, greed and despair.

The second type of ritual belongs to the domain of *religiosity*, understood not as a lifeless ethical code sanctified by a dreary belief system, but as *appreciation of the magnitude of life*.

In this type of ritual, the ego is subservient. The individual acquires meaning only as he willingly surrenders to a repetitive act whose significance lies in the repetition itself, in the abandonment of any individual claim: "Spirit" will then be present and enacted *via* the individual. Thus "transmission" takes place, from an empty vessel to another, and the integrity of the Dharma is ensured through a lineage.

Understanding religious rituals enables us to appreciate the myth of eternal return as the highest affirmation of life and becoming.

Aware of the perishable nature of our individual life, we nevertheless joyfully embrace the life of the whole. We affirm our involvement with a wondrous and bountiful (but also chaotic and terrifying) world through our active participation in rituals.

There is also an intermediate state, or more precisely, a space where one of these two forms of ritual can turn into the other. This ritualistic limbo applies to the double, the *Doppelgänger*, whose very appearance is, as we have seen, an insurance against the destruction of the ego.

It also applies to reflections in mirrors, shadows, guardian spirits, and to the belief in the soul. It applies to the unfathomable realm of the *uncanny*.

It is not possible to draw a neat line between ego-ritual (demonic, driven by greed and attachment) and religious ritual (pious, altruistic, in the service of higher forces and the higher good). In both cases, we serve a God. We know from the Greeks that *there is no occurrence in life where a God is not present* in some form or other. Our own experience teaches that poison can turn into elixir, and that the bondage may lead one to liberation.

We cannot kill our double: that would mean suicide. And what we have learned in limbo testifies of a *vital need for unconsciousness*.

If *Dorian Gray* is a remarkable portrait of our deeply embedded dualism and delusion, it does not match up, however, with the more profound implications of the Double as portrayed by Dostoevsky, Poe, Maupassant and Nietzsche. In Edgar Poe's *William Wilson*, the protagonist kills his double, and in so doing kills himself:

> In me didst thou exist; and in my death see by this image, which is thine own, how utterly thou hast murdered thyself.[73]

In Nietzsche's *Zarathustra*, the double appears in solitude:

> This phantom that runs along behind you, my brother, is fairer than you; why do you not give it your flesh and bones? But you are afraid and you run to your neighbour.[74]

And in Maupassant's tale "He", quoted by Otto Rank, the double make a furtive and terrifying, appearance:

> He pursues me incessantly – That's madness! Yet it is so. Who, he? I know very well that he does not exist, that he is unreal. He lives only in my misgivings, in my fears, in my anxiety! – But when I am living with someone, I feel clearly, yes, quite clearly, he will no longer exist. For he exists only because I am alone, solely because I am alone.[75]

Is it possible for us, after 2000 years of Judaeo-Christian conditioning, to experience our life in the mode of the eternal return? Is the eternal return an archaic, antiquated cosmology belonging to the dawn of History?

The existence of meaningful rituals, the compulsion to repeat, the double, and the uncanny, all demonstrate that modern man is perfectly capable of experiencing life in the mode of eternal return. *He is capable of entering Hades*, the realm of *as if*.

> There are . . . no facts in or according to Hades, only fictions to be enacted in life. There is also no need for proof of whatever is said from the standpoint of Hades. All that is required for something to be an underworld reality is a semblance of believability. The whole Nietzschean view of truth as a matter of appearance and sheer appearance belongs under the sign of Hades.[76]

146 *In the Name of Hades: Notes for a psychology of eternal return*

Using Nietzsche's investigational approach alongside the timeless wisdom and compassion of Zen Buddhist teachings, we are ready to experiment with a new psychology.

We are ready for an *antiscientific, metaphoric* psychology, for a psychology that does its work "in the name of Hades", a psychology that is prepared to explore beyond the denial of death, beyond the ego, and within the wider realm of *psyche*. Nietzsche recognized the urgent need for such psychology many years ago:

> All psychology so far has got stuck in moral prejudices and fears; it has not dared to descend into the depths.[77]

It is difficult to try to define what this new psychology is, for its development is unfolding as we speak. It might be easier, for the time being, saying what it is *not*. It is not ego-therapy; it does not endeavour to bind up a pummelled ego, nor to limit itself in keeping the ego's demands in check so that it can perform better in the wider theatre of State-sponsored delusion.

It is not magical thinking, "trans-personal" psychology, or any of those modes of thought that constitute what Adorno, referring to occultism, called "metaphysics for dunces".[78] Sound psychological enquiry cannot bypass and gloss over the nitty-gritty of love and work, nor can it afford a flight into "divine", "cosmic" consciousness.

It does not serve a system of metaphysics, nor a Procrustean set of beliefs that the person must fit into.

It does not hide its agenda behind capitalized concepts borrowed from Existentialism and ultimately the philosophy of the Enlightenment – of which Existentialism is a by-product – nor does it endeavour to re-instate the monistic decrees of Reason illicitly enthroned at the heart of the psyche.

It does not identify itself in a hierarchical church, where power and prestige are bought and sold for hard cash through a long, complex and ritualized system of proselytism and secular guru-worship, therefore it cannot recognize itself with any particular school of psychology, yet it might operate within the existing schools, and can be identified by its experimental nature, and by the integrity and honesty of its methods and approach.

What is required of the practitioner of this psychological art is a direct involvement with the practice of *not-knowing*, rooted in philosophical enquiry and existential investigation.

Not-knowing is *non-Gnostic* more than explicitly *agnostic*, for the latter implies the worship of meek doubting at the altar of desiccated, pseudo-scientific values.

Modern psychology is still at its infancy, as authentic, in-depth work in the field is marginalized from the established canon, while compartmentalized packages of the self-help variety are flooding the mental health industry in search of customers.

What is required is a new spirit of exploration. We need to climb those mountain peaks again, and courageously enter the caverns of the psyche, cleansing them from the stench of life-denigration, from the pollution of the ideal and the misgivings of dualistic thinking.

> Who before me set foot deep inside the caverns from which the poisonous fumes of this type of ideal – *slander of the world* – are rising? Who even dared to suppose that they *are* caverns?[79]

A psychology of Hades is based on *images*; it admits in its field of attention what Jung called "the little people"; it moves beyond the *narrative* limitations of the ego; it moves into *oneiros*, the Greek word for dream, whose meaning is *image*. Images, therefore, guide us in our picaresque, wonderfully purposeless journey. No longer a factual *story*, nor pilgrim's progress, nor ego-trip.

To assume that we *produce* dreams is an act of arrogance, the same as assuming that sitting here in this room one hears the voice of a passer-by *out there,* in the street. Philemon's insight, when he appeared to Jung during an "active immagination" process, was: "there are things in the psyche which I do not produce, but which produce themselves and have their own life".[80]

Metaphorical, *unsystematic* enquiry goes beyond mere "introspection": we open up to the infinite possibilities of *psyche*, we approach *the middle region* between the relative and the absolute, a humbling experience that invites us to reconsider the very foundations of our search for truth, knowledge and realization.

"Know thyself" assumes a wider meaning: learning from Nietzsche (and later from Jung), *know thyself* will mean *becoming familiar with daemons*.

Opening up to psyche transports us beyond rationalistic introspection, beyond the self-absorbed investigation of the Cartesian ego, where the same old *I* examines and re-examines itself, re-creating itself every step of the way. Although due respect must be given to their thorough-going, uncompromising approach, both existentialist philosophy and the humanistic psychological schools deriving from it rarely move beyond the human and its subjectivity. Long before existentialism and humanistic psychology was born, Nietzsche warned us of the limitation of a mode of introspection limited by the ego:

> Direct self-observation is not nearly sufficient for us to know ourselves: we need history, for the past flows on within us in a hundred waves.[81]

We need to move beyond the Cartesian and Kantian ego, beyond its struggle with "abstract dualisms".

147 *An Ambassador of Hades*

The Nietzschean daemon, who made his first appearance in the *Joyful Science,* is an ambassador of Hades. A *daemon* is not necessarily a *demon*, and Hades is not necessarily Hell; they might appear thus, however, every time our vision becomes blurred by dualistic thinking.

One of Christianity's negative contributions was the destruction of Hades and the creation of Hell. Symbolically, we owe it to Christ's descent into the underworld if we no longer can access the language of Hades as easily as it might have been for the pre-Socratic Western world.

According to Heraclitus, "nature loves to hide"; and nature loves Hades, which by definition is the hidden world, the underworld, *chton* – not to be confused with *ge*, the underground. As Hillman points out, it is very easy to blur the distinction between the two. *Ge* is *Gaia*: material, maternal, fertile earth. *Chton* is dark and void, the carrier of "black winged dreams". It is a sign of anthropocentric fallacy to credit *Gaia* with functionality subservient to our aims of self-preservation. It is naïve to employ *Chton* as our munificent dream-provider whose creations we pillage ("interpret") to the sole advantage of the ego.

According to Greek mythology, Hades' cap makes the wearer invisible. Hermes wears it; Athene puts it on to beat Ares, and Perseus to overcome the Gorgon. The "truth" of the eternal return comes from Hades; *its meaning is hidden, its nature symbolic.* Like a dream, it cannot easily be reduced to the dictates of *logos*, to a manufactured interpretation that might soothe our discomfort. If we venture there, we must abandon all hope, as when entering Dante's Inferno. We also abandon despair, for both hope and despair belong to the world of delusion.

The daemon's visitation has brought us gifts in the form of *images*, set free since the moment that its primary message, the eternal return, was conveyed. Our task is to work through the images, understand their implications fully, and revert our attention to the mirror.

This new psychology embraces the polymorphous nature of the psyche, and it does so through *image work*. In the words of Daniel Chapelle,

> [It has] little interest in measuring psychological life by quantitative means or in changing it or improving it or healing it or making it healthier or more ethical or just or fair or tolerable or pleasant. The primary objective of an archetypal psychology that does its work in the name of Hades is a positive valuation of life's polymorphous self-imagination by means of images that render existence visible to itself. Hence the work of such a psychology is image work.[82]

On one crucial point, however, I do not agree with Chapelle. He states that a psychology based on the eternal return, has also

> little concern for the mechanics of perception, for questions about the correspondence between perception and reality, for distinctions between fact and illusion, for the physical and physiological basis of experience, for cognitive operations.[83]

This is a mistake, as we do need to work with the *totality* of the psyche. It is true that in this day and age materialist, determinist psychology has turned perception into mechanics. It is true that we have gone as far as to reduce even the significance of dreams to the activity of neurotransmitters in the brain. However, doing away with perception altogether means missing out the one golden gate to reality. We would fail to attend to Blake's enticement, of finding "the universe in a grain of sand". *We would be turning a sound exploration of the psyche into modern-day Platonism.* In dismissing perception, we would be repeating the mistake of decadent thought, thus doing away with what makes us human.

That would be a disservice to a psychology that draws its inspiration from Nietzsche's *gravest thought*. Nietzsche's critique of Platonism is still valid; it cautions us against the danger of elevating mere concepts to heavenly "Forms", for both are devoid of true existence.

> In Plato, as a man of overexcitable sensuality and enthusiasm, the charm of the concept had grown so strong that he involuntarily honoured and deified the concept as an ideal Form. Intoxication by dialectic: as the consciousness of excercising mastery over oneself by means of it – as a tool of the will to power.[84]

For Hillman, existential psychology is based on *concepts*, and he sees the *archetype* as different from a concept, for it is based on *images*. Could the Platonic Idea itself be a deified concept? Its validity would be confirmed only in terms of a fictional attempt to exercise mastery, but to presuppose its existence *outside* becoming is preposterous.

Epicurus, a man of great sobriety and balanced judgment, considered Plato a *Dionysoskolax*, an "actor of Dionysus", in other words a flatterer, a meddler involved in histrionics.

For Nietzsche, Plato is responsible for the falsehood of mainstream philosophy and psychology:

[Plato] reversed the concept 'reality' and said: 'What you take for real is an error, and the nearer we approach the 'Idea', the nearer we approach 'truth' [. . .] ![85]

And it is in Plato that he sees the roots of the dangerous avoidance of integrity that has become common practice in Western philosophical discourse.

In all ages, one has taken 'beautiful feelings' for arguments, the 'heaving bosom' for the bellows of divinity, convictions for a 'criterion of truth', the need of an opponent for a question mark against wisdom: this falsehood, this counterfeiting, permeates the whole history of philosophy. The sceptics – respectable but rare – excepted, an instinct for intellectual integrity is nowhere evident. At last even Kant tried in all innocence to make this 'practical reason': he invented a reason expressively for those cases in which one would not need to bother about reason: namely, when the needs of the heart, when morality, when 'duty' speaks.[86]

148 *Birth of Soul*

The *faux pas* of decadent thought over the centuries is to have systematically chosen what is most harmful: since then religion, ethics, philosophy and psychology have all been persistently involved in *fighting the instincts*, thus creating the ideal ground for the proliferation of horrors.

Every mistake, in every sense, results from a degeneration of instinct, a disgregation of the will – which is almost a definition of the *bad*.[87]

Nietzsche anticipated many of Freud's ideas, albeit using a different terminology. In harmony with the Darwinian *atmosphere* of the time, but at variance with the ambition to elevate the "evolution of the species" to metaphysichal heights, he proceeded to strip down human psychology of its spiritual make-believe and to bring it back to its animal origin.

In the *Genealogy of Morals*, human psychology is at first seen as a complicated instance of "animal psychology":

All animals, including *la bête philosophe*, strive instinctively for an optimum combination of favourable conditions which allow them to expend all their energy (*Kraft*) and achieve their maximum feeling of power (*Machtgefuhl*); equally instinctively, and with a fine sense of smell which is 'higher than any reason', all animals loathe any dint of trouble-maker or obstacle which either acutally obstructs their path to this optimum combination or could do so.[88]

Unlike Jung, Freud was to honour Nietzsche's influence. One finds several striking similarities; a significant one is the recurrent Freudian motif of the prize humankind had to pay for the sake of civilization. The very birth of the "soul" is ascribed in the *Genealogy* to a *de-naturalization of the instincts*, to their turning inward, a by-product of the inhibition of their expression. "Soul", in this phase of Nietzsche's inquiry, is akin to *bad conscience*, an idea that mainstream monistic religions have refined to perverse perfection.

Here is to be found the source of what Nietzsche calls *decadence*. Contrary to the popular meaning we ascribe to the term today, *decadence* is understood as an abating of the life force, engendering a revengful attitude to anyone or anything that is vibrant, healthy, endowed with strength, courage, and generosity. In other words, *decadence is the very root of what we have commonly considered "religious" or "spiritual"*. Its source has its roots within *bad conscience*.

In 1888 Nietzsche introduced the important distinction between *Trieb* (impulses, drives) and *Instinkt* (instinct). Similar to Freud's later experiential relation between the unseen goings-on of the unconscious drives and an established data of observable phenomena, Nietzsche had deduced, by painstakingly watching an individual's external instinctual behaviour, "the principle of organization (or lack thereof) that governs the individual underlying substructure of drives and impulses".[89]

In opening up philosophy to the domain of psychology, Nietzsche also honoured the latter's primary felicitous entanglement with the passions and the emotions. *That rare thing, the passionate life in philosophy, was again made possible.*

With Nietzsche, philosophy is reborn as radical *critique* of all established shrines of dominant modes of thought: Platonic, Aristotelian, Cartesian, Hegelian. Time, the self, morality, fate and the "will", community and the state, health, normality, and sickness; everything is re-visioned, re-visited. Nothing can be seen any longer in the same light after such re-evaluation. Not only Reason, the Goddess dear to the philosophers of the Enlightenment, comes here under attack; not just the Socratic tyrant of logic, undisputed autocrat at the heart of our western History. If Nietzsche had stopped there, he would have been nothing more than a late-Romantic, and this is how some have indeed interpreted his work. Romantic notions, however, also come under attack, for the Romantics, according to Nietzsche, often "muddy the waters to make them look deep".

149 *Dream On*

It is a mistake to reduce Zen and Buddhism to humanism. True, the chore teachings of the Buddha deal with the suffering of humans, with the paradox of the human condition. His path to liberation provides one with means to end suffering. We also tend to forget, however, that one of the fundamental causes of suffering is our unchallenged belief in our self-importance *as humans*. Buddhism is an attempt to relieve humans of their self-importance, and also to relieve "nature", by de-humanizing it.

Nietzsche is unique in undertaking a similar task. His tragic but profoundly meaningful example, was similar to the fate of Pasisteles, a great Greek sculptor who lived in the 1st century BC: he was devoured by a panther he was using as a model.

No matter how broad the scope and breadth of humanism, its wings end up flapping against the walls of the human cage. Religion, philosophy and psychology have been made subservient to secular and religious humanism. The same is happening with Zen and Buddhism on a wide scale: they are being amalgamated into the illness of the century, a degenerative by-product of humanism: *Titanism*. Titans were giants in Greek mythology. Our modern-day Titan is the ego, sustained by our absolute belief in the self, by the *inflation of the "personal"*. He rules over our prayers and meditations, our love of the East and our psychotherapy.

If, however, we sincerely embark on the path of Zen, the self is sooner or later forgotten. Looking into the small mind, we find that *Mind is Buddha.*

Zen practice does away with humanism, for humanism's confinements are narrow, limited to the self-supporting interests of a small, transient species. Its work is in connivance with the work of depth psychology: *not an attempt to cure, but instead "dreaming the myth onward"*, as Jung said. What does "dreaming the myth onward" mean? A practitioner becomes an apprentice of the great teaching of the wide universe, coming forth every moment in shining brilliance. He is not merely "improving himself", although improvement may come as a by-product.

It means that the psychotherapy "client" is a *patient of psyche herself*, not of some human-based psychological system to whose definitions of "normality" and "pathology" she has to conform.

For Zen, there is nothing holy. *Vast emptiness, nothing holy*, was

Bodhidharma oft-quoted reply to emperor Wu when asked what the essential message of Zen was.

The implication is also that *everything is holy*, that everything is sacred. For Zen, as for depth psychology, there is "no place without Gods, and no activity that does not enact them". It is unfashionable in a secular world to portray Zen and depth psychology as essentially non-secular. But even scientific secularism is as "mythical" as any of the other activities of the psyche. Science relies on the Goddess Reason and on empirical research; it is endowed with a profound sense of wonder and rigorous means of analysis.

It would nevertheless be a mistake to attempt at presenting Zen and depth psychology as "scientific", but this is exactly what has happened. Psychology has managed to believe itself to be a science. For example, reference is sometimes made to "the science of meditation", for fear of alienating a scientifically-minded culture and society. This leaves the potential open for an intensification of the polarization *religion versus science*, and for the crystallization of reactionary, magical and infantile beliefs in the name of religion.

150   *Each Thing is a Fairy*

There is no redemption – in the dualistic sense – to be found in Zen or in Nietzsche. However, both are *salvations*, or forms of salvation, in the sense Ortega gives to the word in his *Meditations on Quixote*: 'salvation' as *search for the fullness of meaning*, obtained by placing the koan of our life in relation to common humanity. Once interwoven with them, our particular concern is transfigured, transubstantiated, *saved*.

We are provisionally "saved", for example, when "passing" a koan during formal Zen training, for we have succeeded in finding a resonance, a subtle unity between those ancient "tales" and our everyday. We are "saved" each time we manage to see through the narrow confinements of what Adler called "private logic", and appreciate that our pain and joy are echoed in the wide universe. We are saved when we succeed in carrying the smallest thing by the shortest route to its deepest meaning.

This is one of the undertakings of psychology; a task that also belongs to love. What love and psychology require of us is to uncover the magnitude of seemingly insignificant objects, by placing them in a light that will bring out all veiled multicoloured reflections.

At the opposite end of decadent aestheticism, it is the everyday, as in *wabi sabi* of Japanese aesthetics, as in the paintings of Rembrandt.

| 5 | *Integration: A new tyranny?*

Plato is criticitized by Nietzsche as a cantankerous play-actor, a tiresome "philosopher of virtue". Above all, the Platonist fallacy amounts to having asserted the need for a supremacy of one drive against others. In this sense, Nietzsche sees Plato as profoundly *anti-Hellenic*.

> Moral fanaticism (in short: Plato) destroyed paganism, by revaluing its values and poisoning its innocence.[90]

Nietzsche does not neglect the importance of having an organization of the drives. On the contrary, he sees a form of tyranny of one drive over others as indispensable in individuals who are to fulfil their life's task (*Aufgabe*), and as paramount within the psyche of gifted individuals.

In the *Republic*, Plato compares the psyche to the assembly of people within the *polis*. What differs in Nietzsche is the picture of what constitutes the best possible regime within that city. Whereas the Socratic and Platonic ideal sees that "each man, practicing his own, which is one, will become not many but one" (Republic, 423d), *Nietzsche advocates multiplicity*, the full employment of one's conflictual energies. A dangerous undertaking, worthy of a "cultured" individual, of someone who has gone beyond the barbarism implied by *monistic* thinking. "Love of one," writes Nietzsche in *Beyond Good and Evil*, "is a barbarism, for it is practiced at the expense of all others. Love of God likewise."[91]

Integration, a buzzword in popular psychology, is a remnant of our abdication to Platonism. It reflects, and reinforces, our cultural dependency to its by-products, Judaism and Christianity. It re-instates the "heroic" supremacy of the human ego – which thinks itself as a monad, a separate, solid entity – over the *naturally polyvalent nature of the psyche*. The ego craves access to various aspects of the psyche, but only in order to incorporate them, *integrate* them within the walls of the fortress erected in the centre of the city. Ego-integration is unfortunately one of the few ways at our disposal for accessing the "order and necessity" indispensable to the life of the psyche. That order is necessary, but it can come about in ways that are different to the heroic dream of domination of the ego, whether expressed through tyrannical denial of passions, affects and emotions, or through indiscriminate capitulation to them.

Nietzsche saw how the two tendencies often fluctuate within the same individual: he noticed that in Wagner, whose self-indulgence would give way to bursts of tyrannical and self-tyrannical behaviour.

Instead, he proposed a courageous summoning up of the darkest, most fierce and unruly forces of the psyche – which is not at all the same thing as indulging them – with the aim of letting them flow in the great economy of the inner life. These *magnificent monsters* must be met squarely, not avoided. Indulging them or repressing them amounts to the same: in Nietzsche's parlance, the end-result would be *decadence*, weakness; both austerity and libertinism *miss the opportunity* of accessing the realm of psyche. Harshness of discipline is to be relaxed, the powerful energies allowed to flow, *without* giving way to, and being drowned by, their mighty current.

> The highest type of free men would need to be sought where the greatest resistance is constantly being overcome: a short step away from tyranny, right on the threshold of the danger of servitude. This is psychologically true, if one understands here by "tyrants" pitiless and terrible instincts which require the maximum of authority and discipline to deal with them.[92]

ON NOMADIC TRUTH

152 Itinerants' Wisdom

Schopenhauer turned the western eye to the east. Multitudes followed, traveling to India and the Far East: it was a liberating way of sidestepping Cartesian obligations and breaking free of the straightjacket of dualism. For some this meant literally flying over the fertile ground of western dreams and nightmares, embracing new conditionings, blissfully entering new prisons, and even wearing new clothes, in spite of Thoreau's warning against any creed requiring a change of attire.

What the West really needed, and still needs, is the *perspective of the foreign*. Journeying is needed, particularly inward journeying: Fernando Pessoa never ventured outside his beloved Lisbon, but nevertheless knew a thing or two about inward travel and the perspective of the stranger.

It is easily forgotten that the cultural and moral values of a modern nation, as well as the foundations of national identity, are built on tribal prejudices of the "us versus them" variety, with one essential difference: modern nations have lost the instinctive religiosity and respect for the earth upheld by the tribal world.

Exploring the foreign (*das Fremde*) is distancing oneself from one's contemporary state of affairs, so as to be able to comprehend the phenomenon of western, and particularly European, modernity. In an unpublished note of 1884 Nietzsche writes:

> I must learn to think more orientally about philosophy and knowledge. Oriental (*Morgenlandischer*) view of Europe.[1]

And in a letter to his sister of 20 October 1885, he writes:

> If only I were in better health and had sufficient income, I would simply, in order to attain greater serenity, emigrate to Japan.[2]

153 Intermezzo

Sitting zazen in Nietzsche's room where the lonely writer sat at his desk, with the same dark green tablecloth, in his half-lit cave.

This would be my home all year round, if winters weren't so cold in Upper Engadin.

Greatness is cultivated in a modest setting. We marvel at the smallness of Hokusai's waves, at the ordinariness of Van Gogh's chair. They bring tears to our eyes.

Enshrined in wood, the room smells of pine incense. Nietzsche and Hakuin meet here today in this fleeting body, on the wooden floor of Zarathustra's cave, greeting the light that sifts through the small window, at half past seven, reflected by the high peaks.

A presence stirs on the old bed, a 'man of nothing', one who became all the names in History.

I bring what I have gathered, and what I have lost. In this cold room in Upper Engadin Nietzsche becomes acquainted with Zen.

The good European meets the wondering monk, and both are set free. Their liberation is freedom from redemption.

This is not a ghostly union: both have fled the bondage of personality and restored the final riddle to its simplicity in an instant of quiet revelation.

> Vast is the robe of liberation
> A formless field of benefaction
> I wear the Tathagata's teachings
> Saving all sentient beings.

Even Zarathustra's laughter is abandoned.

The stranger gets up from his bed, welcomes the faint light, the tall trees; he washes in ice cold water. The body shivers with vigour and delight. A bird salutes the light through the mist. Peaks still covered by clouds. The bell gives its first toll; it's 8 o'clock.

The stranger is free to roam.

154 *Nietzsche and Japan*

There is still something more that makes Nietzsche's perspective the perspective of a stranger. He intuits the common roots of Indian, Greek and German philosophising in the affinities of language. Their philosophy is the common philosophy of Grammar. In all of the above languages the "I" is present, and it represents the epicentre around which the world is being interpreted. He notes that philosophers

> within the Ural-Altaic language, where the idea of the 'self' is less developed, might look at the world differently.[3]

Nietzsche's intuitions are confirmed by travel writer and Zen teacher David Scott in his book *Samurai and Cherry Blossoms*.

> A Japanese who wants to say the Japanese equivalent of "I am hungry" will say "The stomach is empty". This . . . results in the Japanese not having a full aware-ness of the individual or of an independent performer of actions as an objective being.[4]

Nietzsche's fascination with the Far East was brief and accidental, useful in finding a vantage point from where to gaze at Europe, in order to gain a *trans-European eye*.

The Far East's fascination with Nietzsche, on the other hand, and Japan's in particular, has been growing steadily since his death in 1900.

The first interpretation of Nietzsche in the early days was Bergsonian, reflecting a philosophical mode in vogue at the time, which combines Bergson's vitalism with native elements of animism. Prominent among Japanese writers who discussed Nietzsche is Watsuji Tetsuro, a friend of the poet Natsume Soseki. He shows great appreciation of Nietzsche's synthesis of his artistic talents and of his abilities as a scholar and a thinker. Watsuji's interpretation of Nietzsche is vitalist and Bergsonian, and is substantiated by Nietzsche's own assertions, found in some para-graphs of *Beyond Good and Evil,* on the essential unity between philosophical thinking and what is widely regarded as "intuitive" and "instinctive".

> Having kept a close eye on philosophers and read between their lines for a suffi-cient length of time, I tell myself: the greater part of conscious thinking must still be counted among the instinctive activities, and this is so even in the case of philosophical thinking; we have to learn differently here as we have learned differ-ently in regard to heredity and the 'innate'.[5]

Both a confession and an allegation; an unmasking of oneself and others. Demonstrating the indissoluble unity of thought and instinct exposes any claim to objectivity for what it truly is: a naïve fancy. A philosophy is a form of *biography*:

> It has gradually become clear to me what every great philosophy has hitherto been: a confession on the part of its author and a kind of involuntary and uncon-scious memoir; moreover, that the moral (or immoral) intentions in every philosophy have every time constituted the real germ of life out of which the entire plant has grown.[6]

Drawing inspiration from the above passage, Watsuji Tetsuro points to the basic harmony between Nietzsche's philosophy and what he calls the Buddhist idea of "self-negation". What is merely regarded, and gener-ally misunderstood, as Nietzsche's selfishness, refers, according to Watsuji, to what he calls a "deep super-conscious self". In Zen Buddhism this is known as identifying oneself with "Big Mind".

If we understand nirvana not negatively, as Schopenhauer did, but as "pure activity", an activity unhindered by the demands of the small self, or as "life" in the Bergsonian sense, then the affirmation of the self as "Buddha-nature" will not be in contradiction with Nietzsche's self-affirming stance.

However colored, this and other interpretations of Nietzsche by Japanese thinkers reverberate Nietzsche's appeal for a *trans-cultural eye*. Glimpsed from the vantage point of a geographical, cultural and linguistic distance, these interpretations do not stand in the stream of the western tradition that Nietzsche tried to surmount.

One of these examples of mistakenly re-interpreting Nietzsche within the metaphysical tradition of the West is Heidegger's view of the Will to Power.

Nishitani Keji, who was later, under Heidegger's influence, to change his mind, stated at first that there is some danger in trying to interpret the Will to Power metaphysically.

It is not my intention to equate Nietzsche's inherent "foreignness" to the exotic flight of *transcendence* common to contemporary spirituality and transpersonal psychology, for overcoming of the western tradition takes place *within it*; slipping through its crevices, opening up to the abyss.

155 *Statelessness: A new title of honour*

The University of Basel appointed Nietzsche Professor of Philology in 1869, at the young age of 25. He was awarded a doctorate without examination, due to his extraordinary talent. He was already greatly disaffected with his profession. Meeting Wagner in Leipzig in 1868 had been the equivalent of finding an exciting new drug. Illness later on released him from this double bondage. He encloses a brief 'Vita' or biography within a letter addressed to Georg Brandes, dated 10 April 888, at the very end of which he writes:

> Finally, this illness has been of the very greatest help to me; it has set me free; it has restored me the courage to be myself.[7]

When his condition forced him to abandon his academic post in Basel, he started a wanderer's life, living between Sils Maria, in Upper Engadin, during the summer, and in the warmer locations of Genoa, Nice, Venice and Turin in the colder seasons.

His homelessness was not only a legal condition, but also a state of mind. It was, in his own words, an "honorific title", a condition enabling him to possess a "trans-European eye".

Nietzsche's life and the unfolding of his creative thinking could be read in the interpretative key of the hero's journey. We are faced, however, with many contradictions, too many dark rainbows of tragedy and débâcle; and then there is the self-mockery, the shifting of masks by the consummated actor who loves to manufacture controversy, who, perversely, wants to be misunderstood. The hero interpretation does not work; above all because that very ego that sets off in search of itself and in search of truth ends up losing both along the way.

The young philologist escaped the dullness and pressure of academic life resorting to the only strong drugs available at the time: Schopenhauer's philosophy and Wagner's music. But these were merely escapades, facets of a counterfeit religion. His illness finally broke the spell and freed him up.

The monastic vows in Zen are called "homeless vows". The false security of home, the fragility of one's identity and personality, are left behind. In the powerful and moving ceremony of "home leaving", the Kaishi, the holder of the precepts, says to the new monk:

> Since not even heaven can cover you nor earth sustain you, how could you be mistaken for other beings? Already there is nothing to cover your head.

> Your abode is beyond the Three Worlds, and its virtue pervades the Ten Directions.

> Drifting and wandering through the Three Worlds
> It is very difficult to cut off human attachments and ties
> Now you are entering the world of no-birth and non-death
> This is an expression of True Gratitude

Zen Buddhism itself, as a living tradition, is less established Church than Caravanserai. It moves ceaselessly, acquiring and shedding away in the process various cultural hues and shades; always different, always true to its core. From India it moved to China; from China to Japan. And from Japan to America and, gradually, to Europe.

156 *Travellers' Notes*

Why is travel so exciting and pleasurable? Because, unlike prepackaged tourism, it exposes the traveller to otherness. It humbles us, for viewing different ways of life and different landscapes alters the perspective of our own existence. Contact with otherness also stimulates the development of inner life. A real traveller will not be affected by the malaise of nationalism.

Nietzsche was not a keen observer. Not only was he near-sighted to the point of blindness (his gaze, remarked Lou Salomé, was turned inwards), but the outer environment – chosen often out of climatic considerations due to precarious health – was merely the backdrop for his intense inner life. Precisely this inner life was homeless, stateless, unwilling to be tied down to any national sensibility.

A vigorous, healthy inner life is bound to move out of the confinement of tribe, nation and religion; it will inevitably turn its gaze inwards.

Bodhidharma, known in Japan as Dharuma, the first in a long line of Zen ancestors, went from India to China in the 6th century AD in search of someone to whom he could transmit his teaching, a teaching not founded on words and letters, pointing directly to the human mind.

He travelled far and eventually succeeded in finding a successor. By the time Bodhidharma reached China, Buddhism had already travelled far: from the wordless speech of the Buddha at Vulture Peak via a long thread of remarkable Masters and successors who kept the inestimable teachings of the Buddha alive.

In China, it met with the existing living philosophy of Daoism, as taught by Lao-Tzu (6th century BC) and Chuang-Tzu (3rd century BC). There it thrived and produced many great Masters: Hui Neng (637–714 AD), Joshu (778–897) Lin-Chi (866 AD), also known as Rinzai.

By the 12th Century, Rinzai Zen became popular in Japan, but it took another traveller, Dogen (1200–1253), to bring the essence of Zen teachings to Japan. At the age of 24, dissatisfied with his training, he went to study in China. On his return to Japan, after four years, having come back "empty handed", having merely realized – as he put it – that "eyes are horizontal, and the nose is vertical", having returned with nothing to show – no holy truths, not even with "a hair of Buddhism" – he founded the great Soto school.

And so the journey went on . . . In the 20th century, Shunryu Suzuki, Taizan Maezumi and other great teachers brought Zen to the United States, a country which has already produced two generations of Western Zen Masters.

It is not travel *per se* that counts. Introspection, reflection, meditation are forms of travel. The contemplative life requires that we strip away the familiar landscapes and sand-castles of our identity and enter a new territory.

Conscious outer travel – as opposed to hazy, snapshot-driven consumerism – and inner exploration give us a glimpse of our own self, and of the milieu in which it came into life. Both the self and the nation we were born into appear as less solid: they become points of reference, but no longer self-existing entities.

Sitting in zazen, one pierces through the layers and the aggregates that *seem* to constitute the self and finds them inherently empty. In the same way, gazing from an airplane down to Europe, one cannot tell France from Spain.

157 The Eagle and the Slug

Non-attachment to the self and cultural nomadism are eagle-eyed views of one's condition. Greed and nationalism, conversely, are signs of ignorance.

Nationalism as we know it is a relatively new phenomenon. In *Human all too Human*, Nietzsche defines it as "the sickness of the century". He was deeply displeased by the outbreak of anti-Semitism and German nationalism that were to incite the horrors that followed.

Some might legitimately say that it is questionable to link together "healthy" nationalism – a pride in one's native soil and culture – to aggressive "unhealthy" forms of nationalism such as Fascism. Nevertheless, nationalism as such arises whenever a culture has reached the point of nihilism. We know from Nietzsche that it takes great strength and forebearance to dwell in the abyss opened up by nihilism. If we do, a renewal will eventually take place, harboured in the heart of the void. The void of nihilism, of groundlessness, of the complete absence of values, becomes a womb. If a culture is not strong, it will grasp the first thing at hand. Is "something" (a tattered flag, a wobbly anthem) always better than nothing?

From his great philosophical insights, even an individual such as Heidegger plunged into the mire of criminal folly when he supported the Nazis in his Rectoral Address, speaking of "the great task of the German people".

158 Homelessness

Gaining a trans-European gaze, inhabiting the perspective of the foreign is a possibility that some have embodied. In the process, one discovers that one's roots become, paradoxically, more visible under the dead leaves and the hardened soil.

The rescue of roots is seen through as one of the peculiar fictions we choose to believe in. Nevertheless, it has a strong hold on the psyche, and it raises the pertinent question of whether anyone can truly move away and beyond one's roots. At times it is precisely by moving away, transplanting one's roots into new soil, or even in refraining to do so and become nomad, that one fully experiences the depth of one's culture, religion and upbringing.

Some hold the untenable yet compelling view that Nietzsche completed and brought to a conclusion what Luther had started. The impression one gets among neo-liberal, neo Protestant Swiss, for example, is of a general acceptance of Nietzsche's thought within their tradition. Young Christians read Zarathustra in place of the Bible; they find more inspiration in the *Joyful Science* than in the more archaic language of the Old and New Testament.

The truly foreign is perhaps able to penetrate the familiar more deeply. And it might take some dying and subsequent rejuvenation in order to be able to look at the everyday with the receptivity of the unacquainted.

To "get behind" the familiar, to let something obvious appear as something strange . . . In his self-appointed role as *physician* and *psychologist* of western culture, Nietzsche is guided by the hermeneutical intent of appreciating another author's text better than the author himself did.

We do not serve tradition by doggedly recycling its contents. Instead, we honour it by unmasking its motives, by placing it under scrutiny, revealing the dream behind its seemingly solid reality.

Throughout his harsh critique of modern German culture, for example, at one point Nietzsche states that to be a "good" German means "to overcome one's German qualities". Perceiving one's own anew is a process of *necessary estrangement*. Having embarked on a sea journey, we cast a backward glance at the coast, and

> We command a view, no doubt for the first time, of its total configuration, and when we approach it again we have the advantage of understanding it better as a whole than those who have never left it.[8]

From this voluntary estrangement, originality is born: not the gift, born out of luck, of stumbling upon the new, but the ability to see anew what was previously considered unquestionable, and therefore neglected.

Several cultures are summoned as "foreign" and against their backdrop German (and later European) culture is appraised.

159 *On the Authentic Way of Residing*

In *The Infinite Conversation*, Maurice Blanchot discusses, among other things, the *positive* meaning of exodus, nomadism, wandering, and exile – a meaning, needless to say, notably overlooked in our deskbound culture.

> Let us insist now upon a single point. The words *exodus, exile* . . . bear a meaning that is not negative. If one must set out on the road and wander, is it because, being excluded from the truth, we are condemned to the exclusion that prohibits all dwelling? Or would not this errancy rather signify a new relation with "truth"? Doesn't this nomadic movement (wherein is inscribed the idea of division and separation) affirm itself not as the eternal privation of a sojourn, but rather as an authentic manner of residing, of a residence that does not bind us to the determination of place or of settling close to a reality forever and already founded, sure, and permanent? As though the sedentary state were necessarily the aim of every action! As though truth itself were necessarily sedentary!⁹

Eulogizing nomadism and homelessness at every level (geographical, existential) does not entail idealistic repudiation of all things grounded, material and terrestrial. The premeditated displacement encountered by practitioners of the Way, as well as our deliberate uprooting of what constitutes familiar ground, are not performed in the spirit of renunciation but of *exploration*. Coming and going freely, journeying through the four seasons, leaving *home* behind (our own sense of belongingness, motherland, perhaps, or religion, or simply our cherished opinions . . .): this act of *leaving* the dwelling place *affirms* the world as *passage*. It affirms becoming; this life is no longer perceived as mere impermanence, as the coarse facticity of the *visible*, but allows instead the visible "to reign invisibly".

We follow in the footsteps of the great Zen ancestors, and of every fierce and compassionate soul who lived in Europe. We are not the sadhus, fakirs and cave-dweller of the old school, nor the pious, harmless preachers of everyday Platonism, nor are we the misguided hedonists inhabiting a penthouse in Desublimation Broadway. We are not headed for a life on the run, we do not court eternal misfortune. Our existential exile is akin to what Lukacs called "transcendental homelessness": a condition from which modernity cannot prescind. Some simply awake to the fact, others prefer to live "all life as pressed into ready-made forms, prefabricated homes". Some have seen with Adorno that everything we possess is ultimately a mere *commodity*. As surmised by Edward W. Said, "language is jargon, objects are for sale. To refuse this state of affairs is the exile's intellectual mission."[10] Not being at home in one's home is, in this context, a moral act, the reverse of which is, of course, being at home everywhere. *Exile* relates to *existence*, dualistically perceived as the Outside, which is nevertheless the same as the Rilkean *Open Space*, a realm that we, absent-mindedly, inhabit and breathe.

The words exodus and exile indicate a positive relation with exteriority, whose exigency invites us not to be content with what is proper to us (that is, with our power to assimilate everything, to identify everything, to bring everything back to our *I*). Exodus and exile simply express the same reference to the Outside that the word *existence* bears. Thus on the one hand, nomadism maintains, above what is established, the right to put the distribution of space into question by appealing to the initiatives of human movement and human time. And, on the other hand, if to become rooted in culture and in regard for things does not suffice, it is because the order of the realities in which we become rooted does not hold the key to all the relations to which we must respond.

In discussing the potentially liberative notions of exile and homelessness, it would be callous not to acknowledge the tremendous suffering of so many people who have experienced and continue to experience exile. The very existence of refugees, asylum seekers and homeless people is the by-product of nationalism, capitalism, and of the iniquitous distribution of wealth in modern societies. "Civilization" is known for manufacturing tremendous suffering and displacement, thus revealing what lies at its core: barbarism. "Civilization" is the fossilized manifestation of "culture", which is instead a vibrant, polyvalent, often multi-cultural, always unpredictable phenomenon. Its death and subsequent exhumation and canonization engenders civilization, whose by-product is the necessary displacement of those targeted as potential danger to the new status quo.

It is nevertheless significant that modern culture – as we know it – is precisely the product of this tremendous dislocation.

Modern Western culture is in large part the work of exiles, emigré, refugees.[11]

160 *A Mind of Winter*

Exile is "a mind of winter" (Wallace Stevens): the exuberance of summer, the sweet melancholy of autumn are a stone's throw away, yet out of reach. The promise of spring is around the corner, but remains forever unfulfilled. Were exiles and émigrés to return to their "home", they would find a new place, a third space, a town of asphalt and concrete where once were flowers and trees. The exile "moves according to a different calendar" (Said); his life is "less seasonal and settled than life at home".

> Exile is life led outside habitual order. It is nomadic, decentered, contrapuntal; but no sooner does one get accustomed to it than its unsettling force erupts anew.[12]

The ancient Greeks are chief exponents of this strangeness, and this on is because they themselves incorporated alien cultures, Middle Eastern and Indian. Dionysus himself is seen as an Asian deity who transformed "Apollonian Hellenism". From the wider perspective of Asia, the European continent looks very small indeed.

It would be misleading to see Nietzsche as a perpetrator of the classicism in vogue in Europe at several times in History, and whose chief prejudice is that Ancient Greece represents the dawn of Western civilization. It does not. The dawn of the West is a mixture of Northern-European barbarism, Judeo-Christian tradition, and radical misunderstanding of Hellenic culture.

Hellenism has nevertheless dominated western culture diffusely, indirectly, manifesting in some highly creative moments, above all the Renaissance. The inherent barbarism of the ego-oriented attitudes inherent in our western European roots are manifest in the general misunderstanding of the Renaissance. We value it because we interpret it as victory of man over religiosity, but we forget that the Gods played an important role. We forget that, far from being rooted in goodness and virtue, so much creativity flourished in a human soil "beyond good and evil", and with a philosophical outlook rooted in Neo Platonism, in a polytheistic view of the world, thoroughly alien to Europe's official History.

16 | *The Perspective of the Foreign*

The perspective of the foreign has nothing to do with our recurring fascination with the primitive, the magic, and the unspoiled. That is only the colonizer/tourist's old dream, the escape route of the chronically fatigued, the forest soon to be signposted, the mystery soon to be explained, the shark-free ocean where we learn how to communicate with dolphins before ever having attempted at speaking to our fellows.

The perspective of the foreign grants us fluidity. We come to recognize the on-going cross-fertilization of peoples and cultures, the unavoidable multiculturalism of our modern cities. It reveals nationalism for what it is: an anachronistic, outlandish notion based on defective perception, for which cultural nomadism is a sure antidote.

A thriving culture is by definition multiracial, multicultural, a place where creative re-organizations take place in a living organism. The price to pay is often a sense of uncertainty, "alienation", and instability. The journey at sea might be dangerous, but glancing back we discover a vital new perspective. An inner sense of groundlessness is necessary: a transitory stage which soon will find a new footing.

Refusing to go through this uncertainty as a culture (and as individuals) begets monsters. Nationalism, and its degenerative forms – patriotism, narrow-mindedness – is a sign of our refusal to perceive and deal with groundlessness.

162 *Survival of the Weakest*

The overman, or the true person of no rank, is *supra historical*; he does not think of salvation; for him the world is at every moment complete, its purpose accomplished.

The overman dispenses with salvation, for that idea is tied up with future and progress. Humanity is not slowly moving towards so-called "higher consciousness", becoming wiser and more compassionate at every step of the way. "The goal of humanity," writes Nietzsche, "cannot lie in the end but only in its highest specimen".

This highest specimen is not represented by a future breed of shiny, happy people but has always been there and will always be there, its presence made manifest in quiet, strong individuals whose wisdom and compassion grow despite their conditioning. A physician appears where the malaise is at its highest. Tribes, cultures and nations pride themselves for having hosted great souls, forgetting that in order for that type of wisdom to crystallize, those individuals often had to contradict, fight against, or move beyond tribal pettiness, national prejudices, cultural narrow-mindedness.

The overman is not a Darwinian super-ape; he is not the fittest, but in fact the most fragile. It is always the mob that survives, the adaptable ape, the man who has profitably interiorized the lowest common denominator. At a time in History when Western politics move entirely in the territory of bad art (pantomime, operetta, glitzy showbiz), the most mediocre become, as a general rule, and with a very few exceptions, heads of state.

We have come full circle since the time of Nietzsche. The fragile, somewhat pathetic belief in an aristocracy of cast and spirit has miserably crumbled alongside other such Yeatsian dreams and eccentricities.

Mediocrity rules undisturbed, and along with it a high-tech version of that old rotten chestnut: the idea of progress.

Poking fun at "historical man" does not necessarily turn one into a pessimist. The aim here is not of revamping Spengler's ideas that we are essentially doomed and that we are going through the last vestiges of history. There is no time for fancy theories about the end of the world.

163 *European Zen*

A good European is a *trans-European*, one who has enjoyed the privilege to gaze at Europe from a remote vantage point. A good European is a traveler, whose horizons go way beyond the gore and the mean squabbles of Barbarism on whose soil Europe originated.

A good European is not a European at all. His roots lie in *Hellenism*. But what is Hellenism if not a triumphant amalgamation of many cultures and influences honed down to a point of great refinement?

The essence of Hellenism does not lie, as it was believed before Nietzsche, in aestheticism, the cult of the Apollonian form, or in Platonic politics. Its essence is found instead in plurality, within the constellations of forces at play, in the constant flux and unrest of events and their divine and human designs.

The origin of Europe is in ancient Greece. Since ancient Greece is steeped in the East, the origins of Europe are eastern. Peak moments in European culture are oblique homage to Hellenism, for they rest in that sense of plurality, of defiant creativity and tragic affirmation.

From Montaigne on, Europe has also been the home of an exceptional thread of carefree scepticism, which did not always metamorphose into placid pessimism but grew instead into adventurous quest. And Europe has often been inspired by great American thinkers: Nietzsche often walked with a book of Ralph Waldo Emerson in his pocket.

A good European must nevertheless leave home. We understand "home" only having gone through the excruciating pain and breathtaking freedom of home leaving. Previous jibes and sneers at family, nation and conditioning were mere reaction, a form of overgrown resentment. Having gone far enough away from home, we see it for the first time.

THE INNOCENCE OF
BECOMING

164 *The Beautiful Necessity*

In a world freed from being, freedom and necessity become synonymous. The goddess *Ananke* (necessity) is freed from the wax museum that had her cast opposite Aphrodite, Dionysus, Hermes. Pleasure and pain, suffering and joy, are reunited. Necessity is no longer deterministic and Presbyterian in her grim and mesmerizing call to duty, sacrifice, obeisance, but is instead one with freedom. Already for Spinoza freedom and necessity were identical. Freedom without necessity is unthinkable, and unknown even to God; for Spinoza, God does not act from freedom of will. [1] Deep down we recognize that freedom and necessity are one; the result is *beautiful necessity*.

165 *Innocence Regained*

A world of pure becoming is perceived as through the eyes of a child: innocence regained. Such a world is not an "ideal", but this very life, once we succeed in cutting through the dualistic fallacy. Here new possibilities are open to human endeavour. Innocence opens up the will to create beyond oneself. Such creative acts inject new blood into otherwise stale institutions and practices. Innocence is understood not as clinging to a "pure" state, but instead in keeping up with change, loss and transformation.

The first *paramita*, *dana* (generosity), can be appreciated as relinquishment of oneself, dying to oneself again and again, so that the religious creative experience can renew itself and be supported in the place vacated by the ego.

Since the ego is not involved, or has at least loosened its grip, its typically heroic mode is absent, and playfulness can take place. There may be no other way of dealing with great tasks than *play*. Why then not play with the holy?

This is not the playfulness of de-sublimated, reactive freedom, but instead *sovereign play*, a play that *does not shun necessity*, but is endowed, as with Spinoza through Emerson, with inner necessity: not a compulsion from without, nor an interiorized, super-egoic call to duty, but a call from the inner wilderness, a melody arising from the depths.

Necessity is then a throw of the die, and the forbidding goddess now smiles as she inaugurates the games in Pleasure dome. For she is none other than Chance (*Zufall* in German, what *falls* to one). Thus the Dionysian child is continually dismembered at every breath. We shed our skin at every moment.

166 *The Way We Live*

Some equate a lack of goals to nihilism. Both Nietzsche's philosophy and Zen have been charged with such allegation when it is in fact precisely the need for a literal, factual goal outside that sets the atmosphere for true nihilism. Having a factual goal is based on the desire to move away from becoming, from samsara, from this life as it manifests this very moment. Averting our gaze, painting green pastures elsewhere, into a hypothetical future. Nihilism is denigration of life, lack of appreciation for our perfectly imperfect life.

"Life" is not here what is understood by modern humanism and materialism; for in that view it is all too often associated with human life (not as the wider *psyche*), and often human life is identified solely with the survival of the ego.

Stripped of being, life gains a more inclusive, four-dimensional quality. Previously, the fourth dimension had been projected into being, and we lived life as a prosaic allegory penned by a distant creator. We had been both clumsy and heroic in our attempts to achieve an ever-baffling perfection.

When we cut through dualism, and start viewing the world *ab intra*, life becomes instantly endowed with being; it metamorphoses from prosaic *allegory* to poetic *metaphor*. Our tendency is to equate them, but there is a great difference between the two. An allegory – from *allos*, other, and *agoria*, speaking – is *speaking of other*, referring to something else; in our case this imperfect life speaks of, refers to another, perfect life.

A *metaphor*, from the Greek verb *metapherein*, to transfer, carries a symbol, and it is *not subject to interpretative translation*. Its language is *poetry*, its meaning always *ambiguous*.

If we obliterate *being* (which was not there in the first place), *becoming* (*bhava*) acquires the qualities previously attributed to being (qualities it possessed all along). Life thus becomes a metaphor, and each event an *Arcanum*, from the Latin *arcere*, to be silent. Our common tendency rather than being silent, is to interpret and explain away every single event long before it has been digested into experience: the result is an *un-expe-*

rienced life, a life not lived. And an un-experienced life is *shallow*. But this is precisely how we live. We collect events, as snapshots on a package tour, and gain little or no experience. For an event to turn into an experience, the event needs to be processed, recollected in silence. It then becomes food for the psyche: it acquires meaning. Instead, we experience chronic indigestion paired to constant craving, thus inhabiting a realm not unlike that of the *preta*, the hungry ghosts of Buddhist lore. An un-experienced life is not worth living.

Since we *are* becoming, this world of impermanence is indecipherable. What we commonly and proudly call "knowledge" is at the most a form of exegesis, a mode of interpretation: functional, no doubt, even creative and imaginative; but to invest it with the power of knowledge-wisdom is both delusional and an act of hubris.

We can only grasp that which we ourselves have manufactured. According to Nietzsche, the more knowable a thing, the closer it is to a mental construct.

167 *A European Buddha*

"I could be the Buddha of Europe – Nietzsche wrote – though admittedly an antipode to the Indian Buddha".[2]

It was fashionable in his day, for writers and practitioners of dubious "spiritual" schools, to prettify their inane ruminations with quotes from the vast reservoir of Eastern wisdom. "The new purpose of their work – Nietzsche wrote, referring to contemporary scholars and philosophers, is to provide modernism with a fictitious reputation of wisdom". Nietzsche deemed Buddhism *decadent*, a form of *escapism*. He also referred, however, to his own philosophy as *European Buddhism*.

> Let us think this thought in its most terrible form: existence as it is, without meaning or aim, yet recurring inevitably without any finale of nothingness: the eternal recurrence.
> This is the most extreme form of nihilism: nothingness (meaninglessness), eternally!
> The European form of Buddhism: the energy of knowledge and strength compels this belief.[3]

He recognized that the self is only a fiction; that there is no ego. In Buddhism, one learns of *skandas*, aggregates which, converging together, give one the illusion of individuality and substantiality. In a dialogue between Buddhist monk Nagasena and King Menander (1 BC), we find this point illustrated. It was reported in a study by Oldenberg, *Buddha, sein Leben, seine Lehre, seine Gemeinde*, that Nietzsche had read. In the dialogue, Nagasena explains the meaning of *anatta*, no self, using the allegory of a carriage. He says: "Neither the shaft, nor the axle nor the wheels nor the body of the carriage nor the yoke make the carriage. The carriage is also not the combination of all these component parts . . . a mere word, O king, is the carriage".[4]

If in *Zarathustra* Nietzsche seems to settle with the idea that the soul is "something about the body" (Zarathustra I, 4/II, 17), what he calls the *body* is, however, not the *flesh* of religious parlance, not the *machine* of modernist views, but instead an astounding phenomenon, a radiant mystery.

Whilst endeavouring to dismantle preconceived ideas from both religious and materialist thinking, he maintains nevertheless an open-minded approach on the question of body, soul and self.

Not unlike the Buddha, he warns his readers *against literalism*, against the dogmatic interpretation of his ideas; he abhors the idea of turning them into a "hurdy-gurdy song", a slogan, and an easy formula. According to the historical Buddha, those that misconstrue sunyata as a *negative* fact are irretrievably lost. Those who mistake sunyata itself as a theory are incurable.

Similarly, the theory of eternal return has also been interpreted literally, in the attempt to systematize an unruly doctrine. Interpreters are driven by the "will to truth" which Nietzsche interestingly saw as "the impotence of the will to create".

In many ways, Nietzsche's appeal to the altering qualities of suffering, to cultivation of discipline, to experiential dimensions of selflessness, are not dissimilar from essential Buddhist teachings.

168 *Lightweight*

The heaviest burden is also boundless freedom. The four Bodhisattva vows imply both. When taking full responsibility, accepting our human limitations and the brevity of our life on this planet, aware of the infinite ripples a deed causes in the vast universe, we also realize the unchained melody of living, the unity of ballast and free flight, of heaviness and lightness. Kundera saw this relation clearly:

> If every second of our lives recurs an infinite number of times, we are nailed to eternity as Jesus Christ was nailed to the cross. It is a terrifying prospect. In the world of eternal return, the weight of unbearable responsibility lies heavy on

every move we make. That is why Nietzsche called the idea of eternal return the heaviest of burdens (*das schwerste Gewicht*).

If eternal return is the heaviest of burdens, then our lives can stand out against it in all their splendid lightness.[5]

Accepting oneself, equating this self with fate and karma, freedom and necessity . . . The union of *Eros* and *Ananke* is the sovereign way, the way of the Bodhisattva. We carry the weight of the world, hence we become unbearably light.

But is heaviness truly deplorable and lightness splendid? The heaviest of burdens crushes us, we sink beneath it, it pins us to the ground . . .

The heaviest of burdens is therefore simultaneously an image of life's most intense fulfilment. The heavier the burden, the closer our lives come to the earth, the more real and truthful they become.[6]

Commenting on the above passage, Edward S. Casey applies the dual conundrum of lightness and weight to another important human realm: that of memory and forgetfulness.

Could it be that in following the path of forgetting, we have indeed missed one fundamental form of "life's most intense fulfilment"? Have we perhaps lost touch with the "earth" of memory itself, its dense loam? Is not the way of forgetting a way of obscuring, even of renouncing, the sustaining subsoil of remembering?[7]

Here forgetting is akin to idealistic flight from earth, to the lightness of Icarus, and remembering a way of negotiating reality, accepting the burden and the toil, embracing responsibility, and thus achieving a new freedom. The four Bodhisattva vows *are* this heaviest weight:

Sentient beings are numberless; I vow to save them.

What else can one do when opening one's eyes and seeing everywhere the delicate work of death, Indra's tentacles beaming through vast constellations?

Desires are inexhaustible; I vow to put an end to them.

I vow to turn them into aspirations, pale fire in the heart of a snowstorm, rekindling true joy. I vow to see through the veil of Midas and Aphrodite, to honour them both and restore them to dignity.

The dharmas are boundless; I vow to master them. I vow to learn from the dead and the living, from phantoms and ghosts, from the fly journeying on the rim of my coffee cup. I vow to perceive myself as a phantom and let everything shine in the ten directions.

The Buddha Way is unsurpassable; I vow to attain it. I'll happily dig my own grave, travel to the furthest star and discover the impossibility of saying a single meaningful word.

Likewise, the Verse of Atonement implies the same infinite burden and the boundless freedom of innocence regained – not from the stain of sin, but from the error of conceiving time in linear fashion.

When innocence is regained, time retreats endlessly backward into the past, it moves endlessly forward into the future. In the eternal return the past and the future meet in the now.

With the "unbearable lightness of being" set against the backdrop of the heaviest burden, life is re-experienced as a game of chance metamorphosing into necessity. With heightened awareness, we see this occurring at every moment, from the willful throwing of the die to their freezing into a combination.

A good player is willing to do what must be done, will his or her own past backward, realize existence as Icarus' burnt feather forever drifting on blue sea-water. A "good player" is another name for a Bodhisattva.

169 Instant Heroes

The condition of the overman, or of the true person of no rank, is a state achieved for an instant and then lost.

The goal is to attain the overman for one moment. This experience of "true" (or "higher", if you will) reality is worth an entire life of toil and struggle. And later, it might be forgotten. Indeed, in Zen the experience must be forgotten, or else one is stuck in paradise, unable to move on to the next stage, the path of the Bodhisattva, or, as it has been named by Genpo Merzel Roshi, *the path of the human being.*

> It's tempting to cling to the transcendent state, to try to remain distant from the world and its suffering. As our realization deepens, however, we see that we really can't separate ourselves from the pain and suffering of others. We are all interconnected, and the suffering of the world is our own suffering. So we are faced with making a conscious choice to return to the world if we want to help relieve the suffering of all beings.[8]

Failing to understand the necessary step of becoming again an ordinary human being, a Bodhisattva, one falls prey of several ghastly, erroneous conceptions, the most popular of which in the current spiritual supermarket are the following two:

a) *The pseudo-Darwinian super-ape.* This is the widespread, if not explicitly held belief that our human race is moving ahead at every step of the way, toward ever-increasing wisdom and compassion. The pseudo-evolutionary "progress" will culminate one day in the transformation from mere humans to supra-conscious beings. One only needs to browse a new-age bookshop to find many variations on this theme. No matter how wild, far-fetched and close to science fiction this belief might be, it is nonetheless grounded on the modern doctrine of historical progress, whose foundations are as groundless.

b) *Enlightenment*. The other belief is the belief in enlightenment, understood as a "once-and-for-all" experience, which guarantees permanent bliss.

Both in Nietzsche and in Zen we find a radical refutation of evolutionism and of the perfected, fixed state of ultimate wisdom.

We move way beyond the popular brand of 19th century positivism, with its wide array of messianism and liberalism, that crystallized into Marxism, and which conceived of history as a twisted but assured course towards freedom and well-being. We leave behind the technological barbarism of the 20th century and the communication overload of the beginning of the 21st century. We move towards what George Steiner calls "the disinterested passions" where humanity finds its dignity anew, all of those activities that magnificently exist "without use", in the sphere of the pure gift.

> In the midst of the inhumanity and indifference of history, a handful of men and women have been creatively possessed by the compelling splendour of the useless . . . This constitutes the eminent dignity, the 'princeliness' of our brutal kind.[9]

Maybe a true gift is possible after all; for all the admiration Adorno deserves, it is a blessing to prove him wrong on this point.

170 *Elective Affinities*

Alongside these, we also find affirmative similarities between Nietzsche's thought and Zen thought. An awareness of the nature of suffering, seen as ontological anxiety and disquiet; the refusal of purely doctrinal knowledge; the recognition of an order in the cosmos, based on causality – not in the Western sense, or in the Aristotelian sense, but as "dependent origination" (in the language of Buddhism), and "absolute commentaries of the Will to Power" (in Nietzsche's language). Last but not least, the denial of substantiality, of the self, of the "immortal, individualized soul", of the universal, of duration.

A posthumous fragment (XIV: 286) suggests what could have been the direction undertaken by Nietzsche had he not been so unlucky:

> Light, peace, no exaggerated longing is happiness in the eternalized moment rightly applied.[10]

One single instant of acceptance and joy affirms not only that single moment, but all eternity. This moment does not exist for the sake of another moment, and its full acceptance affirms all existence. In Nietzsche's words:

> The first question is by no means whether we are content with ourselves, but whether we are content with anything at all. If we affirm one single moment, we thus affirm not only ourselves, but all existence. For nothing is self-sufficient, neither in us nor in things, and if our soul has trembled with happiness and sounded like a harp string just once, all eternity was needed to produce this one event – and in this single moment of affirmation, all eternity was called good, redeemed, justified, and affirmed.[11]

In meditation practice one discovers that there is no self. In *shikantaza* (just sitting) one has a close look at what is called self, and finds none such thing. It happens in moments of reflection too, of heightened awareness. Nietzsche saw it clearly:

> But then it [the individual] discovers that it is itself something changing and has a changing taste. It discovers in its freedom the mystery that there is no individual, that in the smallest moment it is something other than in the next moment . . . The infinitely small moment is the higher reality and truth is a lightning flash out of the eternal flux.[12]

1 7 1 *From Perspectivism to No Perspective*

The first to coin the word *overman* was Lucian, in the 2nd century AD: he wrote of the *hyperanthropos*. In the idiom of Zen, we say *true person of no rank*. Whatever the word, what such a person embodies is an all-encompassing alteration, which moves even further than the radical shift of perspectivism. By embracing perspectivism, 20th century's thought has stressed the fact that all one can do is to hold one perspective or other. The next move is from perspectivism to *no perspective*.

The very existence of a true person of no rank contradicts Darwin's dogma of the survival struggle. It is no longer a question of preservation of the species, of striving for existence, but instead of reaching out for more intensity and brilliance.

The *hyperanthropos* mirrors the generosity of nature.

> Life as a whole is *not* need, a state of crisis or hunger, but rather a richness, a luxuriance, even an absurd extravagance.[13]

The overman's perspective is no longer the Romantic perspective, which identifies the Dionysian experience with intoxication, but is instead close to the *ordinary mind* of Zen. There is no gap between the peaks of ecstasy and the valleys of ordinary experience, but the two are integrated and gradually unified.

In his later years Nietzsche distances himself from the "fanatical intoxicates", the "insatiable sowers of the weeds of discontent with themselves and their neighbours, of contempt for their age, and the world". The Dionysian spirit is no longer embodied in the orgiastic consummation of sex, war and religion, but instead by the individual, who personifies the "genius of the heart".

> Nietzsche sees the Dionysian soul in the person who, in the most complete self-abandonment, approaches and is capable of absorbing everything; the one who, by transforming himself instead of conquering the other, becomes everything that appears actual to him and who attracts everything essential, giving himself to it without losing himself.[14]

The overman, the true person of no rank, is not the "higher man", the Yeatsian aristocrat. This is because his state is beyond the dichotomy of mind and body. The true person of no rank is not necessarily endowed with either a super-healthy, strong and beautiful body, or with a highly sophisticated mind. This individual is perfectly at ease in a world devoid of God, of meaning, of moral or religious values. He or she is an artist at heart – although they might not possess artistic talent: their main creativity consists of being able to create from the very heart of groundlessness a new set of values, to sculpt reality from peronsal impermanent being, out of the blue lake of eternally recurring, eternally present time.

The task is that of undoing, unmasking: *non-constructing*, rather than (fashionably) de-constructing. That means refraining from constructing a separation between mind and body, a delusional view that is at the core of the Cartesian fallacy. Undoing also means negating the separation between self and others, our incessant, eager work of erecting barriers, an occupation alien to both animals and Angels. The overman lives in pure immanence, in a non-transcendent world; he bathes in the Heraclitean river of pure becoming, where being and becoming are equally dissolved. He walks on groundless ground, passes through the gateless gate, and realizes that nirvana is none other than living-and-dying.

This does not lead one to "pantheism", to a world where the Gods are hiding in the all-too-human affairs of the everyday, but to an infinitely subtle vision of poetic ambiguity.

God is dead, not because He is everything, but rather because He is in every moment. Every moment calls for a different constellation of dynamic forces, for a specific God, in relation to other Gods and humans. Overriding anguish persuades us to attempt the introduction of human law and order into elemental chaos. Only the aesthetic temperament of the overman, the experimental outlook of the person of no rank allows for enough appreciation of living-and-dying.

> This, my Dionysian world of the eternally self-creating, the eternally self-destroying, this mystery world of the twofold voluptuous delight, my 'beyond good and evil' without goal, unless the joy of the circle is itself a goal.[15]

Nietzsche's perspectivism reveals the ultimate inconsistence of all points of view. It undermines the very idea of objectivity, on which western knowledge rests. It creates vertigo: one no longer senses any solidity in one's point of view; it engenders humility, for one realizes that what one calls "truths" are simply fossilized opinions.

The danger now is that no point of view is converted into a new point of view, a new perspective to which we become attached.

How to get out of this labyrinth? One of the keys is found in contemporary Zen teachings, where we find a high level of fluidity, a constant shift between the relative and the absolute realms.

At first we come to learn – through widening our perspective, by gaining the eagle's view that Zen calls *Big Mind* – that all truths are perspectives.

At the same time, because we live in the relative world, we are bound to hold a point of view, given by the very fact that our human form inhabits a particular place, and from there looks out at the world of phenomena.

We are bound to a perspective, but this time we hold it lightly. This makes humour and detachment possible.

172   *Life is a Bitch (and then you die)*

The antidote to cynicism is the ability to worship and admire greatness.

When faced with true greatness, a cynic will highlight the person's shortcomings, her human weaknesses. The rotten fruit of modern-day cynicism has reduced Zen to *Buji Zen*, to *anything-goes-Zen*.

Sunyata, the groundlessness of existence, has often been mistranslated, as "life is a bitch, and then you die". This has nothing to do with the Dharma, but a lot to do with our mediocre minds.

For the ordinary person – Nietzsche reminds us – cynicism is the only glimpse into reality. When paired with innocence, on the other hand, scepticism becomes true greatness.

Having recognized the animality in man, having denounced all previous "high values" as hypocritical, Nietzsche pursued a path toward the overman, toward the true person of no rank, without falling prey to cynicism and pessimism. Having unmasked the utter void behind high-sounding religious beliefs, or worse, their utilitarian and meretricious nature, Nietzsche found transcendence within immanence, and great meaning in the midst of meaninglessness.

173 *North and South*

Within Western experience, we find a Southern and a Northern perception of reality. The former is distinctly Mediterranean, solar, connected to the luminosity in the atmosphere, to the sharp contrast between darkness and light, to the near absence of twilight. The latter is enveloped in mist, overshadowed by thick forests. The South is visionary, collective, infused with spirit. The Northern experience is understood through symbolism, through the dramatic and magical effect of music. More importantly, the South is polytheistic, tragic, profoundly life affirming, whereas the North is stark, monotheistic, sombre. Nietzsche is not the first writer to have ventured in search of the Southern dream, the visionary journey through the layers of the Southern psyche. He is also not the first to have *idealized* the South. His idealization of the South did not prevent him from identifying something truly essential, buried underneath a veneer of Catholicism. As others before and after him, he sensed the polytheistic nature of the Southern psyche going back to the ancient Greeks, to the roots of Western philosophy and psychology.

There has been a more influential thread that came out of Northern roots, reaching its peak in Hegel's philosophy and in Freud's psychoanalysis: in the triumph of deleterious sophistry with Hegel, of dualistic opposition between life and death in Freud.

Philosophers at the time of Hegel felt powerless against the growing influence and prestige of science, and thus resorted to the muddled argumentations of dialectics in order to counteract it. That very same world failed to recognize the great genius of Hölderlin.

This kind of short-sightedness continues to this day, thanks to an attachment to the artificial separation between knowledge and the art of living, between life and philosophy. Within the world of psychology, we find an equally artificial, even more powerful separation: the separation between the life principle and the death principle. Freud could not truly grasp at the roots of ancient wisdom. He stopped at the Oedipus complex, and even that he only intended symbolically. If he had gone further, he would have found with Heraclitus that *Dionysus and Hades are one and the same God*. For the wisdom of old, which Heraclitus embodies like no other Greek philosopher,

death is only the long wavering shadow projected by life; it expresses the finitude within the heart of the immediate.[16]

Understanding Heraclitus prevents one from vainly chasing after the
absolute, from hubristic presumptions of totality, from the transgression
of unbounded greed. Hegelian knowledge is a form of greed, an indispo-
sition, and a sublimated eating disorder: it's the solitary, invisible worm
eating at the mind of every philosopher who is unwilling to undergo a
radical shift of perspective. The shift of perspective is aligned with
Heraclitus, via Nietzsche, and it provides us with the instruments required
to approach the profound teachings of Zen.

174 *Iridescent Uncertainties*

There are many aspects to Dionysus. He is a God of many dances and
many voices. One could say that he is one and the same, and it is our
perception of him that changes according to our degree of understanding.

When we first meet the God Dionysus, whether accidentally or through
ritualized, purposeful action, he manifests as rapture, ecstatic dance, and
dissolution of the self through the orgy of sex or the orgy of war.

But to a mature devotee, such as Nietzsche was in later life, Dionysus
embraces Apollo. In terms of human passions, drives and instincts, this
level represents their refinement and spiritualization, or sublimation.

> The spiritualization of sensuality is called love: it is a great triumph over
> Christianity.[17]

Dionysus also manifests as female, or strongly related to the feminine.
One of his female doubles is Baubo. Nietzsche mentions this great character in passing:

> One should have more respect for the bashfulness with which nature has hidden
> behind riddles and iridescent uncertainties. Perhaps truth is a woman who has
> reasons for not letting us see her. Perhaps her name is, to speak Greek, Baubo?[18]

In the *Eleusian Mysteries*, Baubo appears to comfort the Earth
Goddess Demeter, who has lost her daughter Persephone, and who, driven
by pain, has not drunk, eaten, bathed or adorned herself for nine days and
nine nights. Baubo shows up, and makes her laugh; she does so by lifting
her skirt and displaying her belly where a figure had been drawn, that of
Iaachoos, child of Demeter, a little-known god sometimes identified with
Dionysus.

At the sight of Dionysus, Demeter finds her joyfulness again, for Dionysus will be reborn, he will recur eternally; her joyfulness is the ancient Greeks' *serenity*.

Baubo's message is identical, or at least parallel, to Dionysus': *life cannot be understood by logic, for life is neither depth nor surface.*

One veil uncovers another veil, and so to infinity. It encourages us to step out of the pessimism and scepticism normally associated with regarding life as appearance. It invites us to a profound affirmation of life: the dance carries on, even though individual dancers may whither and fall.

175 *When the Music's Over, Turn Out the Light*

The Nietzschean id is – at least in the first half of his creative life, until the *Joyful Science* – *music*. From *The Birth of Tragedy* to the *Joyful Science*, Nietzsche's writings are dominated by the dynamic feminine in the form of music, particularly Wagnerian music.

Bayeruth had not yet materialized into the monstrous supermarket that was to become, and which also provided a model for the omnivorous, shallow and widespread cultured philistinism of the late 20th and early 21st century, for the universal *dumbing down* that was to constitute the essential characteristic of our post-modern world. What inspired Nietzsche was music in its raw magnificence, before the advent of the musician as histrionic tyrant, before the birth of pop celebrities and papier-mâché psycho-pomps. Music gives wings to thought. One becomes a philosopher the more one becomes a musician.

Without music, life would be a mistake.[19]

A winged philosophy, a quest for knowledge that is not rooted in aggression, but one that triggers a subtle dance in every cell of our body/mind; no longer the grey sky of predatory logic, but a poetic tongue that frees the spirit from the catatonia of dead words.

The early Nietzsche did not write as an *I*, but as a *force of nature*, and as a highly refined one: music. The late Nietzsche – the one who underwent the discipline and the cold sobriety of positivist thought – wrote as a different, a more mature, but equally compelling voice: *the voice of the Master*, the higher octave of the Dionysian spirit; a force grown wiser by the incorporation of Apollonian teachings.

Music, intimately related to the *dynamic feminine*, invokes otherness, conjures up altered states. It breaks *logos* into *melos*, discourse into song. And every song is a swansong.

Eternity is praised through transience, but using a radically different register than the one utilized by decadent art. Wagner will not allow the swan to fly away, or die. The swan has to be *embalmed* and commodified for eternity, employed *ad nauseam* for the unedifying spectacle of an art infested by jumbled ideology and cut-price religion. He will codify and literalize eternity for the sake of the performer, and in so doing he will revert to a maladjusted pessimism which borrows its moods (but not the depth of insights) from Schopenhauer.

Fear of music is dread of impermanence. Early Nietzschean thought is imbued with the wisdom of the ephemeral and the defiance of a Dionysian adept, dancing in wild abandon, tearing down the walls of the old citadel of philosophy, of all systems that fail to affirm life and becoming. And *all systems are bound to denigrate life.*

The Birth of Tragedy, received with hostility by the academic establishment, marks Nietzsche's *watery initiation*, his first night-sea journey, accompanied by the first severe bouts of sea-sickness, by a premature end to his brilliant career as a young, gifted philologist. That work had upset academia because it destroyed its foundations through a distinctly feminine, and pointedly aesthetic, overview.

His second creative phase is marked by the *fiery initiation* caused by the rigorous, positivist thought which will relentlessly tear apart both his own and humanity's cherished values.

It was his own path towards painful, self-inflicted individuation, of voluntary removal from the "unhewn block", the undifferentiated matrix, the "Great Mother" who gives life, but who also binds and imprisons.

Nietzsche's self-induced fiery initiation has contributed gifts to philosophy, art and psychology. Such initiation was, however, incomplete, for it lacked a crucial element, *community*. I am not suggesting that Nietzsche did not contribute to the vast society of human beings, for he certainly did so *sub specie aeternitatis*, and also within his circle of friends and acquaintances. He longed for a community, and we know through Adler that this entails a willingness to accept one's place in human society, an act of humility echoed in the ritual subjugation of dynamic masculine energies for the benefit of society.

Nietzsche often talked of community in disparaging terms, as the *herd*; and we should bear in mind that contributing to a community does not mean abdicating to blinding, and sometimes criminal, conformity.

Of the *static feminine* he seems to have known only the shadow aspect, embodied by his mother, and especially his sister. He did not (and perhaps could not) integrate the positive aspects of the static feminine. This is testified, I would like to suggest, by the eruption of the destructive manifestation of the Dionysian after his forty-fourth birthday, with the crisis in Turin.

Shortly before the catastrophe, his last work, *Ecce Homo*, testified that he had reached a peak-moment in his creativity, for that book is both a heart-rending harvest and a moment of contemplation and repose. He had brought his tremendous task to successful completion. It also provided us with the first vertiginous hints of an abysmal slide into darkness.

We know that from that point onwards he intended to articulate his ripest thought of the "will to power"- certainly not in the ominous form of the book of the same name – and to give shape to his insights on the subject.

One senses that all he had produced until that point had been a prelude before Act One. A child of Romanticism, he could not but fall back into the bosom of the Great Mother; it's equally true that no one else in the 19th century roamed so freely *out* of his own century, and of the one that followed. Unlike a typical Romantic, he was not a *sorcerer*; he did not simulate pains he did not feel; he understood that suffering is nothing to boast of. He did not fake greatness.

176 Buddha is Dead

Buddhists are the greatest hindrance to the spreading of the Dharma in the West. Buddhism is dead and gone, with no hope of resurrection. It has become a new religion, with sects swarming like flies around a carcass, each claiming an imaginary orthodoxy. What's more, Buddhism has been plundered and pillaged by ego-therapists who chant all the way to the bank. Buddhism's saving grace is that it contains its own undoing within itself, that it does not cling to anything, including its own duration.

177 W. B. Yeats and Aristocracy

Nobility is the dignity and graciousness evoked by a *true person of no rank*, by the *overman*.

In the Western tradition, this is sometimes called "fertilization of the soul", a view that conceivably relies on idealism and spiritualism, on the idea that the immaterial moulds and orders materiality; an idea that poets and artists turned into optimistic faith in the power of art.

Nevertheless, in natures such as W. B. Yeats', the thirst for nobility reflects the *profound aspiration for self-mastery*. According to this view, one is not *born* an aristocrat, one *becomes* it by reshaping one's personality, by re-orienting drives and instincts at one's disposal, by summoning up those *magnificent monsters* and re-directing their numinous energies.

This is not the same as the vulgar aspiration, popular in new-age circles, of building inner power in order to *master events* and turn them in one's favour. This attitude belongs to the child – not to the Heraclitean child of innocence regained, but to the immature child who has yet to face up to the "fiery initiation" into the social world.

True nobility does not consist in being able to master one's environment, but to master oneself, and subsequently, out of that newly acquired strength, the readiness and ability to *form* values.

Nobility is decidedly *anti-utilitarian*. The utilitarian view belongs to the mob mentality, where everything is transaction, intercourse, bargaining, and *scoring*. An aristocratic community, and a noble society are on the other hand characterized, in the Yeatsian view, by civility, reverence, rivarly for honours and above all *little regard for utility*.

The only power that truly matters is, for both Nietzsche and Yeats, *cultural power*; in the long run, *cultural influences tend to overrule military might*. Paradoxically, the ideal ground for culture is that very same which technological and political force tries to combat in the service of the much-loved abstraction called *progress*.

Buddhism uses a similar metaphor: the lotus flower, growing out of the mud. If we were to endeavour in cleansing and destroying the mud, the lotus flower would not grow. That is precisely what we do when obeying the "modern style" and grow into prosperous, vacuously cheerful individuals who resent their fate and hide their heads into the deep sands of virtually-enhanced denial.

Nevertheless, Yeats' belief in the superiority of spiritual nobility is still miles away from both Zarathustra and the overman. Yeats' aristocracy belongs to the level of those who Zarathustra calls "the higher men", naïve and comical in their hopeless disdain of democracy. Honourable in many ways, opposed to social climbing, money-making and other such vulgar activities, the higher humanity is nevertheless trapped in the relative values of social hierarchy, status, and time-honoured principles.

178 *Hungry Ghost Boulevard*

Life as a rapturous, tragic festival, life as *anti-humanist* . . . In a letter to his father dated 1910, Yeats writes:

> The world being illusive, one must be deluded in some way if one is to triumph in it.[20]

Pursuing power, money and status on Hungry Ghost Boulevard,

careering with great gusto down a dead-end tunnel; all the while, trading in our natural genius for living into a "shopkeeper's affair".

If there *is* such thing as secular, non-cynical disdain for mankind, that is merely the condescension of what Nietzsche calls "the higher men". Extraordinary as they may be, their very specialness is a hindrance to *the glorious nadir of the person of no rank*. They still conceive of an "external" world as a backdrop to their fabricated, and often melodramatic, "realizations".

Money and power are of little importance to the noble person. Power can be accepted solely in terms of *creative ability*, not as vulgar *force* or as tasteless craving for *status*. And money is only a means to *resourceful exchange*.

In the first book of the *Joyful Science*, Nietzsche expounds the noble person's characteristics:

Feeling intensely and passionately about things that leave all other people cold; divining values for which no scales have been yet invented; sacrificing on altars dedicated to an unknown *god*; bravery without any desire for honours; an inner sovereignty that overflows and gives itself to all things.[21]

179 *Angels and Sailors*

The true person of no rank does not flee into a utopian future, nor settles with ready-made consolations borrowed from religious traditions. Instead, she consents to the inexplicable unfolding of becoming, riding the blazing stream of the dragon's flames, staying with its *unceasing* motion, for, as Rilke reminds us in the first of his *Duino Elegies*, we make a "too sharp distinction" between the living and the dead, who are both part of the "eternal torrent". And in his customarily startling fashion, Nietzsche reverses the human predicament when he writes:

The living is merely a type of what is dead, and a very rare type.[22]

Rilke and Nietzsche are alike in seeing the limitations of human culture, and both are unique in creating new mythologies compatible to the crisis of the West. Whereas Nietzsche dismantles and opens up uncharted routes, Rilke injects an intensely *new* life into images of old. His *Angels* are such creatures, infused with a new, radiant energy: no longer God's waif-like employees; instead, inscrutable beings inhabiting the eerie, unfamiliar *middle realm* so neglected by religions.

Rilke's Angels are at home in the world, endowed with animal naturalness, and at the same time conscious and aware, poised and graceful.

The Angel Gabriel in Pasolini's wondrous *Gospel according to Matthew* is such an undefinable creature, both human and non-human. [23]

If the overman is no angel, as it were, if no mortal can justifiably inhabit the middle realm which is the home of soul, or *psyche*, he nevertheless unceasingly *aspires* towards *perfection* by embracing *imperfection* and cultivating *no aspiration*. Not wishing to become a Buddha, or to escape delusion.

180 *Les Saltimbanques*

We do not evade the terrifying meeting with the Angel, for the creative joy of the true person of no rank allows us to welcome what is normally perceived as hostile and alien. We are on our way to become acrobats and travellers, forever fleeting, embracing pain and fear, beyond the spirit of revenge which demands of us that we uproot those feelings, and also beyond the Kafkian horror and comedy of the absurd.

181 *The Dogma of Evolution*

In re-establishing the importance of engaging in the noble art of genealogy, Nietzsche defines it as the reverse of an idea that has dominated and continues to dominate our culture: *evolutionism*. He writes of two essential models of evolutionism. The first one is a "German" model, as established by Hegelism, according to which evolution unfolds through *contradiction* – the now formulaic model of thesis, anthithesis and synthesis, or, as in Marx's example, through *struggle*. Paradoxically, Hegel's and Marx's great contribution was to *delay* the death of God. Their "achievement" was to swiftly resuscitate Him through the phantom of History. In so doing, they embalmed Christian morality in layman's garments, they breathed new life into the moribund concept of the "ideal": the 20th century later manifested such ideal to abominable perfection. The result was totalitarianism, genocide, hi-tech barbarism, and in an increasingly explicit fashion, its underlying component of "religious" fanaticism. For evolution is but a shadow of the expiring God. In unmasking the underlying Christian element in Hegel's thought, Nietzsche wrote:

Looking at nature as if it were demonstration of the goodness and care of a God; interpreting history in honour of some divine reason, as a persistent testimony of a moral world order and ultimate moral intent; interpreting one's own experiences in life in the way religious people have long interpreted theirs, as if everything were sympathetic, a kind of inkling, conceived and predetermined for the sake of wellbeing of the soul – all that is *over and done with* now.

It has conscience against it; every refined conscience considers it to be coarse, dishonest, a deception, a kind of effeminacy, weakness, cowardice. It is on account of this thoroughness that we are in fact good Europeans and heirs of Europe's longest and most daring self-overcoming. As we thus discard Christian interpretation, by condemning its 'meaning' as bogus, Schopenhauer's question: 'Does existence have any meaning at all?' immediately looms over us in a terrifying way. A few centuries will be needed for this question to be understood and experienced in all its depth.[24]

The second model of evolutionism is the English one, which could not have come into being without the first. "Without Hegel," Nietzsche wrote in the *Joyful Science*, "there could be no Darwin." The key words of the English evolutionary model are *profit* and *interest*. What determines progress and evolution, according to this view, is no longer the "higher" synthesis achieved through conflictual elements, but instead *utility*. Such need for advantage and utility betrays mediocrity, and is the very opposite of the attitude of a true creator, of an artist/philosopher. It might be deemed as "pragmatic", but that is misusing the word, which in its origin is a *manifestation of love*, the product of shared labour and endeavour. This utilitarian model of evolutionism is the product, in Nietzsche's words, of "respectable but mediocre Englishmen – I name Darwin, John Stuart Mill, and Herbert Spencer".[25]

Their ideas gained pre-eminence among the European middle-classes in the second half of the 19th century and still dominate in secular Anglo-Saxon societies.

Indeed, who could doubt that it is a useful thing for such minds to have ascendancy for a time? It would be an error to consider the highly developed and independently soaring minds as specially qualified for determining and collecting many little common facts, and deducing conclusions from them; as exceptions, they are rather from the first in no very favourable position towards those who are 'the rules'. After all, they have more to do than merely to perceive: – in effect, they have to *be* something new, they have to *signify* something new, they have to represent new values! The gulf between knowledge and capacity is perhaps greater, and also more mysterious, than one thinks: the capable man in the grand style, the creator, will possibly have to be an ignorant person; – while on the other hand, for scientific discoveries like those of Darwin, a certain narrowness, aridity, and industrious carefulness (in short, something English) may not be unfavourable for arriving at them.[26]

And in the preface to his *Genealogy of Morals*, Nietzsche wrote:

... the Darwinian beast civilly extends a hand to the morally meek and mild, the ultra-modern soul who has learnt 'not to bite'. In the latter's expression a certain good-humoured and refined indolence is joined by a grain of pessimism and fatigue: as if all these things – the problems of morality – were really not worth taking so seriously. On the contrary, it seems to me now that there is nothing which better repays serious consideration: to such rewards belong for example the possibility of one day being entitled to approach the problems of morality in *high spirits*.[27]

182 *What Progress?*

With Rilke, as with Nietzsche – in spite of the latter's use of hyperbolic and epic tone – we are in the presence of truly *elegiac* natures: there is no resorting to religious consolations, nor to those offered by secular beliefs in *progress*. The idea of progress is nonsense. Believing in progress is only possible if we take on board the naïve credos of mechanization, which are based on the idea that humans are "essential social or biological components", inhabiting a world of limitations, misery and struggle. We would need to agree with the physics lecturer Dr. Frankstone, a fictional character in D. H. Lawrence's *The Rainbow*, when, in a conversation with one of the protagonists of the novel, Ursula Brangwen, she says:

"No really", Dr. Frankstone had said, "I don't see why we should attribute some special mystery to life – do you? We don't understand it as we understand electricity, even, but that doesn't warrant our saying it is something different in kind and distinct from everything else in the universe – do you think it does? May it not be that life consists in a complexity of physical and chemical activities, of the same order as the activities we already know in science? I don't see, really, why we should imagine there is a special order of life, and life alone . . . "[28]

Alongside the mainstream belief in the limitations of matter, which modern biology has taken as a given, no longer making a hard distinction between the organic and the inorganic, we miracolously find thinkers like Spinoza who, in the Volume II of his *Ethics*, writes:

Every substance is necessarily infinite.[29]

"His proof of this proposition," writes Keith M. May, "was that a substance can be limited only by another substance having exactly the same attributes. I may be limited only by another me, not by some other person or process."[30]

Belief in progress is a symptom of *decadence*. Its twin notion is the concept of mental and physical *health*. Both ideas of *progress* and *health* are based on the decadent dream of a perfect world – one free of conflict.

Nietzsche redefines *health not as absence of sickness, but as the strength to overcome it*. Both in the individual and in society, true health does not shy away from sickness, but makes use of it, transmuting its poison into nectar. A noble society produces flowers from chaos and discord. It uses everything as fertilizer for the creation of an enlightened society, a vision opposed to self-indulgent floundering in the mud, or escape into delusional ideas of enlightenment understood as *egohood*.

D. H. Lawrence expresses something remarkably similar when, through his alter ego Birkin in *The Rainbow* talks of the radical difference between two modes of living; one he calls *synthetic creation* and the other *destructive creation*.

The first, as embodied by Ursula's entire existence, is life-affirming. It rejects the decline of the West, and it counteracts through positive affirmation.

In Gudrun, Ursula's sister, we find an embodiment of darker forces: *destructive creation*, or *the dark river of dissolution*, a *black river of corruption*. Lawrence being Lawrence, and not Dickens or Manzoni, the forces of good and evil are not clearly defined in Manichean fashion. We cannot say that Ursula is *good*, and Gudrun is *bad*. His being a *tragic* tale in the unfashionable sense, not a moralizing novel, the two pairs, Ursula and Birkin, Gerald and Gudrun, are interconnected, not opposed, to one another.

We do recognize in Gudrun, though, the all-too-familiar, "modern" *delight in decay*. We recognize that narcotic revelling in slow descent. Gudrun and Gerald are *decadent*, in the Nietzschean sense: they share a *hatred of life*, a *desire for extinction*. They are thoroughly *modern*: Gudrun is lured by what destroys her self-reliability, hence her freedom; Gerald loves the mechanical, *because* it lacks internal conflict.

In this motion too there is creation, says Lawrence, albeit of a different kind – vulgar and coarse; transgressive, perhaps, but in a compulsively *downward* motion.

Later manifestations of these same energies gave us Hitlerism, and more recently, de-sublimated, de-motivated, utterly bamboozled environments such as contemporary Italian society.

Birkin and Ursula *do not avoid crossing this wasteland, but they do not get stuck there*. They are people of no rank. They do not avoid nature, but embrace it: that same nature we love to loathe because it is so treacherous, lavish, irrational, luxuriant, and, above all, *pluralistic*. Birkin prophetizes *the end of individuals*, a future as either purely sensual or abstract. That future is now here, and it has turned out to be even worse than what Birkin expected, for it is both sensual *and* abstract: *abstracted sensuality* (without mystery, mystique, romance and, above all, without love), and *sensualized abstraction*: virtual reality, *sexyness* as all-pervading high-street value and commodity.

Birkin valued the painful individualist route, and knew how easy it is to convince people that, since it is difficult, it is also wrong. What he could not foresee was the late 20th century's triumph of individualism as new, supreme banality achieved by the mob.

At the time of writing *The Rainbow*, Lawrence believed in the communion between man and woman, and in the lineage of profound experience transmitted from the man who is about to die to the survivor, as part of an endless chain of cultural heritage. This is known in Zen as the *blood lineage*, an uninterrupted transmission proceeding from the historical Buddha to contemporary practitioners of the Way.

183 *Mustn't Grumble*

At present, we only possess vague indications of how a true person of no rank might operate. We have inklings of what he or she might say or do. To a bodhisattva, a Zen practitioner on the path of the Great Vehicle, those traits are fingers pointing to the moon, representing one's aspiration to accomplish the Way.

We need to realize, however, how deep the spirit of revenge has imbued our thinking. The spirit of revenge, which engenders *ressentiment* and bad conscience, is an integral part of our genealogy. We do not really know what a person devoid of *ressentiment* would be like. Would one still think like a human, who does not in anyway accuse, chastise, depreciate existence? A person who is capable of *supreme affirmation*? A person who no longer blames anyone or anything, a bearer of what Nietzsche called *glad tidings*, a will to create, to contribute, someone imbued with a feeling of tragic joy, a joy that encompasses both pain and happiness?

The true person of no rank does not bet but *plays*. The true person of no rank does not leap but *dances*. Even great thinkers such as Pascal and Kierkegaard do not play, do not dance. First they bet, and then leap.

The overman is not interested in gain. As a bodhisattva, his actions are beyond deluded notions of gain and loss. If the dice throw decrees that he is to be born in the hell realms for countless lives, he will not complain, he will hold no grudge. Hell might be a more interesting place, who knows? Moreover, there is where he finds countless beings who need his help. His very attitude will transform hell into heaven, for every fibre of his being is a refutation of the spirit that has dominated humanity: the spirit of revenge.

The spirit of revenge poisons the most praiseworthy aspirations, for it instills in them the Satanic seed of hubris, the pretence of owning for oneself what instead belongs to the Gods, and to the totality of the psyche, of that totality which is *beyond the human realm.*

We "moderns" have dismantled some of the most pernicious view of institutionalized religion and subsequently mourned the death of God. We must now duly attend to the burial of that other, more insidious fallacy, the human ego. History, the nightmare from which we are still trying to awake, rests on this one construct, on this illusory notion of a distinct "I".

No sins are being denounced here, nor expiations of any kind are called for. But there are two gigantic errors which our culture as a whole urgently needs to rectify: the illusion of separation (the idea that "I" exist separately from the rest of existence), and the added insult of *hubris.* If we fail to understand these two crucial points, we also fail to grasp the deeper meaning conveyed by both Heraclitus and Nietzsche.

Hubris (superbia, egoic pride) is the acid test for every true disciple of Heraclitus. For everything in Heraclitus points to *psyche* rather than the human and the human ego. Similarly, if we reduce Zen solely to a way of dealing with the human condition, and reduce Buddhism to a form of existentialism, we are exposed to the danger of equating buddhahood with egohood. Some of the most recent interpretations of Buddhism in secular societies tend to see it as a form of humanism. This is in my opinion a reductionist view of the Dharma. It is true that one can find virtually anything in the teachings of the Buddha. They work wonderfully when applied as a behavioral methodology for healthy, balanced living. They provide a philosophical corpus with remarkable similarities with existentialism, post-modernism as well as modern physics. There is also a more esoteric, mystical aspect to Buddhism which has a lot more to offer than exotic lure and spiritualist platitudes. Whatever the approach, it is undeniable that in the midst of authentic practice *psyche itself* is affected, and the changes set in motion are reflected in the life of the individual. When psyche is affected, for better or for worse, so is the human sphere, and human life. *It is, however, a mistake to identify the totality of psyche with the human.* Buddhist practice works in mysterious ways, and it would be a mistake to reduce its modus operandi to the human realm only.

84 *Against Humanism*

Latter-day agnostics are new exponents of old-time atheists, expounding vague agnosticicism and innocuous atheism. They are *humanists* at heart (Nietzsche's term was "free thinkers"): they foolishly believe in the "redemption of mankind". They do love the Church, it's just that they can't stand the smell of incense . . .

In place of the triviality of so-called free thinkers, Nietzsche volunteers the only worthwile alternative: the audacity of those he calls *free spirits*.

A free spirit moves beyond the *facts,* and *human* facts in particular, which are the untenable precepts of, respectively, positivism and humanism. "There are no facts, nothing but interpretations", he famously noted in his posthumous writings, a stance which has been largely misused by late 20th century's philosophy and metamorphosed into mere perspectivism.

The problem with positivism, humanism and latter-day "agnosticism" is twofold: they are fairly rigid positions from which little exploration is possible. Secondly, *they do not admit to anything greater than the human ego*. Conversely, the true person of no rank, or the Nietzschean free spirit, which for me are one and the same, acts as vehicle and attendant of greater – one might say *archetypal* – forces.

Superficial agnosticism is the new church of modernity. Its characteristically bleak claims and the generally cynical posturing paved the way to the birth of its spoiled offspring, the *faux* radicalism of post-structuralism and deconstructionism.

A free spirit also soars above the *obsession for improving humans' content*, always a trait of Hegelism and its offshoots, and a tendency which has greatly impaired religious and psychological enquiry. However, rejecting is not equal to advocating passive resignation, or fatalism. "I saw my fate without its mask", wrote Emily Brontë, which implies *embracing* one's fate with courage, from thrilling uncertainty of the dicethrow to the graceful acceptance of the outcome. Fatalism, on the other hand, is rooted in pessimism, resentment, inability to see events and the world as an integral part of the "self". Acceptance of the *beautiful necessity* is an act of gratitude, a quality harboured through spiritual discipline in the recesses of a noble heart.

185 *Snoring Mindfully within a Safe Environment*

Another offshoot of superficial agnosticism is a current popular brand of pop psychology offhandedly combining watered-down Buddhist teachings with Pavlovian platitudes on the human condition. The "product" is then delivered in an overtly "sensitive" and unthreatening fashion, so as not to scare away potential patrons. Were one to challenge it slightly, however, the soft exterior will quickly unsheathe sharp teeth from its rock-solid interior. All one has to do to turn *metta* (kindness), and "mindfulness" into plain, old-fashioned hostility is to mention the words *God* and *religion*, for every group has its set of dogmas, and the worst cases are those where dogmas are implied, unspoken, left to slumber in the shadows.

To be sure, there is no harm in following these prescriptions: they are designed for professional psychologists, some of which bask in the dream of turning institutions into benevolent kindergardens and rest homes where the harsh truths of the human condition are kept at bay. Left to their devices, they would turn life into a "safe environment", a place devoid of challenge, and consequently devoid of growth.

Their task is hubris per excellence: restoring the self to sanity, building an "aware ego", an up-right citizen who will be able and willing to serve the corporations in whatever collective idiocy might present itself under the banners of "duty" and "service". An impossible task, for we have learnt from existentialism and from Zen that *self-estrangement and anguish are not fortuitous to the self, but essential to its configuration.*

186 *Learn to Forget*

There is forgetting and forgetting. We subconsciously remove from our memory unpleasant experiences, and we tend to "forget" by sheer inertia. On a super-conscious level, however, we keep consciousness fresh and vibrant by *actively forgetting. The noble person knows how to forget*, not solely out of compassion ("forgive and forget"), but also because

> there could be no happiness, no cheerfulness, no hope, no pride, no *present*, without forgetfulness.[31]

Life would drag on, forever unresolved, the life of a man who "cannot 'have done' with anything", a life of *ressentiment*, a sick life. For Nietzsche, *ressentiment* is sickness, and sickness itself is a form or *ressentiment*.

We need *active*, deliberate *forgetting*. Such forgetting is a manifestation of the will to power, and it counteracts the reactive forces of bad conscience and guilt, which are animated by the spirit of revenge. It was Otto Rank who wrote of the need of relying on the *active* forces present within the Freudian "unconscious", on *creative* and *artistic* ways of erasing mnemonic traces. The inability to put up any resistance – against the flood of memories, against sickness – is a sign of surrendering to *fatalism*.

> The sick person has one great remedy – I call it *Russian fatalism*, that fatalism without rebellion, by which a Russian soldier for whom war has become too

harsh, ends up surrendering himself to the snow. Above all . . . no longer coun-
teracting . . . The great reason for this fatalism, which is not always just the
courage to die . . . consist in a lowering of metabolism, in its slowing down, in a
kind of wish to hybernate . . . Since one would burn up too quickly, if on the
other hand one were to counteract, then one does not act anymore: this is the
logic behind.[32]

A prodigious memory is the chief quality of the man of *ressentiment*.
There is a profound link between *revenge* and *memory*, a chronic inability
to digest and properly *metabolize events*. One reason might be that a
particular *event* is never allowed to upgrade, as it were, to the rank of
experience. An *event* is forever replayed in the theatre of memory and
never properly processed, never allowed to become *experience*. Thus it is
being eternally repeated in the rituals of compulsion and any form of
addiction, from substance abuse to "love" and sex. The event is re-enacted
in a slightly different scenario, and never properly *digested*.

187 *It's All Your Bloody Fault*

The true person of no rank actively forgets, and creatively counteracts
signs of sickness in the soul. Conversely, the reactive type – what
Nietzsche calls the "slave" – possesses the memory of an elephant: no
insult, discourtesy, or impertinence is ever forgiven. Nothing is ever
forgotten: unlike the aristocratic spirit, the reactive type has no respect for
the causes of misfortune, no understanding of the context in which they
manifest. Happiness to him is a narcotic. He *cannot* admire, respect, let
alone *love* anyone, or anything. The reactive type is immediately identifi-
able by the fact that he *wants to be loved*. His morality is *utilitarian*: what
is good is merely what is useful. One of his chief concerns is the distribution of responsibility, and his tone is of perpetual *accusation*. Passions and
assertive pathos are muted into vengefulness and rancour. His all being
screams: "It's your fault! You did this to me!"

Passions and emotions are not spiritualized or sublimated, as in the
case of the "master", of the committed practitioner of the Way. They are
falsified, deprived of their conditions of operation. They are *turned
against themselves*; internalized, but perversely; they are not properly
experienced and understood. Pre-Socratic Greece taught us that when one
of this *magnificent monsters* is not honoured, it turns against us and
causes havoc not only in the psyche of those involved, but they in turn try
to spread the psychic pestilence among the healthy.

They are all men of *ressentiment*, these deformed and maggot-ridden men, a whole tremulous realm of subterranean revenge, inexhaustible, insatiable in its outbursts against the fortunate and also in masquerades of revenge, in pretexts of revenge: at what point would they really attain their ultimate, finest, most sublime triumph of revenge? Without doubt, once they succeeded in forcing their own misery, the whole of misery as such into the *conscience* of the fortunate: so that these latter would one day begin to feel ashamed of their good fortune and perhaps say to one another: 'It is a disgrace to be fortunate! There is too much misery!'[33]

88   *The Squalid Workshop*

We live in a world turned upside-down, where *active* forces have been exiled and forced to turn against themselves. How many live and die consciously? How many lead a fulfilled, serene life? How many escape the worship of ignorance, hatred and stupidity? Good people kill their time by worshipping buffoons. The silver river of life turns muddy: a supremely sad act of self-violation, an act of cruelty.

This secret self-violation, this artistic cruelty, this desire to give a form to the refractory, resistant, suffering material of oneself, to brand oneself with a will, a criticism, a contradiction, a contempt, a No, this sinister labour, both horrific and pleasurable, of a soul voluntarily divided against itself, a soul which makes itself suffer for the pleasure of it . . . [34]

Gilles Deleuze calls this uniquely modern fashion of manufacturing misery by turning active, healthy forces against themselves *the squalid workshop*; the way in which it operates is twofold:

1) By the *interiorization of active forces*. This is not the same as sublimation, but rather the topological aspect of *bad conscience*, whereby a natural instinct is perverted and interiorized, turned against itself.

Bad conscience is the conscience that multiplies its pain, which has found a technique for manufacturing pain by turning active force back against itself: the squalid workshop. *The multiplication of pain by the interiorisation or introjection of force —* this is the first definition of bad conscience.[35]

2) By the *interiorization of pain itself*. This is not the existential suffering expounded by the historical Buddha in the first noble truth, but instead the humanization and the contamination of suffering by ideas of sin, guilt, *ressentiment*, and the whole accoutrement of the spirit of revenge. Religion has played an important role here, and its influence has not always been constructive.

The implications are clear from Nietzsche's writings that we should consider the fact that there are in fact two types of religions: a *mature* religion, suitable for the "strong" (active, life-affirming) and, conversely, a *nihilistic* one, a religion for the "weak", based on the denial and the denigration of life.

"Strength" and "weakness" here are not intended reductively, as moral and psychological judgments, but mainly as *cultural*. Entire cultures are subject to this kind of value judgement, as well as the philosophies and ethics which sustain them. The entire edifice of *metaphysics* seen in this light is a *symptom of weakness*, due to its persistence in affirming that there might be something else behind the curtain. Its outlook betrays the inability to embrace the imperfection of what is unfolding at this very moment: *impermanence,* in all its transient glory.

The same applies to the exaggerated importance given by the modern era to *reason* (always a sure sign that *unreason* has taken hold and overruled human impulses) and *politics* (the distorted expression of will to power by reactive, inferior forces).

The final by-product of the squalid workshop is the *reactive man*: we see his statue erected in all the main squares of our cities, peering through varied façades, honoured and respected for many forms of endeavour, but all united by one element: their reactive, inferior nature. Reactive man has superseded the many Gods of Greece, and the one God of the Jews and the Christians. He might be a footballer, a supermodel, a statesman, a movie star or a comedian. What he or she stands for are all the grand illusions of our peculiar era: passive adaptation, progress, evolution, amusement; all commonplace, reactive qualities that feed on and multiply our sense of misery, inferiority and estrangement. Above all, these illusions rely on the *fundamental lie of facts and events*, particularly of so-called "great historical events".

Values change, fashions come and go. What seems to remain is the nihilistic perspective, the denigration of life based on denial and *ressentiment*. Zen practice and Nietzsche's philosophy can undermine the nihilistic perspective that dominates our world. New values can be discovered, if we are willing to undergo a necessary transformation. We might even find happiness – not empty-headed buoyancy – but instead the Rilkean joy that is the unexpected reward for having gone through the *Land of the Lamentations.*

189 *When Happiness Falls*

Every instant is chaos and necessity, and out of the strident paradox, meaning is born, as expounded in the "Orphic" ninth elegy.

Why, when this span of life might be fleeted away
as laurel, a little darker than all
the surrounding green, with tiny waves on the border
of every leaf (like the smile of a wind): – oh, why
have to be human, and, shunning Destiny,
long for Destiny?
Not because happiness really
exists, that precipitate profit of imminent loss.
Not out of curiosity, not just to practice the heart,
that could still be there in the laurel . . .
But because being here is much, and because all this
that's here, so fleeting, seems to require us and strangely
concerns us. Us the most fleeting of all. Just once,
everything, only for once. Once and no more. And we, too,
once. And ever again. But this
having been once, though only once,
having been once on earth –
can it ever be cancelled?[36]

As "value-conferring animals", we humans need to *create* meaning and thus *justify* our existence. We do not exist for the sake of happiness, we do not *look* for happiness: "only Englishmen do", Nietzsche wrote mischievously. Human search for meaning is forged in the fire of "Primal Pain":

Lone he ascends to the mountains of Primal Pain.
And never once does his step sound from the soundless fate.[37]

That pain is "primal": inborn within our incongruous condition. It is the same suffering the Buddha speaks of when expounding the First Noble Truth. It is the same primal pain Nietzsche speaks of, urging us to use it as a *great tonic*. This pain is "woven into the writhings and blossomings of every life-form". If we try to minimize our primal pain – which has been precisely the chief endeavour of the human race – we do so at a high cost: we deprive ourselves of the possibility of true joy, and settle instead with bland amusements and spiritual sterility.

It is only natural that one would wish to practice Buddhism out of a need for solace and relief from anguish. Indeed, the Buddha himself showed that a way out of suffering *does* exist. But there seems to be no way around it, nor *above* it. We might need to go through it, descend, and eventually *fall*.

Zen is not an *ascensionistic* path. It does not share the attitude of denial inherent in the flight of so-called "transpersonal" psychologies. It is instead a *descent* into the land of the shadows, an encounter with one's most frightful fears and demons.

It shares, in its fierce determination, the task of authentic western depth psychology, the one that finds its roots in Heraclitus, and in our western anti-tradition.

Nietzsche and the great masters of Zen invite us to a great descent, to the most difficult of all affirmations, the affirmation of sorrow and suffering. The rewarding outcome is the startling emotion of a happiness that *falls*, as Rilke says, in the final verses of his 10th Duino Elegy:

> *And we, who think of ascending*
> *happiness, then would feel*
> *the emotion that almost startles*
> *when happiness falls.*[38]

NOTES

Opening Quotes

1 *La Gaia Scienza,* 5:343, p. 194, my translation.

2 Montaigne, Essays 3:2, p. 613.

3 Adorno, *Minima Moralia: Reflections from a Damaged Life,* p. 111, # 72 'Second Harvest', pp. 109–13.

4 Salomé, *Nietzsche,* p. 136, 'Nietzsche's System', pp. 90–159. The whole passage reads: "The old Hindu teaching or reincarnation through the migration of the soul, a curse to which everyone is heir until one has achieved an extinction of the self, is completely turned upside down by Nietzsche. Not *release* from the duress of the recurrence cycle but a joyous *conversion* to it, becomes the goal of the highest ethical striving; not Nirvana but Samsara is the name of the highest ideal."

5 Merzel, *The Path of the Human Being,* p. 75, 'Put the Mind to Rest', pp. 74–7.

6 Nagarjuna, *Madhyamaka Karika* 22, XIII, Raniero Gnoli, p. 42; my translation.

Introduction

1 Rilke's letter quoted in May, *Nietzsche and Modern Literature,* p. 50, 'Rilke's Angels and the Ubermensch', pp. 45–78.

2 Blanchot, *The Infinite Conversation,* pp. 140–1.

3 Dostoevsky, *Crime and Punishment,* Epilogue, Chapter 2, p. 428.

4 *Hsin Hsin Ming* quoted in Soeng, *Faith in Mind,* p. 14, translation by Richard B. Clarke.

Part I
Mission: Untimely
The True Task of Philosophy

1 R. J. White (ed.), *Political Tracts of Wordsworth, Coleridge, and Shelley.* Shelley, 'In Defense of Poetry', pp. 195–206.

2 *On the Genealogy of Morals,* 3:11, p. 95, 'What is the Meaning of Ascetic Ideals?', pp. 77–136.

3 Ortega, *Meditations on Quixote,* p. 152, 'Tragedy', pp. 152–5.

4 Yeats, *The Poems,* p. 214, 'The Phases of the Moon', pp. 213–17.

5 *Untimely Meditations* 3, p. 181, 'Schopenhauer as Educator', pp. 127–94.

6 Adorno, *Minima Moralia: Reflections from a Damaged Life,* # 41 'Inside and outside', pp. 66–8.

7 Blanchot, *Friendship,* p. 191, 'The Detour Toward Simplicity', pp. 188–200.

8   Ibid.
9   Quoted in Blanchot, *The Siren's Song*, p. 49, 'A happy end is out of the question', pp. 45–51.
10 Blanchot, *The Siren's Song*, pp. 49–50.
11 Deleuze, *Nietzsche and Philosophy*, p. 103, # 15 'New Image of Thought', pp. 103–10.
12 Nietzsche, *Untimely Meditations*, 3:8, pp. 193–4, 'Schopenhauer as educator', pp. 127–94.
13 Ibid., p. 191.
14 Schopenhauer, *Parerga and Paralipomena*, Vol. 1, p. 139, 'On Philosophy at the Universities', pp. 139–97.
15 Ibid., p. 153.
16 *Untimely Meditations III, 3*, p. 137 'Schopenhauer as educator', pp. 127–94.
17 Ibid.
18 Ibid.
19 Blanchot, *The Infinite Conversation*, p. 152, 'Nietzsche and fragmentary writing', pp. 136–71.
20 Ibid.
21 Magee, *The Philosophy of Schopenhauer*, p. 9, 'Schopenhauer's Life as Background to his Work', pp. 3–27.
22 Goethe's couplet quoted in Magee, *The Philosophy of Schopenhauer*, p. 17, 'Schopenhauer's Life as Background to his Work', pp. 3–27.
23 Schopenhauer, *The World as Will and Representation*, quoted in Magee, *The Philosophy of Schopenhauer*, p. 25.
24 *The World as Will and Representation*, III, pp. 164–5, quoted in Magee, *The Philosophy of Schopenhauer*, p. 53, 'The Great Tradition', pp. 49–72.
24 Ibid.
25 Ibid.
26 Ibid.
27 Ibid.
28 Goethe's *Faust* Part I quoted in *Parerga and Paralipomena*, p. 142.
29 On the subject of Nietzsche and music see Curt Paul Janz, 'The Form-Content Problem in Nietzsche's Conception of Music', pp. 97–116 in T. Strong and M. A. Gillespie (eds), *Nietzsche's New Seas*.
30 Schopenhauer, *Parerga and Paralipomena*, Vol. 1, p. 141.
31 Deleuze, *Nietzsche and Philosophy*, p. 77 in 'Critique', pp. 73–110.
32 For the similarity between Nietzsche and the Vedanta's idea of the cosmic play see Glen T. Martin, *Deconstruction and Breakthrough in Nietzsche and Nagarjuna*, in *Nietzsche and Asian Thought*, pp. 91–111.
33 Heraclitus, # LVIII, Kahn, *The Art and Thought of Heraclitus*, p. 55.
34 Ibid., # LXXXVII, p. 69.
35 Ibid., # CXIV, p. 81.
36 V. Woolf, 'Montaigne' in *The Common Reader*, quoted by G. Parkes, *Composing the Soul*, p. 384n.
37 Nietzsche, *Assorted Opinions and Maxims*, # 408 quoted in Parkes, *Composing the Soul*, p. 330, 'Dreams and Archaic Inheritance', pp. 327–34.
38 Heraclitus, # CXIV, Kahn, *The Art and Thought of Heraclitus*, p. 75.

39 Emerson, *Prose Works*, p. 498, 'Fate', pp. 493–505.
40 Ibid.
41 Ibid.
42 Ibid.
43 Colli, *Dopo Nietzsche*, p. 48, 'Un disguido della fama', pp. 47–8.
44 *On the Genealogy of Morals*, 3:15, p. 105.
45 Cf. Graham Parkes *Nietzsche and Jung: Ambivalent Appreciation*, p. 207.
46 Ibid.
47 Cleary (trans.), *Book of Serenity*, p. 86, "Dizang's 'Nearness'", pp. 86–90.
48 Adorno, *Minima Moralia: Reflections from a Damaged Life*, 126, 'I.Q.', pp. 196–7.
49 Aitken, *The Practice of Perfection*, p. 2.
50 Ibid.
51 *Human all too Human*, 515, 'A Nietzsche Reader', p. 198.
52 Jaspers, *An Introduction*, p. 213.
53 Camus, *The Rebel*, pp. 65–6, 'Absolute Affirmation', pp. 57–71.
54 Ibid., p. 66.
55 Quoted in Klossowski, *Nietzsche and the Vicious Circle*, p. 191, 'The Euphoria of Turin', pp. 159–94.
56 See Karsten Harries' book, *Metaphor and Transcendence*, quoted in Bibliography.
57 *Twilight of the Idols*, pp. 16–17, V, 2, " 'Reason' in Philosophy ", pp. 16–25.
58 Deleuze, *Nietzsche and Philosophy*, p. 3, *The Tragic*, pp. 1–38.
59 *Thus Spoke Zarathustra*, III, 'Of the Apostates', 2, p. 201.
60 Deleuze, *Nietzsche and Philosophy*, p. 5 'The Tragic', pp. 1–38.
61 Adorno, *Minima Moralia*, # 151, 'Theses against occultism', pp. 238–44.
62 Ibid.
63 *On the Genealogy of Morals*, 3:8, pp. 89–90.
64 Ibid., 3:10.
65 Deleuze, *Nietzsche and Philosophy*, p. 4, 'The Tragic', pp. 1–38.
66 Blanchot, *The Infinite Conversation*, p. 152, 'Nietzsche and fragmentary writing', pp. 136–71.
67 *Thus Spoke Zarathustra*, p. 297, 'Of the Higher Men', 4:3.

Part II
Great Doubt and the Death of God

1 Quoted in Janz, *Vita di Nietzsche*, Vol. 2, p. 65, 'Ritorno al Rifugio dell'Engadina', my translation.
2 *Gaia Scienza*, 4:276, my translation.
3 Nishitani Keji, *Religion and Nothingness*, p. 232, 'Sunyata and History', pp. 218–85.
4 Rose, *On not being able to sleep*, p. 73, 'Virginia Woolf and the Death of Modernism', pp. 72–88.
5 Ibid., p. 73.
6 Mathiessen, *Nine Headed Dragon River*, pp. 15–16.
7 *Twilight of the Idols*, II, 24, p. 7, 'Maxims and Barbs', pp. 5–10.

8   *Twilight of the Idols*, II, 7, p. 13, 'The Problem of Socrates', pp. 11–25.
9   *Twilight of the Idols*, II, 9, p. 14, 'The Problem of Socrates', pp. 11–25.
10 Janz, *Vita di Nietzsche*, Vol. 2, p. 284, 'Il cammino suo proprio', my translation.
11 Janz, *Vita di Nietzsche*, Vol. 2, p. 293, 'Ammiratori', my translation.
12 Tobden, *The Way of Awakening*, pp. 330–1.
13 Loy, *Non-duality*, p. 249, 'The Clôture of Deconstruction', pp. 248–60.
14 Ibid.
15 Nagarjuna, *Madhyamaka Karika* XXIV, 18, quoted in Loy, p. 251.
16 Nagarjuna, *Madhyamaka Karika* 25, VIII, 8, in Luetchford, *Between Heaven and Earth*, p. 107.
17 Loy, *Non-duality*, p. 253, 'The Clôture of Deconstruction', pp. 248–60.
18 *Untimely Meditations*, 2:9, p. 113, 'On the uses and disadvantages of history for life', pp. 59–123.
19 T. E. Wood, *Nagarjunian Disputations*, p. 2, Introduction.
20 Nagarjuna, *Madhyamaka Karika* 17, XXXIII, in Luetchford, *Between Heaven and Earth*, p. 78.

Part III
The Will to Power and Generosity

1   See Nishitani Keji, *Religion and Nothingness*, 'Sunyata and History', pp. 218–85.
2   Hakuin, *Zen Words for the Heart*, p. 9, translated by Norman Waddell.
3   Ibid., pp. 17–18.
4   Goethe, *Faust*, Part 2, 'Classical Warpulgis Night'.
5   *On the Genealogy of Morals*, 2:17 & 18, pp. 66–8.
6   *Thus Spoke Zarathustra*, I, p. 78, 'Of the Flies of the Market Place', pp. 78–81.
7   *Thus Spoke Zarathustra*, II, p. 111, 'On the Blissful Islands', pp. 109–12.
8   Deleuze, *Nietzsche and Philosophy*, p. 15, 'The Tragic', pp. 1–38.
9   *Thus Spoke Zarathustra*, III, p. 208, 'Of The Three Evil Things', 2, pp. 205–9.
10 Ibid.
11 On Lawrence's idea of "synthetic creation" and the "silver river of life", see May, *Nietzsche and Modern Literature*.
12 Nishitani Keji, *Religion and Nothingness*, p. 234, 'Sunyata and History', pp. 218–85.
13 Ibid., p. 251.
14 *The Will to Power*, 692, p. 369.
15 Nishitani Keji, *Religion and Nothingness*, p. 251.
16 Ibid.
17 It is rather sad that often the sheer complexity of Nietzsche's thought is simplified, in contemporary attempts at philosophical discourse, to mere 'perspectivism' and 'relativism'.
18 Deleuze, *Nietzsche and Philosophy*, p. 128, 'From Ressentiment to the Bad Conscience', pp. 111–45.
19 *Beyond Good and Evil*, 261, pp. 179–80.
20 *Daybreak*, p. 68. 2:113, 'The striving for distinction', pp. 68–9.

21 *On the Genealogy of Morals*, 2:10, pp. 53–4.
22 *Beyond Good and Evil*, 260, p. 178.
23 *Daybreak*, 3:202, p. 203, 'For the promotion of health', pp. 201–10.
24 *Minima Moralia*, 21, pp. 42–3.
25 Locke, *Second Treatise of Government*, p. 13, Chapter V, 'Of Property', pp. 12–23.
26 Gregory, *Gifts and Commodities*, p. 19, 'The Competing Theories', pp. 9–28.

Part IV
The Crooked Path of Eternity: Time and the Eternal Return

1 On this subject, see Joan Stambaugh's rigorous study, *The Formless Self*. Details in Bibliography.
2 Blanchot, *The Infinite Conversation*, p. 148, 'Crossing the Line', pp. 143–51.
3 Salomé, *Nietzsche* p. 133, 'Nietzsche's System', pp. 90–159.
4 For an in-depth discussion on the theme of the 'enigma', see Paul Ricouer: *Freud and Philosophy: An Essay on Interpretation*.
5 Batchelor, *At the Crossroads* – Interview in *Tricycle, The Buddhist Review*, Fall 2002.
6 Janz, *Vita di Nietzsche*, Vol. 2, p. 106, 'Lou'.
7 Michelangelo, *Sonnet 38*, my translation. See also Sidney Alexander (editor, translator), *The Complete Poetry of Michelangelo*, p. 43.
8 Stack, *Lange & Nietzsche*, p. 39n, 'Eternal Recurrence', pp. 25–50.
9 Quoted from Leonard, The Silent Pulse, in Mu Soeng, The *Diamond Sutra*, p. 45.
10 *The Will to Power*, # 577, p. 310.
11 Loy, *Lack and Transcendence*, xv, Introduction.
12 Ibid., xv–vvi.
13 Ibid., p. 103, 'The Meaning of It All', pp. 102–32.
14 Ibid., pp. 121–2.
15 Ibid.
16 Swain, *A Place for Strangers*, pp. 17–18, 'Worlds to Endure', pp. 13–68.
17 Ibid., p.18.
18 Ibid., p. 19.
19 Ibid., p. 19.
20 F. S. Perls, R. Hefferline, P. Goodman, *Gestalt Therapy Excitement and Growth in the Human Personality*, p. 293, 'The Compulsion to Repeat'.
21 Ibid.
22 W. B. Yeats, *Autobiographies*, quoted in May, *Nietzsche and Modern Literature*, p. 23, 'Yeats and Aristocracy'.
23 *La Gaia Scienza*, 4:341, p. 192, my translation.
24 Salomé, *Nietzsche*, p. 102, 'Nietzsche's System', pp. 90–159.
25 *Beyond Good and Evil*, 56, pp. 63–4.
26 Deleuze, *Nietzsche and Philosophy*, p. 81 in *Critique* pp. 73–110.
27 Lawrence quoted in May, 'Nietzsche and Modern Literature', p. 128.
28 *Thus Spoke Zarathustra*, p. 332 'The Intoxicated Song', 11, 326–36.

29 *Thus Spoke Zarathustra*, III, p. 178 'Of the Vision and the Riddle', pp. 176–80.
30 *Will to Power*, 1060, pp. 545–6.
31 *Thus Spoke Zarathustra*, III, p. 177, 'Of the Vision and the Riddle'.
32 Madhyamika karika, XXI, 14–15 in Luetchford, *Between Heaven and Earth*, p. 89. I substituted 'annihilationism' with 'nihilism'.
33 *The Poems of W. B. Yeats*, p. 301, 'Vacillation, IV'.
34 *Beyond Good and Evil*, I, # 1, p. 15.
35 N. O. Brown, *Love's Body*, p. 199, XII, 'Resurrection', pp. 191–214.
36 Shakespeare, *King John*, Act 3, Scene 4.
37 Freud, *Beyond the Pleasure Principle*, 28, quoted in Chapelle, *Nietzsche and Psychoanalysis*, p. 105.

Part V
Beyond the Dream of Change: Towards a Zen Psychology

1 Jung, *Psychological Types*, Chapter 1, quoted in Parkes, p. 209, 'Nietzsche and Jung: Ambivalent Appreciation', in *Nietzsche and Depth Psychology*, pp. 205–27.
2 *Human, all too Human*, 13 quoted in Parkes, ibid., pp. 208–9.
3 *La Gaia Scienza*, I # 54, p. 75, 'La coscienza dell'apparenza', my translation.
4 Jung, *Memories, Dreams, Reflections*, p. 102–3 quoted in Parkes, p. 203, 'Nietzsche and Jung: Ambivalent Appreciation' in *Nietzsche and Depth Psychology*, pp. 205–27.
5 Jung, *Memories, Dreams, Reflections*, p. 289, quoted in Parkes, ibid., p. 213.
6 Shakespeare, *Hamlet*, p. 226 Act I, Scene V, vv. 172–5, Hamlet, The Arden Shakespeare.
7 Berry, *Echo's Subtle Body*, p. 139, 'Hamlet's Poisoned Ear', pp. 127–61.
8 Chapelle, *Nietzsche and Psychoanalysis*, p. 5 'A Demonic Thought for a Start', pp. 1–14.
9 Ibid., p. 5.
10 Ibid., p. 8.
11 Ibid., p. 9.
12 *Beyond Good and Evil*, 70, p. 73.
13 Freud, *Beyond the Pleasure Principle*, # 23 quoted in Chapelle, *Nietzsche and Psychoanalysis*, p. 97, 'Eternal Return in Everyday Life', pp. 95–102.
14 Ricouer's quote in Chapelle, *Nietzsche and Psychoanalysis*.
15 Camus, *The Myth of Sisyphus*, particularly Chapter 1 'An Absurd Reasoning', and Chapter 2, 'The Absurd Man'.
16 John Donne, *The Complete English Poems*, pp. 272–3, 'The First Anniversary' vv. 86–92, from 'An Anatomy of the World'.
17 Chapelle, *Nietzsche and Psychoanalysis*, p. 99–100, 'Eternal Return in Everyday Life, pp. 95–102.
18 *Twilight of the Idols*, p. 9, 1:34, 'Maxims and Barbs', pp. 5–10
19 Waddell, Abe, *The Heart of Dogen's Shobogenzo*, p. 8, II, 'Bendowa – Negotiating the Way', pp. 7–30.

20 Ibid., p. 8.
21 Ibid., p. 63, VI, 'Bussho – Buddhanature', pp. 59–98.
22 Ibid., p. 22, II, 'Bendowa – Negotiating the Way', pp. 7–30.
23 Ibid., p. 22.
24 Ibid., p. 40, IV, 'Genjokoan, Manifesting Suchness', pp. 39–45.
25 Ibid., Waddell, p. 33 'Ikka Myoju, One Bright Pearl', pp. 31–7.
26 Ibid., pp. 33–4.
27 *Thus Spoke Zarathustra*, p. 331, 'The Intoxicated Song', pp. 326–36.
28 Reed, *Half of Life: Versions of Holderlin*, p. 12.
29 *The Will to Power*, # 933, p. 492.
30 *Ecce Homo*, p. 32, 'Prologo', my translation.
31 Jones, *The New Face of Social Buddhism*, pp. 113–26, 'Social Awareness: the opening of the fourth eye'.
32 *Human all too Human* (Hollingdale's translation), Vol. 1, p. 12, I, 1, 'Chemistry of concepts and sensations'.
33 *Daybreak*, p. 561, V, 560, 'What we are at liberty to do'.
34 *Human all too Human*, Part 2, 'The Wanderer and his Shadow', # 53, p. 323.
35 *Beyond Good and Evil*, # 206, p. 113–14.
36 Quoted in Parkes, p. 221, in *Emotions in Asian Thought: A Dialogue in Comparative Philosophy* 'Nietzsche and Zen Master Hakuin on the Roles of Emotion and Passion', pp. 231–3.
37 Ibid., p. 223.
38 *Thus Spoke Zarathustra*, III, p. 230, 'Of Old and New Law-Tables', pp. 214–32.
39 Hakuin, quoted in Parkes, p. 224, 'Nietzsche and Zen Master Hakuin on the Roles of Emotion and Passion', pp. 231–3.
40 *Ecce Homo*, 9 'Perchè sono un destino', p. 96, my translation.
41 Adorno, *Minima Moralia*, # 2 'Grassy seat', pp. 22–3.
42 Marcuse, *One Dimensional Man*, p. 56, Chapter 3, 'The Conquest of the Unhappy Consciousness: Repressive Desublimation', pp. 44– 61.
43 Ibid.
44 Hillman *Insearch: Psychology and Religion*, p. 114, 'Inner Femininity: Anima, Reality, and Religion, pp. 95–126.
45 Hillman *Insearch*, p. 115.
46 Hillman *Insearch*, p. 117.
47 *Ecce Homo*, II, 9, 'Perchè sono così accorto', pp. 49–50, my translation.
48 H. L. Ansbacher & R. Ansbacher *The Individual Psychology of Alfred Adler*, p. 32, 'Transformation of Drives, pp. 32–3.
49 Berry, *Echo's Subtle Body*, p. 37, 'The Dogma of Gender', pp. 35–51.
50 Ibid., pp. 37–8.
51 Ibid., p. 38.
52 Deleuze, *Nietzsche and Philosophy*, p. 17, 'The Tragic', pp. 1–38.
53 *The Will to Power*, # 1050, p. 539.
54 *The Birth of Tragedy*, p. 120, # 22, pp. 117–21.
55 Freud, *Beyond the Pleasure Principle*, quoted in Chapelle, p. 8, 'A Demonic Thought for a Start', pp. 1–14.
56 Rank, *The Double*, quoted in Chapelle, p. 8.

57 Nietzsche, *Selected Letters*, p. 174.
58 Ansbacher & R. Ansbacher, *The Individual Psychology of Alfred Adler*, p. 153.
59 *Human All too Human, Preface*, 1, my translation.
60 *Twilight of the Idols*, p. 21, V, I 'Morality as Anti-Nature', pp. 21–5.
61 Parkes, 'Nietzsche and Zen Master Hakuin on the Roles of Emotion and Passion', p. 213–14 in *Emotions in Asian Thought: A Dialogue in Comparative Philosophy*.
62 Plato, *Gorgia*, # 484a, p. 187, my translation.
63 Plato, *Gorgia*, # 492, p. 196, my translation.
64 See Vattimo, *Terza Pagina*, pp. 125–8, 'Hanna Arendt: La Verità nell'Apparenza'.
65 Freud, *The Dynamics of Transference*, 108, quoted in Chapelle, *Nietzsche and Psychoanalysis*, p. 109.
66 Ibid., p. 110.
67 Freud quoted in Chapelle, p. 110.
68 Freud, *Civilization and its Discontents*, VI, pp. 74–5.
69 *Twilight of the Idols*, p. 18, III 6, 'The Problem of Socrates', pp. 10–15.
70 Freud, *Remembering, Repeating, and Working Through*, quoted in Chapelle, p. 107, 'Eternal Return in Transference', pp. 103–11.
71 Eliade, *Cosmos & History: the Myth of Eternal Return*, pp. 3–4, 'Archetypes and Repetition'.
72 Ibid.
73 Poe quoted in Otto Rank, *The Double*, p. 27, 'Examples of The Double in Literature', pp. 8–33.
74 *Thus Spoke Zarathustra*, p. 87, 'On Love of One's Neighbour', pp. 86–8.
75 Maupassant quoted in Otto Rank, *The Double*, p. 22, Examples of The Double in Literature', pp. 8–33.
76 Chapelle, *Nietzsche and Psychoanalysis*, p. 227, 'Soul and Image: Archetypal Psychology', pp. 225–39.
77 *Beyond Good and Evil*, 23, pp. 35–6.
78 Adorno, *Minima Moralia* # 151 'Theses against occultism', pp. 238–44.
79 *Ecce Homo*, XIII, 6, p. 94 my translation.
80 Jung, *Memories, Dreams, Reflections*, pp. 102–3 quoted in Parkes, p. 203, 'Nietzsche and Jung: Ambivalent Appreciation' essay in *Nietzsche and Depth Psychology*, pp. 205–27.
81 *Assorted Opinion and Maxims*, 223, quoted in Parkes, *Composing the Soul*, p. 124.
82 Chapelle, *Nietzsche and Psychoanalysis*, p. 236, ' Soul and Image: Archetypal Psychology', pp. 225–39.
83 Ibid., pp. 235–6.
84 *The Will to Power*, 431, pp. 235–6..
85 *The Will to Power*, 572, p. 308.
86 *The Will to Power*, 414, p. 223.
87 *Twilight of the Idols*, VI, 2, p. 27, 'The Four Great Errors', pp. 26–32.
88 *On the Genealogy of Morals*, III, 7, pp. 85–7.
89 Conway, 'The Birth of The Soul: Towards a Psychology of Decadence', in

Nietzsche and Depth Psychology, p. 60, 'The Birth of Soul', pp. 51–71.
90 *The Will to Power*, 438, p. 242.
91 *Beyond Good and Evil*, 67, p. 72, 'Maxims and Interludes', pp. 72–89.
92 *Twilight of the Idols*, IX, 38, p. 65, 'Reconnaissance Raids of an Untimely Man', pp. 43–75.

Part VI
On Nomadic Truth

1 Colli/ Montinari, 'Scelta di Frammenti Postumi' in *La Gaia Scienza*, pp. 378–9.
2 Ibid.
3 A firm grounding in the practice of philology gave Nietzsche an unusual angle to his philosophy, even though he was later to repudiate his former profession of rummaging through old books.
4 Scott, *Samurai and Cherry Blossoms*, in Hazy Moon Zen Review, Vol. 1, issue 6, 2001.
5 *Beyond Good and Evil*, 1:3, 'On the Prejudices of Philosophers', p. 3.
6 *Beyond Good and Evil*, 1:6, p. 19.
7 *Selected Letters*, p. 342.
8 *Human all too Human*, 1:616, p. 195 (Hollingdale), 'Estranged from the present'.
9 Blanchot, *The Infinite Conversation*, p. 127, *Being Jewish*, pp. 123–30.
10 Said, *Reflections on Exile and other literary and cultural essays*, p. 184; 'Reflections on Exile', pp. 173–86.
11 Ibid., p. 173.
12 Ibid., p. 186.

Part VII
The Innocence of Becoming

1 Spinoza, *Ethics*, p. 25, 'Concerning God', Proposition XXXII, 'Will can be called a necessary cause, not a free one', Corollary 1.
2 Nietzsche, KGW, VII, I:4 (2), quoted by F. Mistry, *Nietzsche and Buddhism*, p. 1.
3 *Will to Power*, 55, pp. 35–9.
4 Quoted in Mistry, *Nietzsche and Buddhism*, p. 56, 'The analysis of personality and universe', pp. 51–79.
5 Kundera, *The unbearable lightness of being*, p. 5.
6 Ibid.
7 Casey, *Remembering: A Phenomenological Study*, p. 3, 'Remembering Forgotten'.
8 Merzel, *The Path of the Human Being*, Preface, xiv.
9 Steiner, *Errata: An Examined Life*, p. 113, Chapter 8.
10 *Frammenti Postumi*, Colli/Montinari, *La Gaia Scienza*, p. 388.
11 *Will to Power*, # 1032, p. 532.

12 Ibid.
13 *Twilight of the Idols,* IX, 14, p. 50, 'What the Germans Lack', pp. 36–75.
14 Jaspers, *Nietzsche: An Introduction,* p. 344, 2:6: 'The Basic Thoughts of Nietzsche'.
15 *Will to Power,* # 1067, pp. 549–50.
16 Colli, *Dopo Nietzsche,* p. 51, my translation, 'L'accordo finale'.
17 *Twilight of the Idols,* V, 3, p. 22, 'Morality as Anti-Nature', pp. 20–5.
18 Nachlass 9, pp. 261–9.
19 *Twilight of the Idols,* p. 9, 'Maxims and Barbs', 33.
20 Quoted in Richard Ellman, *The Identity of Yeats,* p. 109.
21 *La Gaia Scienza, I,* # 55, my translation.
22 *On the Genealogy of Morals,* Preface, # 7, pp. 8–9.
23 The Angel in Pasolini's Gospel: androgynous, numinous, an apparition within a black and white canvas.
24 *La Gaia Scienza,* 357, pp. 217–18, my translation.
25 *Beyond Good and Evil,* # 253, pp. 165–6, 'Peoples and Fatherlands', pp. 151–72.
26 May, *Nietzsche and Modern Literature,* p. 126, 'Lawrence: Becoming What One Is', pp. 111–43.
27 *On the Genealogy of Morals,* Preface, # 7, pp. 8–9.
28 D. H. Lawrence, *The Rainbow,* p. 408.
29 Spinoza, 'The Ethics' in *Works of Spinoza,* Vol. II, Part I, p. 48.
30 May, *Nietzsche and Modern Literature,* p. 126.
31 *On the Genealogy of Morals,* 2:1, pp. 39–40.
32 *Ecce Homo,* 1:6, p. 37, 'Perchè sono così saggio'.
33 *On the Genealogy of Morals,* p. 103, 3:14, pp. 100–4.
34 *On the Genealogy of Morals,* 2:18, pp. 67–8.
35 Deleuze, *Nietzsche and Philosophy,* p. 129 'From Ressentiment to the Bad Conscience', pp. 111–45.
36 Rilke, *Duino Elegies* p. 83, IX Elegy, vv. 1–18.
37 Ibid., p. 99, X Elegy, vv. 104–6.
38 Ibid., vv. 107–13.

BIBLIOGRAPHY

Nietzsche's Works

Beyond Good and Evil, trans. R. J. Hollingdale. Penguin, 1973/1978.
The Birth of Tragedy, trans. Douglas Smith. Oxford University Press, 2000.
Daybreak – Thoughts on the prejudices of morality, trans. R. J. Hollingdale. Cambridge University Press, 1997.
Ecce Homo Come si diventa ciò che si è. Tascabili Newton, 1993.
La Gaia Scienza – Idilli di Messina – Scelta di Frammenti Postumi. Giorgio Colli and Mazzino Montinari (eds.). Mondadori Editore, 1978.
On the Genealogy of Morals: A Polemic, translated with an introduction by Douglas Smith. Oxford University Press, 1996.
Human, all too Human, translated by Marion Faber and Stephen Lehmann. Penguin, 1984.
Human, all too Human, trans. R. J. Hollingdale. Cambridge University Press, 1986.
Philosophy in the Tragic Age of the Greeks, trans. M. Cowan. Chicago Gateway, 1962.
Thus Spoke Zarathustra, trans. Walter Kaufman. Viking Press, 1954.
Thus Spoke Zarathustra, trans. R. J. Hollingdale. Penguin Books, 1961.
Twilight of the Idols, trans. Duncan Large. Oxford University Press, 1998.
Untimely Meditations, edited by Daniel Breazeale, translated by R. J. Hollingdale. Cambridge University Press, 1997.
The Will to Power, trans. Walter Kaufman. Weidenfeld and Nicolson, 1967.
Selected Letters, translated by A. N. Ludovici, edited with an introduction by O. Levy. London: Soho Book Company, 1935.
A Nietzsche Reader, trans. R. J. Hollingdale. Penguin Classics, 2003.

Selected Sources

Theodor Adorno, *Minima Moralia – Reflections from a Damaged Life*, trans. E. F. N. Jephcott. Verso, 1978.
S. Alexander (editor, translator), *The Complete Poetry of Michelangelo*. Athens: Ohio University Press, 1991.
H. L. Ansbacher and R. Ansbacher, *The Individual Psychology of Alfred Adler*. Allen & Unwin, 1958.
Hannah Arendt, *The Origins of Totalitarianism*, 1951.
Robert Aitken, *The Practice of Perfection – The Paramitas from a Zen Buddhist Perspective*. Washington: Counterpoint, 1997.
Robert Aitken, *The Mind of Clover: Essays in Zen Buddhist Ethics*. North Point, 1984.
Stephen Batchelor – *At the Crossroads*. Interviewed in *Tricycle, The Buddhist Review*, Fall 2002.

Bibliography

Maurice Blanchot, *L'Entreteien infini (The Infinite Conversation),* translated and with a foreword by Susan Hanson. University of Minnesota Press, 1993.

——, *Friendship,* trans. Elizabeth Rottenberg. Stanford University Press, 1997.

——, *The Siren's Song,* selected essays, ed. G. Josipivici, trans. Sacha Rabinovitch. The Harvester Press, 1982.

Patricia Berry, *Echo's Subtle Body.* Dallas: Spring Publications, 1982.

Norman O. Brown, *Love's Body.* New York: Random House, 1966.

Albert Camus, *The Rebel,* trans. A. Bower. London: Penguin, 1971.

——, *The Myth of Sisyphus.* New York: Vintage Press, 1955.

Edward S. Casey, *Remembering. A phenomenological study.* Bloomington and Indianapolis: Indiana University Press, 1987.

Daniel Chapelle, *Nietzsche and Psychoanalysis.* Albany, SUNY Press, 1993.

Giorgio Colli, *Dopo Nietzsche.* Adelphi, 1974.

Thomas Cleary (trans.), *Book of Serenity.* Lindisfarne Press, 1990.

Daniel Conway, The Birth of The Soul: Towards a Psychology of Decadence, in *Nietzsche and Depth Psychology,* edited by Jacob Golomb, Weaver Santaniello, and Ronald L. Lehren. SUNY Press, 1999.

John Donne, *The Complete English Poems.* Penguin, 1996.

Master Dogen. *Shobogenzo,* translated by Gudo Nishijima and Chodo Gross. Windbell, 1994.

Giles Deleuze, *Nietzsche and Philosophy,* trans. Hugh Tomlinson. London: Athlone Press, 1983. Originally published in France in 1962.

Fiodor Dostoyevsky, *Crime and Punishment.* Penguin Books, 1997.

R. M. Eaton (ed.), *Descartes Selections.* New York: Scribners, 1955.

Mircea Eliade, *Cosmos & History: the Myth of Eternal Return,* trans. W. R. Trask. Princeton University Press, 1971.

Richard Ellman, *The Identity of Yeats.* Faber & Faber, 1964. First published by Macmillan, 1954.

Ralph Waldo Emerson, *Prose Works.* London, New York and Melbourne: Ward, Lock & Co., 1889.

Sigmund Freud, *Beyond the Pleasure Principle,* trans. J. Strachey. Bantam, 1959.

——, *The Complete Introductory Lectures on Psychoanalysis,* trans. J. Strachey. New York: Norton, 1966.

——, *The Standard Edition of the Complete Psychological Writings of Sigmund Freud,* trans. J. Strachey. London: Hogarth Press, 1955.

Goethe, *Faust,* trans. George Madison Priest, hosted by the Alchemy website: <http://www.levity.com/alchemy/faustidx.html>.

John Gray, *Straw Dogs.* Granta Books, 2002.

C. A. Gregory, *Gifts and Commodities.* London Academic Press, 1982.

Hakuin, *The Zen Master Hakuin: Selected Writings,* trans. I. Yampolsky. Columbia University Press, 1971.

Karsten Harries, *Metaphor and Transcendence.* Chicago Press, 1979.

Gareth Hill, *Masculine and Feminine: The Natural Flow of Opposites in the Psyche.* Shambhala, 1992.

James Hillman, *Re-visioning Psychology.* HarperCollins, 1992.

——, *Insearch: Psychology and Religion.* Spring Publications, 1994 edition. First published in 1967.

——, *Healing Fiction*. Station Hill, 1983.

——, *Inter Views – Conversations with Laura Pozzo*. New York: Harper & Row, 1983.

——, *The Soul's Code*.

Curt P. Janz, *Vita di Nietzsche*, 3 volumes, 1980–1982. Roma–Bari: Laterza.

Karl Jaspers, *Nietzsche: An Introduction to the Understanding of His Philosophical Activity*, trans. C. Wallraff. Johns Hopkins University Press, 1997.

Ken Jones, *The New Social Face of Buddhism: A Call to Action*. Boston: Wisdom Publications, 2003.

C. G. Jung, *Memories, Dreams, Reflections*, edited by Aniela Jaffe, translated by Richard and Clara Winston. London: Fontana, 1963.

——, *Collected Works of C. G. Jung*. Princeton University Press, 1961.

Charles H. Kahn, *The Art and Thought of Heraclitus*. Cambridge University Press, 1979.

The Zen Teachings of Huang Po on the Transmission of the Mind, trans. John Blofeld. The Buddhist Society, UK, 1959.

Walter Kaufman, *Nietzsche: philosopher, psychologist, Antichrist*. Princeton University Press, 1950.

Milan Kundera, *The unbearable lightness of being*. London, Boston, 1984.

Lin-Chi, *The Record of Lin-Chi*, trans. Ruth F. Sasaki. Kyoto: Institute for Zen Studies, 1975.

D. H. Lawrence, *Women in Love,* intro. by Richard Aldington. Phoenix Edition, William Heinemann, 1961. First published, 1921.

——, *The Rainbow*. Penguin Books, 1995. First published, 1915.

John Locke, *The Second Treatise of Government and A Letter Concerning Toleration*. New York: Dover Publications, 2002.

M. Lowenthal (editor and translator), *The Autobiography of Montaigne*. Routledge & Sons Ltd, 1935.

David Loy, *Lack and Transcendence*. Prometheus Books, 1996.

——, *Non-duality*. Yale University Press, 1988.

Michael Eido Luechford, *Between Heaven and Earth: From Nagarjuna to Dogen – A Translation and Interpretation of the Mula madhyamaka karika*. Windbell Publications, 2002.

Taizan Maezumi, *Appreciate your Life*. Shambhala, 2001.

Bryan Magee, *The Philosophy of Schopenhauer*. Oxford & New York, 1983.

Herbert Marcuse, *One Dimensional Man*. Abacus, 1972.

J. Marks & R. T. Ames, *Emotions and Asian Thought: a dialogue in comparative philosophy*. SUNY Press, 1995.

Peter Mathiessen, *Nine-headed Dragon River*. Collins Harvill, 1986.

Keith M. May, *Nietzsche and Modern Literature*. Macmillan Press, 1988.

Dennis Genpo Merzel *The Path of the Human Being – Zen teachings on the Bodhisattva Way*. Edited by Wynn Seishin Wright. Boston and London: Shambhala, 2003.

——, *Beyond Sanity and Madness*. Boston: Tuttle, 1997.

——, *Dharma 24/7*. Boston: Tuttle, 2001.

F. Mistry, *Nietzsche and Buddhism*. De Grutier, 1981.

Montaigne, Michel de., *The Complete Essays of Montaigne,* trans. Donald M. Frame. Stanford, 1958.

Jose Ortega y Gasset, *Meditations on Quixote,* with introduction and notes by Julian Marias; translated from the Spanish by Evelyn Rugg and Diego Marin. New York, London: Norton & Co. , 1963.

Nagarjuna, *Madhyamaka karika,* trans. Raniero Gnoli. Boringhieri, 1961.

Nishitani Keji, trans. J. V. Bragt. University of California Press, 1982.

Platone *Gorgia,* Traduzione, Introduzione e Commento a cura di Stefania Nonvel Pieri. Napoli: Loffredo, 1991.

Graham Parkes, *Composing the Soul. Reaches of Nietzsche's Psychology.* The University of Chicago Press, 1994.

—— (ed.), *Nietzsche and Asian thought.* The University of Chicago Press, 1991.

F. S. Perls, R. Hefferline, and P. Goodman. *Gestalt Therapy – Excitement and Growth in the Human Personality.* The Julian Press, 1951.

Otto Rank, *The Double.* New York Library, 1979.

Jeremy Reed, *Half of Life: Versions of Holderlin.* Rivendale Press, 1998.

Paul Ricouer, *Freud and Philosophy: An Essay on Interpretation.* New Haven: Yale University Press, 1970.

——, 'The History of Religions and the Phenomenology of Time Consciousness' in *The History of Religions: Retrospect and Prospect,* edited by J. M. Kitigawa. New York: Humanities Press, 1961.

Rainer Maria Rilke, trans. J. B. Leishman and S. Spender, *Duino Elegies.* Chatto & Windus, 1975.

Jacqueline Rose, *On not being able to sleep: Psychoanalysis and the Modern World.* Vintage, 2004.

Rudiger Safranski, *Nietzsche – A philosophical biography.* Granta, 2002.

Edward W. Said, *Reflections on Exile and other literary and cultural essays.* Granta, 2001.

Lou Andreas Salomé, *Nietzsche.* University of Illinois Press, 1988. Translated and edited by Siegfried Mandel.

Schopenhauer, *Parerga and Paralipomena,* Vol. I, trans. E. F. J. Payne. Oxford University Press, 1974.

Ofelia Schutte, *Willing Backwards: Nietzsche on Time, Pain, Joy, and Memory,* an essay in *Nietzsche and Depth Psychology,* edited by Jacob Golomb, Weaver Santaniello, and Ronald L. Lehren. SUNY Press, 1999.

David Scott, *Samurai and Cherry Blossoms.* London: Century Hutchinson Ltd., 1987.

William Shakespeare, *Hamlet.* The Arden Shakespeare, edited by H. Jenkins. T. Nelson & Sons Ltd.

——, *King John,* The Complete Works of William Shakespeare, <www.shakespeare-literature.com>.

Mu Soeng, *Diamond Sutra: Transforming the Way We Perceive the World.* Boston Wisdom Publications, 2000.

——, *Trust in Mind: The Rebellion of Chinese Zen.* Boston Wisdom Publications, 2004.

Susan Sontag, *Under the Sign of Saturn.* Vintage, 2001.

Benedict de Spinoza, *Works of Spinoza,* Vol. II, trans. and introduction by R. H. M. Elwes. New York: Dover Publications, 1951.

George J. Stack, *Lange & Nietzsche.* De Grutier, 1983.

Joan Stambaugh, *Thoughts on the Innocence of Becoming,* in *Nietzsche-Studien* Band 14. De Gruiter, Berlin, 1985.

——, *The Formless Self.* SUNY Press 1999.

W. H. E. Stanner, 'The Dreaming' in *Traditional Aboriginal Society: A Reader,* ed. W. H. Edwards. Melbourne: Macmillan, 1987 (1956).

George Steiner, *Errata: an examined life.* Weidenfeld & Nicolson, 1997.

Tracey B. Strong and M. A. Gillespie (eds), *Nietzsche's New Seas.* University of Chicago Press, 1988.

Tony Swain, *A Place for Strangers – Towards a History of Australian Aboriginal Being.* Cambridge University Press, 1993.

Geshe Yeshe Tobden, *The Way of Awakening – A Commentary on Shantideva's Bodhicharyavatara,* trans. Manu Bazzano and Sarita Doveton. Boston: Wisdom Publications, 2005.

Gianni Vattimo, *Le Mezze Verità.* Terza Pagina, 1988, Torino: La Stampa.

Norman Waddell and Masao Abe (translators/editors), *The Heart of Dogen's Shobogenzo.* SUNY Press, 2002.

Norman Waddell (trans.), *Zen Words for the Heart Hakuin's – Commentary on the Heart Sutra.* Shambhala, 1996.

R. J. White (ed.), *Political Tracts of Wordsworth, Coleridge, and Shelley.* Cambridge University Press, 1953.

Thomas E. Wood, *Nagarjunian Disputations – A philosophical journey through an Indian looking-glass.* University of Hawaii Press, 1994.

Philip Yampolsky, trans., *The Zen Master Hakuin: Selected Writings.* New York: Columbia University Press, 1971.

The Poems of W. B. Yeats: A New Edition, edited by R. J. Finneran. Macmillan, 1961.

W. B. Yeats, *Autobiographies.* Macmillan, 1983.

INDEX

Index

Index

Index

Index

Index

Index

Index

Index

Index

Weimar, 25
Westminster Review, 17
Wilde, Oscar, 152, 168
will, history of, 71
will to art, 76
will to give, 76, 80, 107, 131, 136
will to knowledge, 57
will to power, 71–84, 88, 141, 213
   and the ego, 78, 94, 96
   forgetting, 223
   Heidegger's view, 186
   instinct of preservation, 122
Will to Power (Nietzsche), 88
will to truth, 41, 76, 202
William Wilson (Poe), 169
wisdom, 34, 132, 133, 136–8
Wittgenstein, Ludwig, 90
woman (*das Weib*), 134
Women in Love (Lawrence), 106–7
Woolf, Virginia, 23
work, 31, 32, 106, 164
The World as Will and Representation
   (Schopenhauer), 17
Wu, Emperor, 160, 177
wu-wei, 137

yang wisdom, 133, 137
Yeats, William Butler, 6, 42, 103–4, 112,
   213–14
yin wisdom, 133, 136–7

Zarathustra, 26, 31, 35, 39, 43, 59
   compulsion, 124
   dignity of the earth, 132
   enigma of time, 107–8
   generosity, 80
   higher men, 27, 214
   scientific seeker of truth, 135
zazen, x, 127
zeal, 34
Zen Buddhism
   actualization, 79
   as affirmative art, 39
   affirmative similarities with Nietzsche,
     205–6
   as an art, 131–2
   anti-humanist insight, 129–30
   appreciation of one's life, 89
   Big Mind, 185, 208
   continuous refinement, 77

   and death, 158
   depth psychology, 20, 227–8
   descent, 60, 227–8
   desiderata, 53
   and doubt, 23, 65
   down to earth quality, 72–3
   emotions, 141
   eternal return, 110
   evolutionism, 205
   existential edge, 43
   experience of true reality, 204
   experiential nature of, 160
   femininity, 138, 155
   fetishism, 40
   and Heraclitus, 22
   and holiness, 176–7
   homeless vows, 187
   and humanism, 176
   immanence, 91–2
   individual versus the State, 26
   investigation of truth, 20–1
   koan study, 33, 90
   liberation, 44, 176
   misunderstandings of, 143
   mui shinnin, 156
   nihilism, 67, 200, 226
   ordinary mind, 27, 54
   passions, 141, 143, 157
   poetic ambiguity, 73
   redemption, 177
   salvation, 177
   satori, 102
   scope and breadth of, 67
   self and not-self, 79
   self-estrangement, 223
   social engagement, 138
   sublimation, 141–2, 143, 144
   training, 130
   transcendence, 22, 92
   travel to different states, ix, 1, 187, 188
   true person of no rank, 24–5
   universe as a bright pearl, 129–30
   wearing a mask, 44–5
   zazen, x, 127
   see also bodhisattva vows; Dharma;
     Dogen Zenji; Great Doubt; Hakuin
     Zenji
Zen Masters, 20, 52, 92, 132, 188
Zimmern, Helen, 59